About this volume:

The distinguished British and American contributors to this book believe that language is a broadly-based means of communication with contested and consensual meanings, that such meanings must be revealed and evaluated by precise historical contextualization of language and proper attention to established rules of historical method, and that we must rethink the connections between the linguistic and the social.

The book aims to move beyond the despairing and unproductive fragmentation and relativism, the narrow textual range, and the literal and anti-realist readings of the postmodern 'linguistic turn', to offer a rigorous approach to the study of language and the subject of history.

About the editors:

John Belchem is Professor of History at the University of Liverpool. Neville Kirk is a Reader in Economic and Social History at Manchester Metropolitan University.

Languages of Labour

Languages of Labour

Edited by

JOHN BELCHEM and NEVILLE KIRK

Ashgate

Published by
Ashgate Publishing Limited
Gower House
Croft Road
Aldershot
Hants GU11 3HR
England

HD
4813
.L36
1997

Ashgate Publishing Company
Old Post Road
Brookfield
Vermont 05036–9704
USA

British Library Cataloguing in Publication Data

Languages of Labour
    1. Labour movement—History.
    I. Belchem, John. II. Kirk, Neville.
    322.2'09

    ISBN 1–85928–428–0

Library of Congress Cataloging in Publication Data

Languages of labour/edited by John Belchem and Neville Kirk.
        p.   cm.
    Includes index.
    ISBN 1–85928–428–0
    1. Labor—Terminology—Congresses.   2. Labor—History—Congresses.
    I. Belchem, John.   II. Kirk, Neville, 1947– .
    HD4813.L36   1997
    331'.01'4—dc21   97–18807
                                                                         CIP

ISBN 1 85928 428 0

This book is printed on acid free paper

Typeset in Sabon by Manton Typesetters, 5–7 Eastfield Road, Louth, Lincolnshire, LN11 7AJ and printed in Great Britain by

Printed in Great Britain by The Ipswich Book Company, Suffolk.

Contents

Notes on contributors

John Belchem is Professor of History at the University of Liverpool. He has published widely on popular politics, including a recent survey of *Popular Radicalism in Nineteenth-Century Britain* (1996). His present interests include ethnicity and Irish migration, the modern history of the Isle of Man, and the cultural history of Liverpool.

Roger Fagge is a lecturer in History at the University of Warwick. His publications include *Power, Culture and Conflict in the Coalfields: West Virginia and South Wales, 1900–1922* (1996). He is currently working on a study of the Labour Party in inter-war Britain.

Leon Fink is Professor of History at the University of North Carolina at Chapel Hill and the author of *In Search of the Working Class: Essays in American Labor History and Political Culture* (1994), and *Progressive Intellectuals and the Dilemmas of Democratic Commitment* (forthcoming).

Karen Hunt is Senior Lecturer in Economic and Social History, Manchester Metropolitan University. She is author of *Equivocal Feminists: The Social Democratic Federation and the Woman Question 1884–1911* (1996), and is currently conducting further research into women and socialism.

Neville Kirk is a Reader in Economic and Social History, Manchester Metropolitan University. His recent works include *Labour and Society in Britain and the USA*, 2 vols (1994) and, as editor, *Social Class and Marxism* (1996). He is currently working on the ideologies of labour movements and workers in Britain, the USA and Australia.

Susan Levine is Associate Professor of History at East Carolina University in Greenville, North Carolina and is author of *Degrees of Equality: The American Association of University Women and the Challenge of Twentieth-Century Feminism* (1995), and *Labor's True Woman: Carpet Weavers, Industrialization and Labor Reform in the Gilded Age* (1984).

Richard Price is Professor of History at the University of Maryland, College Park. He is author of *An Imperial War and the British Working Class* (1972), *Masters, Unions and Men* (1980), and *Labour in British Society 1780–1980* (1986 and 1992).

Melanie Tebbutt has taught in adult, further and higher education. The work for her contribution to this volume was completed while she was a Research Associate in the Manchester School of Management, UMIST. She is now Research Fellow at the Regional History Centre, Manchester Metropolitan University.

Eileen Janes Yeo teaches at the University of Sussex and is currently chair of the Society for the Study of Labour History. She has written a number of articles on Chartism and radical culture more generally. Her most recent book is *The Contest for Social Science: Relations and Representations of Gender and Class* (1996).

Introduction

John Belchem and Neville Kirk

This book developed out of the Spring 1996 conference of the Society for the Study of Labour History, held at Manchester Metropolitan University in late April. The invited paper-givers were requested by the conference organizers, John Belchem and Neville Kirk, to address themselves to the broad theme of 'Languages of Labour'. Beyond the common aims of demonstrating the unduly neglected existence among labour historians of concerns with the important and currently fashionable topics of language and identity and the theoretical and empirical engagements of such historians with the recent 'linguistic turn' in historical studies, neither the conference organizers nor the speakers wished to observe strict uniformity of assumption, method, interest or purpose. Rather, a key aim of the conference was to demonstrate the varied ways in which current work among British and US labour historians has maintained, advanced, and challenged and changed the 'traditional' interests in language, identity and consciousness pioneeringly established by such distinguished labour and social historians as E.P. and Dorothy Thompson, Eric Hobsbawm, Asa Briggs, Herbert Gutman, Eugene Genovese and David Montgomery.[1]

By the close of the conference there was general agreement that its aims had been successfully realized. The papers delivered and the informed, lively and constructive discussions to which they gave rise lent themselves to two conclusions. First, that there do indeed currently exist continuing and vital areas of interest and debate concerning language and identity *within* 'modernist' labour and social history – a conclusion which challenges both the assumed novelty of the 'linguistic turners" 'invention of language'; and postmodern dismissals of 'traditional' labour and social history as hopelessly outmoded in matters substantive and methodological.[2] Labour history, indeed, remains at the forefront of historical research and methodology, eschewing the crude polarities of socio-economic reductionism and linguistic determinism. Second, that every possible effort should be made to bring the papers to the attention of a wider audience. Alec McAulay of Scolar Press accepted enthusiastically this conclusion and kindly agreed to publish. Subsequently all the original eight conference papers were revised for publication and now appear in *Languages of Labour*. The duties of joint editorship have been undertaken by the conference organizers.

As will be evident from the opening paragraph, in both their conference-organizing and editorial capacities Belchem and Kirk have consciously eschewed the imposition of substantive and methodological straitjackets upon contributors and their material. The essays which make up this volume should accordingly speak to the reader in their richly diverse and distinctive ways. Equally conscious endeavours have, however, been made by both the contributors and editors to ensure that the book is not a jumble of totally disconnected individual pieces, devoid of common foci, threads, conclusions and guiding assumptions and principles. In fact an attempted balance has been struck between, on the one hand, elements of unity and similarity and, on the other hand, distinctiveness and difference. As we will see below – in our outlines of the overall structure of the book and in our brief descriptions of the individual chapters – these dualisms of unity and diversity are closely linked throughout this study rather than organized statically in separate sections. However, it is important to alert the reader at the very outset to those shared assumptions and points of view which inform, to varying degrees, all the essays. It is also important to note that such assumptions and 'positions' have manifested themselves most clearly and strongly in the course of contributors' advised 'critical and constructive engagement' with the 'linguistic turn'. Undertaken from a variety of positions and within different historical and geographical contexts and periods of time, this process of engagement has yielded the following common results.

First, all the contributors agree that there is 'more to language' than 'mere words'. Language is employed in a wide sense to refer to a means of signification and communication, both verbal and non-verbal in character. Second, in opposition to postmodernist 'non-referential' or largely 'free-floating' usages of language and discourse (the latter being defined in this volume as 'systems of knowledge or meaning', a set of rules, as it were, about what you can and cannot say[3]), there is a shared concern fully to *contextualize* language – that is, to situate language within and investigate its complex and changing links with social structure. Third, there is a common emphasis both upon the complex and non-reductionist character of these links – of language shaping as well as being shaped by its structured context, and of people as being the active creators, or 'agents' of systems of language and discourse, rather than the predominantly passive 'bearers' or 'carriers' of cultural messages and discourses. Within this complex interaction, multiple identities are constructed and thence prioritized through differentiation and displacement, processes of inclusion and exclusion which operate and alter according to context. Fourth, the meanings of language and discourse are revealed, as a result of rigorous pursuit of the 'rules of

historical method' – of the dialogue between concept and evidence, and
of due attention to context and chronology – as frequently contested
and fractured rather than consensual and uniform – especially along the
lines of race, gender and class – and subject to change over time.
Looking beyond the paradigms of 'classic' texts, labour historians investigate language in action as mediated through 'contentious reper-
toires' (to use Charles Tilly's term), the changing codes and conventions
of public space and collective behaviour interposed between utterance
and representation, intention and perception.[4]

Finally, and although made more explicit in that first part of the book
entitled 'Theory' than in the less abstract parts which follow, the book
as a whole is informed by a pronounced 'realist', as opposed to a
'postmodernist' or 'anti-representational', methodology and epistemology.[5] For example, in maintaining that the study of language should be
socially contexualized, and as such rendered fully sensitive to issues of
power and domination, class, gender and race, and to the popular
receptions afforded to (in, for example, demotic or vernacular speech)
as well as the nature of the linguistic messages put out by élites and
establishment sources, all the contributors are claiming that there is
more to reality than postmodernist historical notions of 'culture' and
the predominantly public–political 'official word'.[6] A central tenet of
realism is that aspects of culture, such as words, consciousness, and
norms and values, coexist and interact with political, economic, social
and other structures and processes which come into being and develop,
albeit partly rather than totally, 'out there', 'behind people's backs', in
unintended and unexpected ways. Accordingly, the study of reality
involves close attention to, and the interplay of, both 'culture' and
'structure', meaning and existence, and the internal and the external
and the intended and the unintended nature and consequences of human thought and action. Realism's epistemological and methodological
credentials and procedures can thus be seen to be diametrically opposed
to those employed by postmodernists who see nothing beyond subjectivity, no lurking or hidden external material and other structures and
interests beyond what is captured by self-referential and more or less
fully autonomous languages and discourses. In the latter case the link
between 'representation' and the 'real', language and the social world,
is dissolved: the 'real' becomes, *in toto*, 'representation', as manifested
in language and discourse. It is this deeply-rooted antithesis between the
assumptions and procedures of 'modernist' history and much
postmodernism which has partly led Richard Price fundamentally to
question in this study the extent to which postmodernism is compatible
with, and useful to, the very pursuit of history as a discipline.

As indicated, the book is organized in such a way as to reflect the coexistence among the contributions of shared assumptions and view-points and distinctive traits, emphases and, in some instances, points of difference. In Part One, entitled 'Theory', both Richard Price and Eileen Yeo take vigorous issue with those 'linguistic turners' who have offered largely decontextualized, unitary and uncontested notions of language. Insisting that language is plastic, multivalent and contestable, Yeo nicely illustrates her case with reference to changing and conflicting linguistic appropriations of the term, 'the People', from Chartism to Thatcherism. Price offers a careful, detailed and compelling 'critical interrogation' of the epistemological and methodological claims of postmodernism. His conclusion – 'I have yet to be convinced that postmodernism can deliver the promise of a better kind of historical practice' than 'traditional', 'modernist' historiography – can be seen as indicative of the book's findings as a whole. But Price and Yeo are not in complete accord. The latter historian, for example, generally perceives there to be more of value for historians in *some* postmodernist writings, especially those of Michel Foucault whose notion of discourse is, according to Yeo and Ali Rattansi, socially situated rather than non-referential or fully autono-mous in character.[7] In a similar way, and without by any means accept-ing the full body of ideas and assumptions associated with the postmodernist 'linguistic turn', the overall work of three of our con-tributors, Yeo, Karen Hunt and Susan Levine, does recognize the impor-tant, if by no means sole, influence of the postmodernist 'turn', associated particularly with Joan Scott, in focusing attention upon the partial genderblindness of 'traditional' labour history.[8]

The interplay of similarity and difference is also manifest in Part Two, entitled 'Gender'. In their very different yet equally perceptive chapters, the contributors to this part of the book, Hunt and Levine, draw attention to the ways in which, respectively, the language of British socialism – especially that of the Marxist Social Democratic Federation – before the First World War and the 'living wage' debate in early 1920s USA were heavily gendered. Hunt skilfully explores the contradiction between, on the one hand, socialism as a message of inclusiveness and universal emancipation and, on the other, its simulta-neous limitations or fractures along the lines of gender and race. The persuasive argument presented is that the primacy afforded by the SDF to class-based issues and forms of emancipation effectively marginalized important concerns and debates revolving around sex, feminism, and race. For example, and notwithstanding the formal commitment of many socialists to sexual equality, patriarchal attitudes and practices remained very strong within the SDF, and the party's stance towards the 'woman question' was ambivalent. Similarly, albeit in a less pronounced manner, the SDF failed fully to tackle racist, and especially anti-semitic, sentiments among some members.

In Levine's chapter the focus switches to contested definitions and measurements of a 'living wage', and especially the gendered dimensions underpinning such definitions, between employers and workers in early 1920s America. During the massive, bitter and protracted 1922 railroad shopcraft strike workers and their unions put forward the demand for a 'living wage' which was seen as consistent with the 'American standard' and with the rights of 'republican citizenship and welfare' – rhetoric which continued to exclude the black 'other'.[9] While the unions and workers articulated the classic 'family-wage' argument, equating the 'living wage' solely with the earnings of the male head of the household (which 'should be sufficient to support a family'), the employers adopted the opposing viewpoint that, in reality, the income of most working-class families was composed of the earnings of more than one member of the family. At the same time, however, both owners and workers agreed that the value of the family's wage 'depended upon the skills of the wife and her ability to negotiate an uncertain consumer market'. In effect, and notwithstanding their major economic and cultural differences of opinion, both organized labour and capital shared the same gendered assumption that working-class women were to be seen *primarily* as wives (and mothers) rather than as wage-earners.

Whether this assumption amounted, at least from the points of view of male and female shopcraft workers, to the primacy of patriarchy over class – of male power and domination and female dependency, support and inferiority overriding bonds of mutuality between the sexes – is open to debate. The evidence unearthed by Levine, and especially the material relating to the 'voices of women' (absolutely crucial, if much neglected subject-matter in the history of gender), would, however, strongly suggest that the priorities of the wives of shopcraft workers lay far more with their positive and rewarding contributions to family life and the support provided to their striking menfolk than with denouncements of patriarchy and the promotion of advancement for themselves by means of wage earning. As such, Levine's class-based conclusions provide a nice point of contrast, and a suitable springboard for critical engagement with, the predominantly 'patriarchy-first' emphases offered by Hunt.

Part Three switches the focus towards concentrations upon 'Community and workplace'. John Belchem is concerned historically to reconstruct and decode scouse – that 'blend of truculent defiance, collective solidarity, scallwaggery and fatalist humour which sets Liverpool and its inhabitants apart'. This endeavour involves due attention to, and analysis of, not only a pattern of speech but also of individual and social identity, of 'a micro-culture in historical formation', in which 'the ambivalence and tension between cultural representation and socio-economic materialism' is clearly revealed. Belchem's chapter is strongly informed by emphases upon the necessary contextualization of language, the complexity of the interplay between the 'linguistic' and the 'social', attention to the importance of demotic speech as well as the public–political text, and the questioning of Liverpool's 'proverbial exceptionalism' in terms of the development of modern British history. Unlike cockney – which has recently been superbly reconstructed historically by Gareth Stedman Jones[10] – scouse is revealed to lack 'a long and changing history', being seen, in important and challenging ways by Belchem, rather as 'a recently invented tradition, a cultural response to the city's decline'. Herein lies an invitation to historians to undertake further work on the narratives of social identity, both in relation to Liverpool and other modern British urban centres.

While scouse has frequently been associated with Liverpudlian humour, togetherness and defiance, then gossip, which forms the subject-matter of Melanie Tebbutt's innovative and stimulating contribution, has been described as the 'politics of the dispossessed and powerless'. Based upon participant observation and interviews, Tebbutt's chapter examines, through the medium of gossip, lecturers' responses to the profound and extremely unsettling changes (such as the onset of 'macho' management and budget cuts, mounting job insecurity, redundancy and 'proletarianization') which have affected the Further Education (FE) sector in England and Wales since 'incorporation' in 1993.

Largely focusing upon lecturers' evaluations of their managers in a single FE college, the author clearly shows both that the managerial rhetoric of empowerment, consultation, harmony and opportunity is fundamentally at odds with daily practice, and that overwhelmingly negative perceptions and experiences prevail among the teaching staff. The result has not been 'to eradicate opposition'; but neither has there so far occurred a massive upsurge in collective solidarity, militancy and radicalism. Rather, cynicism, demoralization, and mounting individualism and competition have characterized, alongside predominantly 'underground dissent', staff responses to change in the college under review. Tebbutt's finely nuanced, micro-study of the *complex* nature of 'worker' reactions to change should serve as an indispensable point of reference for scholars wishing more fully to understand the nature of workplace relations and change, and 'worker consciousness' in contemporary Britain.

In Part Four, 'Labour movements', Leon Fink and Roger Fagge also demonstrate the historical complexities of labour-movement development, language and worker consciousness. Forming part of a larger

project on intellectuals and organized labour in the USA, Fink's concern
rests with the nature and promise of social democracy offered to American labour in the inter-war years by W. Jett Lauck, economist and long-
time policy adviser to John L. Lewis, leader of the United Mine Workers
of America and 'father' of the mass-unionist Congress of Industrial
Organizations. Fink's elegant chapter skilfully traces the development
and nature of Lauck's social-democratic vision, combining 'democratic
planning' of the economy with rising living standards (the 'living wage'),
and the ways in which this vision increasingly assumed a position of
relevance and strength within the ranks of organized labour – as against
the older claims of 'voluntarism' – within the contexts of war, prosperity, depression and partial recovery. In turn, by the end of the Second
World War Lauck's progressive vision had lost much of its former
appeal in the face of the new economic orthodoxy of 'high consumption
divorced from structural economic reform'. Ironically, concludes the
author, 'the tables have turned again', the current era of globalization,
deregulation, downsizing and falling living standards for the once affluent US middle classes bestowing renewed relevance and promise upon
Lauck's call for 'minimum living standards, controls on investment
capital, and even an "economic United Nations"'.

Finally, Fagge's examination of workers' political identities in the
coalfields of West Virginia and South Wales during the first two decades
of the twentieth century makes (along with his book-length study of the
same subject) an important contribution to the development of the
growing field of comparative, cross-national labour history. The author
charts the existence in both coalfields of high levels of industrial conflict. However, whereas such conflict was increasingly accompanied in
South Wales by the development of a strong labourist class consciousness, as made manifest in the growth of the Labour Party, socialist and
independent labour politics made far less headway in West Virginia. In
the latter case, the miners' dominant political allegiances remained with
the two main parties, and their protests were expressed through a
'vague and loosely defined' appeal to 'American rights' and 'Americanism'. Fagge shows that the key to understanding the development of
these different identities 'lies in the contrasting social structures, cultural formations and power relationships within the two coalfields'.
Once again, a sensitively contextualized 'reading' of language and identity is seen to bring rich rewards. It is to be hoped that the work of
Fagge will encourage the much needed expansion of similarly comparative studies in the near future.

In conclusion, the various chapters in this book should convey to the
reader the fact that there exists a continuing tradition within labour
history which 'goes beyond' a narrow, largely male-dominated institu-

tional and descriptive perspective to embrace language and identity, culture and structure, evidence and concept, and description and analysis. Through critical self-interrogation of its premises, labour history stands revivified, displaying a keen awareness of fracture, differentiation and displacement within labour's past.

Notes

1. Neville Kirk, 'The continuing relevance and engagements of class', *Labour History Review*, 60, 3 (Winter 1995), pp. 2–15.
2. Patrick Joyce, 'The end of social history?', *Social History*, 20, 1 (January 1995), pp. 73–91.
3. See Chapter 2 by Eileen Janes Yeo in this volume; Kirk, 'The continuing relevance', p. 3.
4. Charles Tilly, *Popular Contention in Great Britain 1758–1834* (Cambridge, MA, 1995).
5. Kirk, 'Class and the "linguistic turn" in Chartist and post-Chartist historiography', in Neville Kirk (ed.), *Social Class and Marxism: Defences and Challenges* (Aldershot, 1996), pp. 121–6.
6. See Dorothy Thompson, 'The languages of class', *Society for the Study of Labour History Bulletin*, 52, 1 (April 1987), pp. 54–7.
7. Eileen Janes Yeo, 'Gender and class: women's languages of power'; Ali Rattansi, 'Race, class and the state: from marxism to "post-modernism"'; and Neville Kirk, 'Continuing relevance of class' – all in *Labour History Review*, 60, 3 (Winter 1995).
8. Joan Wallach Scott, *Gender and the Politics of History* (New York, 1988).
9. David Roediger, 'Race and the working-class past in the United States: multiple identities and the future of labour history', *International Review of Social History*, 38, Supplement 1 (1993), pp. 127–43.
10. Gareth Stedman Jones, 'The "cockney" and the nation, 1780–1988', in D. Feldman and G. Stedman Jones (eds), *Metropolis London: Histories and Representations since 1800* (London, 1989).

PART ONE
Theory

CHAPTER ONE

Postmodernism as theory and history*

Richard Price

Introduction

The shores of modern British social history have recently been lapped by the tides of postmodernism. During the course of a fierce and extensive theoretical and historiographical debate about the foundational assumptions of social history, an invitation has been issued to shake off the conservative wrap of positivism and 'engage with contemporary discourse on modernity'. There is nothing reciprocal, however, behind this proposal. It is not assumed that positivism has much to teach postmodernism; the task is defined as exploring 'what this discourse can bring to history [rather] than ... what history can bring to it'. That is, we are being invited to replace an epistemology of history that rests upon the idea of an observable, interrelated world of social reality with an epistemology that proceeds from the notion of a world of 'self-constitution, randomness and the reflexivity of subjects'.[1]

Neither modern British social history nor social history alone are unique in feeling the shifting weight of intellectual fashion and perception. Although the categories of social history are the most important target of the postmodernist critique, the whole project of historical study as it has been practised since the nineteenth century is also called into question by the postmodernist method. But British social history is a crucial field of engagement for postmodernism. For British social history in the recent past achieved a particularly successful combination of the empirical method and Marxisant theory. In this respect, then, it is a historiography that reflects the accomplishments of a modernist history, operating through the premises of positivism. As such, it is matched only, perhaps, by the *annalistes* as a standing rebuke to the theory and practice of postmodernism.

Although many historians are tempted to assume the obstinacy of Canute or the denial of the ostrich when faced with epistemological matters, it would be a mistake to refuse to examine what is being offered by this latest philosophical confection. The challenge of postmodernism is a challenge that deserves to be met. Postmodernists have some title to be modern day radicals and there is truth to their claim that historians tend to be conservative in their approaches, suspicious of theory or conceptualization. Those who worked within the Marxist tradition have good reason to know this. But it is also true that we should demand the most convincing reasons to abandon a historiographical tradition that rested on such deep and sturdy theoretical foundations as those provided by Marx and Weber. F.R. Ankersmit, who has some claim to be the most intelligent current philosopher of history and who is himself sympathetic to the new epistemology, has observed how 'no historical theory has guaranteed historical writing greater and better-deserved triumphs than historism'. This body of thought cannot be consigned lightly to the dustbin of history.[2]

Yet it is remarkable how easily the belief in a world that is rhetorically constructed has become received truth and how casually the modernist epistemology of an observable, knowable world has been sacrificed. The assumption that postmodernism has swept aside the reasoning procedures and operating categories of positivist social theory has not been thought worthy of much substantiation. We have been asked to take on faith the collapse of positivist assumptions, the irrelevance of class and the unreality of 'structure'. Indeed, the tone of the move known as the 'linguistic turn' is captured nicely by Patrick Joyce's impatient response to the attempts by other historians to interrogate his arguments. 'Times really have moved on', he claims. But times move in all sorts of curious ways, and any theory that claims to displace (at least) a hundred years of scholarship surely deserves to be tested, assessed and interrogated. It is the purpose of this chapter to explore the claims that postmodernism provides historians with a useful discourse.[3]

I wish to draw out the ambiguities, conceptual implications, and the logic that lay embedded within postmodernist approaches. The only way I know to do that is to adopt an inquiring gaze, to ask questions, to probe and poke the procedures and arguments heralded as insightful by postmodernists. This implies a largely *critical* posture towards the body of postmodernism that I have chosen to examine and the result may very well appear more negative than I intend. I am not concerned to write postmodernism out of our vocabularies of inquiry, even if my rating of its intellectual robustness is lower than is generally assumed. I do believe that postmodernism plays a useful role, if only in causing us to re-examine our epistemologies, in reminding us to beware of claims to absolute or universal truth. I also believe that postmodernism has worthwhile things to contribute to those of us who continue to work in the positivist tradition. But it is not my purpose here to provide a balanced account. I am concerned to test how postmodernist arguments fare against the kind of critical interrogation that we are entitled to apply to all propositions that make large claims.[4]

I shall therefore proceed in the following fashion. My arguments will pivot around the postmodernist thinkers and ideas that seem to be most important in the proposed reinterpretation of British social history, since it is this field that is my main focus of interest. In the process I shall have occasion to tramp discursively (adopting a core postmodernist procedure) elsewhere in the thickets of postmodernist discourse. But I shall make no attempt to confront all aspects of postmodernism nor shall I treat all its thinkers with equal attention. In the first section, I will contextualize postmodernism historically because this has important implications for its posture towards history and its usefulness as a source of historical categorization. In the second section I shall discuss its reasoning procedures as an essential way of evaluating the intellectual armoury and vocabulary of intellectual exchange that postmodernism seeks to deploy. The third section will explore the implications for the writing of history that is implied by postmodernist lines of thought. Finally, in the most important section, I shall address the strength of postmodernist epistemology and the persuasiveness of its theorization.

Contextualizing the postmodern

The idea of the postmodern lurked around the edges of the intellectual world for many years before it was taken up by French intellectuals and then captured by segments of the American academy. The first appearance of the term 'postmodern' in a book was in 1926; it was occasionally used in the 1930s and 1940s, and by the 1950s there was an anti-modernist movement in American poetry that labelled itself as postmodernist. Thus, from the beginning postmodernism was strongly associated with literary criticism. Only in architecture can one speak of a coherent postmodern style and definition. In other disciplines a marked instability attached to its meaning and it is best understood as a collection of intellectual postures towards representation and meaning.

But for historians postmodernism is almost entirely moored to the rejection of positivist notions of representation. This move, associated most notably with the writings of Roland Barthes, Jacques Derrida and Michel Foucault, shifted the idea that knowledge is a reflection of some external reality to the idea that knowledge is a discourse created by language. Although this theory of representation has long roots in Enlightenment thought, it is only under the particular conditions of the late twentieth century that it has been able to attain sufficient credibility to promise a redrawing of the boundaries of knowledge. There is both a political and technological dimension to the viability of this non-referential theory of representation.[5]

At the political level, there is an unmistakable convergence between postmodernism's emergence and the collapse of the belief systems of Marxism and communism. The collapse of viable socialist politics created a crisis of legitimation for many intellectuals. Marxism had begun to lose its political purchase as a critique of capitalism long before this, of course, and a growing political and cultural pessimism spread within left-wing politics beginning after the failure of 1968. Various intellectual fashions marked this path, but the general progression has been away from conventional Marxism and a reversal of paradigmatic assumptions from a system of belief that emphasized determination and possibility, to another that emphasizes indeterminacy and futility. But this shift (which seems to have been accomplished effortlessly by many intellectuals) was eased because it seemed to be in line with the way the world could be shown to work. Even in the sciences the new emphasis on 'chaos theory' contained resonances of the same themes. The end of the cold war marked the end of 'totalizing' nationalism and internationalism and the collapse of Soviet Russia marked the demise of a belief in the possibilities of positivist constructions of society. The linguistic turn was as much a rejection of Marxist structuralism as it was a positive embrace of literary theories of representation and knowledge.[6]

At about the same time, the technological potential and reach of capitalism began to change. Industrial production in the core countries ceased to be the marker of economic might and gave way to a system that was much more flexible and rested on the limitless and uncontrollable potential of electronic transfer and, therefore, on the knowledge that kept this system running. This meant, on the one hand, that goods could be produced without ever passing through a central co-ordinating 'factory'. On the other hand, it meant that the driving force of modern culture was not 'production' but the generation and control of knowledge. The role of capitalist techno-science in reshaping the conditions of modern society and individual identity lies at the heart of all postmodern theorizing. The central narrative of Lyotard's *The Postmodern Condition*, one of the founding documents of postmodernism, was the destruction of modernism by new technologies of knowledge. The Foucauldian focus on knowledge systems follows directly from the contemporary idea that knowledge production has replaced factory production as the centre of the new world political economy. In this context where the computer screen and the internet have added new dimensions to social interaction and communication, it is not surprising that new theories of how reality is represented were able to attain a purchase that they previously had not possessed.[7]

Thus, following from this reading of the technology of late capitalism, postmodernism describes modern society as a system where identity and meaning is *simulated*, where culture is entirely commodified, and where the division between the representational and the real (therefore) has been dissolved. In its most extreme formulation (that of Jean Baudrillard) contemporary capitalism is believed to displace entirely the distinction between the sign and the signified so that it is impossible to speak of reality separate from its own sign. Under this formulation, no distinction may be drawn between real and the hyperreal. Thus, it follows that for Baudrillard 'the idea of representation has become irrelevant. Labour, production, the political [all the things, in other words that historians think important] everything persists, but lacks all referentiality and is reduced to the status of a meaningless sign'. The fragmentation of the real, its reduction to semiological signs and to simulation has, according to Baudrillard, undermined the possibility of modern social theory which operated on the basis of a dialectic between subject and object.[8]

Baudrillard's presentist analysis of contemporary society is thoroughly typical of postmodernist thought. As Frederic Jameson has pointed out, postmodernism is the cultural logic of late capitalism and its particular theory of representation is tightly linked to the contours of contemporary capitalism. The logic of postmodernist arguments about the dissolution of representation by the techno-science conditions of modern capitalism and the subsequent collapse of reality into simulation suggest that it is *only* in late capitalism that a postmodern epistemology is possible. It is only in late capitalism that the opportunity has presented itself of reversing the relationship between the represented and the real so that culture and society themselves become entirely simulations.[9]

But if this is so we cannot assume that such a theory of representation has any meaningful explanatory role beyond our own particular epoch. Thus, in production-dominated modernist capitalism (say of the period *c.*1870–1975) an analysis of representation that privileges simulation will be quite pointless. In other words, until the late twentieth century all the epistemologies that proceed from an assumption that there is a reality to be described may be appropriate ways to explain society. It would be surely a contradiction to argue that a theory of representation that can only exist within the context of a totally commodified contemporary society can be applied to the past when the hyperreal and the commodification of culture in Baudrillardian terms did not describe the perceived relationship between things and signs.[10]

It is no surprise, therefore, that postmodernism does not look to history to understand the present, or to develop epistemologies that allow us to analyse past society. Indeed, in a very profound way, it rejects history as an explanation for anything. In this respect post-modernism represents a significant departure from the intellectual tradition of modernism, whose epistemology was rooted in history and from which it derived conceptual frameworks (metanarratives) for categorizing knowledge. It is these metanarratives that postmodernism insists on rejecting, consigning them to the category of knowledge systems that discipline and control thought, and that contain no essential meaning. In particular, of course, postmodernism is concerned to reject the various tyrannies that flowed from the claims of Enlightenment metanarratives to embody emancipation and reason. It is precisely this aspect of postmodernism that has been most powerfully applied against the conventional study of social history, particularly the notion of class. For Lyotard, there was nothing essential or progressive about the republican idea of the 'will of the people' which was equally capable of justifying the tyranny of Robespierre, Stalin or Hitler as it was the liberal democracies of republican France or America. Indeed, at one point, Lyotard even placed democracy as but one more resting place on a continuum with Nazism – a more 'discreet' totalitarianism, he described it. In postmodernism, then, the Enlightenment has been turned upside down; in place of being the home of emancipatory histories, it has taken its place in the pantheon of terrorism for its attempts to totalize knowledge.[11]

Yet there are very important ways in which postmodernism remains deeply embedded in the modernist tradition. Thus, the language of crisis, even apocalyptic crisis, runs through postmodern literature. But crisis is a concept that can only make sense within the notion of historical linearity. Indeed, the distinction between postmodernism and modernism is a lot less sharp than is usually assumed. The notion that postmodernism represents a new stage either of societal analysis (Baudrillard), or of an epistemological break (Lyotard) therefore grossly overweights the originality of its epistemes. Postmodernists have greatly exaggerated the extent to which they are engaged in a new enterprise. Many of the central assumptions of postmodernism are either already part of modernism or quite compatible with it. The critique of metanarratives, for example, lies at the core of postmodernist epistemology and supposedly represents the key departure from Enlightenment thought. Yet this same strategy was central to the Enlightenment tradition. Marxism, in particular, was always subject to this line of criticism and in history the founder of the modern historical method, von Ranke, was the ultimate postmodernist in his opposition to Hegelian metanarrative.[12]

In fact, it is important to highlight the failure of postmodernism to pay due attention to the space within the Enlightenment tradition for ambiguity, contradiction, and the pluralistic instability of meaning. These supposedly postmodernism values are integral to the patterns of thought we inherited from the eighteenth century. Enlightenment thought established scepticism as a primary conceptual tool, broke the hold of religious-based universalist theories of knowledge and opened the way for pluralistic alternatives of intellectual understanding. Thus, to dismiss the modernist scholarly tradition as the creation of essentialist metanarratives like 'class' or 'capitalism' is to ignore the fact that contention and multiplicity were also central to this intellectual tradition. Indeed, the case for modernism as an open and not a closed system of thought needs to be insisted upon. Pluralistic, dialectical and conflicting interpretations and meanings were integral to modernist narratives. We have only to think of the grand narratives and traditions of modernist thought, such as Marxism, to realize this. Modernism's potential to accommodate multiplicity of meaning, complexity and difference is capacious. These are precisely the values that postmodernism claims for itself but which in fact also belong to modernism.[13]

In this respect postmodern theory reveals its contempt for the past, as well as a thin theoretical shell. Historical themes and phenomena are decontextualized by postmodernism in a mindless coupling between past and present which abandons any sense of historical time. Thus, postmodernism collapses the boundary between interpretation and source, reducing history only to the understanding of the discourse that is revealed by a particular source. It was Roland Barthes who formulated the essential contradiction that allowed postmodernism to dismiss history in this way. For Barthes, history was merely a self-defining discourse that selects its 'facts' and then uses them to prove its various categories of signification. History thus becomes essentially circular: the referent is detached from the discourse and from this aloof perch governs the discourse.[14]

According to this presumption, source and interpretation are collapsed into discourse. The source ceases to be a description of something 'real' and is transformed into merely one more discourse to be deconstructed by the historian. In place of the notion that sources can be used to define the subject, the sources themselves become the subject and reading those sources is no different than reading the interpretations of historians. Historical argument is treated as the creation of a rhetorical structure which in its turn serves to endorse some versions and close out others. The main task of the historian is to expose the systems of power and authorizing that are contained within the particular rhetorical devices used to frame arguments. Thus, the important thing about Lefebvre's *Coming of the French Revolution*, it has been claimed, is the way the rhetorical structure of its opening 'forces the issue of passage [i.e. the 'coming'] in a particular way'. Similarly, the naming of certain periods and historical themes may be seen as an allegorical device designed to compel a certain strategy of choice in interpretation. The notion of class, the *longue durée*, or even the Renaissance may be reduced to this literary trope.[15]

Postmodernism's collapse of the distinction between past and present is part of its claim to read transgressively and to cross disciplinary boundaries. Postmodernism sees the configuration of disciplines as essentially ideological. In this reading nineteenth-century modernism imposed privileged procedures and ways of thinking on our knowledge of the world and marginalized other epistemes. Thus, in this respect, for example, there is no difference between the knowledge systems that gave us such disciplines as sociology, history and psychology and those that gave us astrology and magic. Rather than seeing disciplinary boundaries as practical means of handling the complexities of knowledge, postmodernism treats the hermeneutics of a field as determined by its procedures of inquiry. Postmodernist procedures are therefore designed to free thinking from the tyrannical constraints that characterized particularly positivist and scientific modes of thinking. This does not mean an established interdisciplinarity to reshape the boundaries of knowledge. It demands instead a subversion of established modes of perception and thinking and a refusal to be bound by the conventions and laws of traditional scholarly engagement. It is this that authorizes the practice of argument that pulls from disparate and unrelated sources, disciplines and chronologies.

But this failure to respect disciplinary boundaries ultimately fails to liberate. There are undoubted gains to be had from defying traditional intellectual procedures; it enables us to seek connections that may previously have been undervalued. Historians have always been major borrowers from other disciplines, but generally with due regard for the different procedures demanded by different fields of study. Postmodernism, by contrast, uses the method of the vandal, tramping mindlessly around, picking indiscriminately according to need or desire with no principles of selection that preserve an integrity to the process of interdisciplinarity itself. Postmodernism fails to recognize the multiple meanings behind the boundaries between disciplines. Boundaries between fields of study are not simply frontiers of control or strategies of policing. They speak to different use-interests and the different purposes of particular fields of study. It is not much help to read a novel through a telescope or to use the theories of astronomy to interpret historical documents. By the same token it does not assist meaning to reduce, say, the observable facts of astronomy to discourse representa-

tion. Different fields of experience need different forms of argumentation. Indeed, as Habermas has pointed out, at the end of a lengthy
critique of Derrida on this very point, 'the false assimilation of one
enterprise to the other robs both of their substance'. What is a useful
tool to make aesthetic judgements is not necessarily useful to critique
metaphysics. Neither rhetoric nor the field of study it is being used to
'deconstruct' benefit from this reductionism; both are diminished to the
point of meaningless.[16]

More seriously, perhaps, abandoning disciplinary boundaries also
means abandoning accepted standards of validation. This was both
amusingly and seriously revealed when Alan Sokal, a physicist at New
York University, wrote a satirical article arguing how quantum gravity
was a rhetorical construction. The piece was accepted (unrefereed by
any physicist) by a leading postmodernist journal as a contribution to
its issue on 'science wars'. The fact that Sokal's article was intentionally
nonsensical was completely lost on the postmodernist editors of *Social
Texts* until it was pointed out for them by Sokal himself, although the
title should have given the game away. Even a non-physicist using
modernist tools of logical reasoning and critical readings can detect
something very wrong with Sokal's argument. The fact that such an
article could be treated with profound seriousness by the intellectual
leaders of postmodernism in New York does not suggest any dishonesty
in their reading of this attack on the reality of quantum mechanics. It
followed quite naturally from the editor's contempt for logic and observation as the basis of reason and their elevation of metaphor and
rhetoric as the means by which meaning is secured. But even more
profoundly, the editors were quite comfortable with Sokal's spoof because the absence of logic was not taken to be a disqualification of
intellectual authenticity. The deep context of this episode is provided by
a notion of representation that is defined entirely around subject-based
rhetoric and metaphor. In such a system of belief, validity procedures
that depend upon logic do nothing to certify an argument. The principles of reasoning and validation that most of us live by in our everyday
life and in our scholarly worlds can therefore be avoided by postmodernism.[17]

Reasoning procedures

Systems of thought must be judged in part by the way they deploy
arguments and the extent to which their reasoning procedures can
sustain critical inquiry. The question must be asked of postmodernism:
what is the character of its reasoning procedures? The first thing to

strike one about postmodernism's reasoning procedures is the absence
of any system of refutation. By contrast, modernist metanarratives had
built-in systems for qualification or refutation. Marxism can be con-
futed as a predictive system, as has been endlessly pointed out. Positivism's system of empirical verification allowed for its refutation by the
very failure of its own laws. We do not need to hold postmodernism to
a strict Popperian standard that a hypothesis be entirely refutable to be
respectable. Binary alternatives do not measure the validity of a theory
or explanation. On the contrary, theories are evaluated by the depth
and extent of their explanatory scope and the more complexity and
nuance they allow the more impressive they tend to be. By this standard, the labile openness proudly centred as the prime virtue of
postmodernist writing is auspicious. But even the most casual glance at
postmodern writing reveals how the promise of an intellectual capa-
ciousness turns out to be a deadening system of closure. The problem is
that in abandoning convention, postmodernism substitutes assertion for
reason and denies the possibility of critical engagement and evaluation.

As one of the most influential postmodernist commentators and as a
major source for British social historians who have boldly taken the
linguistic turn, Jean Baudrillard is an appropriate case to examine in
this respect. Baudrillard's writings can accommodate a wide variety of
readings. He can be read as perpetrating one enormous joke – and we
can only dismiss that possibility because there is not one hint of humour
or light subtlety in his writings. Baudrillard himself has been quoted as
remarking how his reflections on America – reflections that are often
read as sociological descriptions of postmodern capitalism – are basi-
cally fictions. At various times his work can claim to be science fiction,
social theory, metaphysics, truth and fiction. But the instability of
Baudrillard's positionings are mirrored through a style of presentation
that is characteristically postmodern.[18]

We cannot call his remarks an 'argument' because they lead us into a
bizarre intellectual world where major terms are left undefined, where
hyperbolic and declarative modes of reasoning prevail with 'a contempt
for facts and definitions, [and] a style that is equally reluctant to give
concessions to the demands of the concrete and a grand vision that
develops distinctly metaphysical overtones'. Baudrillard 'totalizes his
insights, refusing to qualify or delimit his claims. He writes about
particular experiences, television images, as if nothing else in society
mattered, extrapolating a bleak view of the world from that limited
base. He ignores contradictory evidence such as the many benefits
afforded by the new media'. Thus, we are taken through a sustained
series of *ex-cathedra* pronouncements which proclaim, for example,
Disneyland as the 'objective profile of the United States' whose purpose

is to convince us that the rest is real 'when, in fact, all of Los Angeles and the America surrounding it are no longer real, but of the order of the hyperreal and simulation'. In this schema not only is Los Angeles, with its real 12 million inhabitants, its real pollution and its equally real vibrant cultural life, treated as an imaginary, but the rest of America in all its amazing diversity is distilled into a few square acres of commercialized leisure.[19]

Baudrillard's collapse of the real into signs raises the distinction between signified and sign to a new level of arbitrariness and denies the availability of criteria to evaluate his work. There is general consent that Baudrillard's arguments fail the validity test for accuracy, but this does not matter. 'It is no longer a question [for Baudrillard] of the false representation of reality (ideology), but of concealing the fact that the real is no longer real, and thus of saving the reality principle'. Certainly, the reality principle is not much in evidence in Baudrillard's work where impression and anecdote provide the foundations of an argument which is then treated as if it were true. Even sympathetic commentators on Baudrillard agree that, in the words of Rojek and Turner, his arguments are shallow, 'literally out of this world' and that in making them he frequently 'gets away with murder'.[20]

Baudrillard's style of asserting a broad truth without any apparatus of empirical data or reasoning is a mainstream postmodern method even if some formulations are more impressive than others. The Harvard philosopher, Hilary Putnam, has noted how in the work of Jacques Derrida arguments are presented by allusion rather than given and how 'his own writing style consists of one assertion after another'. It is characteristic of postmodern theory, then, to present a series of assertions which possess no serious architecture of reasoning. There are circumstances in which such a procedure may be justified. But the important question for historians is whether such a system of argumentation can be of much help in understanding historical processes? Those historians who find postmodernism insightful and useful for their epistemologies must recognize that this model of historical insight or reasoning at least needs some explanation and defence. Only very infrequently does one find attempts to grapple seriously and extensively with such questions as: when and how exactly did modernist arguments and precepts become falsified or inappropriate? How did class cease to be an economic and political formation?[21]

Indeed, proceeding from postmodern assumptions historians are beginning to make some very large assertions about the end of class and the demise of positivist reasoning procedures. Some examples from a recent reader on *Class* by Patrick Joyce will serve to illustrate the point. Joyce reproves postmodern sociologists Alan Touraine and Zygmunt

Bauman for modestly confining their new sociological concepts to the present and not pushing them into a reinterpretation of history. Joyce claims their work reveals

> a general perspective on the **processual** nature of social reality [which] suggests itself as of as much use in interpreting the past as the present, especially when it so successfully reveals the tendency of traditional accounts to privilege structure over process in interpreting the very past these accounts purported to describe.

This assertion then becomes the authority for a critique of 'traditional notions of the dichotomy of structure and culture, objective and subjective and so on'. Although no explanation is offered of this sweeping away of a massive corpus of history and sociology, Baudrillard is trundled forth as a supporting source. But we have already suggested the problems of using Baudrillard as the source of historical conceptualization: he is, after all, the most presentist of all postmodernist commentators, and anyone who can reduce American culture to Disneyworld (a reduction that might be an effective polemical trick, but hardly qualifies as serious sociology) has well earned his place as the most dubious of all postmodernist 'theorists'.[22]

This tendency to erect large propositions – such as re-writing social history – on rather narrow conceptual foundations is revealed again in the same source by Joyce's use of an extract from Rosemary Crompton's book *Class and Stratification: an Introduction to Current Debates*. At the very end of the extract quoted, Crompton rightly points out that

> in the late twentieth century, a criticism that is made of both authors [Marx and Weber] ... is that such arguments place too much emphasis on the significance of economically determined classes at the expense of other, competing source social identity such as nationality, gender, locality or ethnic group. In short, it is argued, nineteenth-century sociology cannot adequately grasp the complexities of late twentieth-century behavior.

This extract serves as Joyce's authority for the claim that positivist sociology can describe neither nineteenth- or twentieth-century social structures. But Crompton's remarks read more in the nature of an aside, and it is stretching them to suggest as Joyce does 'the possibility of a radical rethinking of the founding propositions of sociology, and social theory more generally, "society" and "class" amongst them'. Nevertheless, proceeding from this basis, Joyce then goes on to make the even more radical claim that 'if [nineteenth-century sociology] does not describe contemporary reality can we be so sure it describes the reality of the times in which it grew up?' Rushing over the admission that Crompton did not really suggest this, Joyce's succeeding qualification that, of course, classical sociology *sometimes* did well describe the society 'that produced them, but the point, precisely, is that they were a historical product and not a neutral analytic' hardly eases the reader's stunned confusion. We have been led to believe that a certain proposition – that positivist social science is invalid as a descriptive force – is the basis for a new, radical sociology. We then encounter the admission that, yes, sometimes positivist sociology **did** describe society well (although no criteria is suggested as to when this was the case), but this admission is immediately neutralized by the assertion that the important thing about sociology is its ideological content anyway.[23]

The absence of principles of validation and the denial, too, of boundary markers and controls within which reasoning and argumentation can take place imposes a formidable barrier between postmodern and other kinds of epistemologies. The consequences can be illustrated by an example from one of the most liberal-minded of the postmodernists, Jean-François Lyotard. In *Toward the Postmodern*, Lyotard raises the accusation against history that it operates on the basis of *exclusions* and that, by contrast, postmodernism assumes *no privileged standpoint*. Thus, in an (interesting) article about the strait-jacket of positivist interpretations of revolution, the argument proceeds to demonstrate history as pure invention. History 'serves the constitution of a performative power' and the historian who categorizes Robespierre (for example) is staking out an exclusionary power position just as Robespierre did when he claimed to speak for the will of the people. Indeed, in his role as the excluder of evidence, the historian is likened to the terrorist:

> in rejecting instinctual processes that he [the historian] deems deviant, superficial, irrelevant, ancillary, or contingent, this reality-definer destroys no less information (be it only by omission) than does the Jacobin politician when the latter rejects as conspiracy, treason, plotting, or at least irresponsibility anything in the information he receives that might force him to modify what he declares to be the reality.[24]

Where does this passage take us as historians? The first thing that strikes us is postmodernism's claim to liberate history from the evaluative responsibility of the 'privileged standpoint'. But what does this mean in practice? It means a freedom from rules and the privilege of arbitrarily borrowing from any sphere or discourse without attention to its relevance. It also means a self-referential approach to history. Having dismissed the historian's tendency to categorize and systematize, Lyotard then goes on to argue that it is futile to label any historical phenomenon in anything except its own terms. Indeed, it is more than futile, it is terroristic and abusive. Thus, the historian's tendency to 'name' social movements prescribes what they are and 'makes decisions for the social body'. But, Lyotard claims, things cannot be labelled beyond their own terms and we 'must stop letting ourselves be abused by the phraseology of Reason. When Robespierre … pronounces Reason, the word affirms order and power'. Yet if we abandon what Lyotard calls history's exclusionary privileges then we cannot adopt an interrogative posture towards historical subjects – they must be taken on their own *subject centred* terms. This it should be noted is precisely what Patrick Joyce does in his postmodernist *Democratic Subjects* where his treatment of Edwin Waugh and John Bright fails to move beyond what they themselves thought of themselves and where explanation occurs entirely within that self-referring context.[25]

The difficulty we have in making this critical observation is that it rests upon a concept of 'reason' that possesses little force for postmodernism. Modernist modes of thought use reason to access our understanding of 'truth'; they depend upon an understanding of reason that allows it to be separated from its subject. Postmodernism refuses to grant reason this status and in this respect draws upon the Nietzschean and Heideggerian traditions where the possibilities of reason are regarded as the myth of the Enlightenment. In this context possession of knowledge is not the condition of liberation or emancipation but merely the identity card of a certain power relationship. Furthermore, the obsession with knowledge as a rational discourse is merely, as Heidegger put it, 'the stiff necked adversary of thought'. It is important to realize the consequences of the denial of reason as a basis for discourse and communication. Two such consequences are worthy of brief mention.[26]

The first is that postmodernism leads inevitably to a total relativism in which there is no difference in quality between any identity, arguments or, as some postmodernists suggest, species. Thus, as Habermas has rightly pointed out, postmodernism's denial of reason as a route to truth (however difficult reason may be to attain), leads to the position that a principle can be accessed only by evocation. But evocation is a deep force which, by its nature, is not subject to demonstration beyond the word of the person proclaiming it. The advantage of this position, of course, is obvious: it is neither subject to verification by anyone else, nor is it necessary to defend by arguments or reasons that are dialogic. Historians who use postmodernism should explain why such a procedure has more power for historical insight than the principle of 'reason'.[27]

Historians cannot practise their trade without some agreement on the notion of truth that reaches beyond just the writer or reader. The same demand does not apply to the writer of fiction, poetry or those who see the world through a series of simulated metaphors. Both Foucault and Derrida in their different ways have thrown into question the possibility of truth: Foucault in his emphasis upon the way truth is a function of the power structure of knowledge systems, and Derrida by his emphasis on the absence of a final signifier and the ultimate instability of meaning. Hilary Putnam has aptly captured the consequences of Derrida in gentle reproving manner when he pointed out that although Derrida may disclaim a nihilist interpretation or intent to his work 'the thrust of [his] work is so negative, so lacking in any sense of what and how we should construct, politically or otherwise, that it is difficult to exonerate him completely from responsibility for the effect of his teaching'. And, in particular, although Derrida may express horror at the way some of his teaching has been used to deny the categories of rightness and truth, the argument that reason is repressive does contain the very clear danger of providing 'aid and comfort for extremists ... of all kinds ... Our task is not to repeat the mistakes of the twentieth century. Thinking of reason as just a repressive notion is certainly not going to help us to do that'. [28]

As Putnam's last sentence suggests, a second consequence of the postmodernist abandonment of reason is to open the way to political nihilism. The boundaries between knowledge and politics are collapsed; no distinction need be drawn between knowledge and politics; the possibility of knowledge controlling politics is denied. The uses to which this procedure may be put can be illustrated by the treatment of Heidegger and de Man's attachments to fascism at various points in their careers. In both cases the defence of their actions rested upon a sophisticated moral relativism. As Habermas has demonstrated, Heidegger evaded accepting responsibility for his actions as Nazi-appointed University Rector by detaching 'his actions and statements altogether from himself as an empirical person and attribute[ing] them to a fate for which one cannot be held responsible'. De Man never spoke of his fascist writings. Once they were discovered an exquisite postmodernist defence was mounted by Derrida in an exercise known as 'strong misreading'. Strong misreading, as it is explained by Dominick La Capra, is a technique which involves reading a text in terms of the multiple possibilities contained within it and that may not even be realized by the writer. Thus, the text 'is indeed rewritten in terms of possibilities that were under exploited or even unexplored by its author and perhaps remained submerged in the text'. In this manner, Derrida was able to read some of the offending pieces as subversive of anti-semitism and fascism, implying that perhaps de Man was a secret resistant and inferring that de Man ceased to write for the collaborationist newspaper once German censorship became explicit. What is especially condemning in both cases is that neither Heidegger nor de Man took responsibility for their actions, nor did they enquire as to the relationship between those actions and their philosophy.[29]

Postmodernism rejects standards of ethics that purport a universality. But this does not have to lead where Derrida seemed perilously near to resting in his defence of de Man. Thus, Zygmunt Bauman has addressed the question of whether postmodern ethics are possible and has arrived at the only possible conclusion – that only in individual particular cases can ethical judgement be exercised in the postmodern world. Bauman's arguments make the strongest possible case for the possibility of a postmodern ethics. But this is not of much help to historians who have traditionally tried to navigate between a recognition of the immediacy of politics and an understanding of its threats to truth and fairness. It is this passage that postmodernism threatens to divert. We can argue about the appropriateness of postmodernism's claim that this traditional perch of the historian is an irrelevant nonsense. What we need to register is the kind of politics that postmodernism injects into our processes of historical reasoning.[30]

Conservatism

As an ideology of late capitalism – the capitalism shaped politically by Ronald Reagan and Margaret Thatcher – it is hardly surprising that postmodernism has strong affinities with conservative politics. It was, after all, Margaret Thatcher who first brought to public attention Baudrillard's claim that there was no such thing as society. The dismantling of the political economy that supported labour rights was the most obvious expression of this philosophy and, indeed, a generally contemptuous attitude towards the popular classes and their politics is increasingly characteristic of Baudrillard's pronouncements. We should not be surprised, then, to find powerful affinities between traditional conservative approaches to history and those who swim in postmodernist streams.[31]

Postmodernism draws from an anti-democratic philosophical tradition. Nietzsche's views on democracy as the triumph of slaves and a slave mentality and Heidegger's Nazism as a reflection of his contempt for western Enlightenment-based thought are both well known. But the main target of postmodernism in modern British history is the hopeful and high-spirited social history of the 1960s whose agenda lay within the tradition of 'modernist' progressive politics. Ironically, the development of this social history opened the way for postmodernist rejection. For the tendency of social history of this era was to highlight alternative and multiple identities which had the unintended result of undermining its metanarrative assumptions like class. But, of course, the discovery of other identities is not in itself a reason for the denial of class which is the purpose of postmodernist social history.[32]

For those who are interested in explaining class as a function of external forces that determine 'its' passivity and powerlessness, Baudrillard is an appropriate intellectual mentor. The emphasis in Baudrillard is on the passivity and controlled nature of the masses and the influence of media whose simulation of reality defines the self, reduces choice and ends notions of free will and liberty. Although Baudrillard's arguments about the end of society refer specifically to contemporary America, his contempt for the 'masses' and the nihilism that underlies his arguments makes him a particularly effective battering ram against the historiography of the 1960s and 1970s whose *raison d'être* was largely the recovery of the 'lost' experience of ordinary people. His silent majorities are victims, denied any 'social referent of the classical kind (a people, a class, a proletariat)', and are reduced to a passivity he perversely and quite absurdly turns into resistance. Similarly, his notion that the social has come to an end means a state of political passivity in which the information of the information age does not allow empowerment, but an even more neutralizing force creating 'an inert mass impermeable to the classical institutions of the social'.[33]

Pessimism and stasis as regards social progress and change underlie the politics of postmodernist thought. Conceptions of social processes that are inflected with postmodernism are similarly limited. Foucault's history, for example, points in this direction. In spite of an impressive intellectual apparatus, Foucault's conception of history is ultimately conservative and constricted in the best postmodernist tradition. Thus, his emphasis is entirely upon the history of power from the standpoint of those who exercise it. In this schema, there is no room for a dynamic reciprocity in the creation of social stability or social relations; the central narrative is subjugation. Foucault is not interested in explaining knowledge systems as the product of a social process; he is interested only in describing the genealogies and the internalities of various discourses. If we are to explain social integration within the context of Foucault's model, we can only do so by seeing power as internalized by every individual. This was precisely where Foucault was moving in his later years with his notion of governmentality which proposes the protean nature of state power in everyday life. This may be an interesting alternative to the Gramscian notion of power. But the trap of governmentality is precisely the trap of all Foucault's history: that it absolves the historian from developing typologies that can explain the differentials in power between individuals and groups, and reduces the problem of state power to a function of the individual rather than history.[34]

Thus, historians touched by postmodernist winds usually end up writing history that forefronts the forces of privilege and established authority even when their subject is supposedly subaltern groups. History that defines representation as proceeding entirely from language will inevitably tend to privilege those who control the major ways in which language meaning is expressed. To admit language meaning as contested is immediately to admit a dialogic view of language which cannot be confined to a bizarre world of signs divorced from social reality. A reluctance to adopt this broadly Bahktinian view of language is the reason why there are powerful affinities in British social history between those who wish to remove class as a social force from nine-teenth-century politics and the overtly conservative political history revisionism of historians like J.C.D. Clark. Clark's view of class, for example, is that it is merely an intellectual construct of language and that the story of classes is as much a story of intellectual biography as of any economic and social reality. Both conservative and postmodern revisionism share a view of history as the unruffled exercise of élite authority.[35]

But the conservative logic of postmodernism's history extends beyond its tendency to privilege the forces of authority and power. In spite of its claims as a radical intellectual challenge, postmodernism's methodological biases parallel in many respects the traditional prejudices of the historian. A truly postmodernist history, for example, is most of all a fragmented history (which does not mean, however, that a fragmented history is inevitably a postmodern history): only the small pieces of previously held metanarratives can be understood. But postmodernists take this narrowed approach to history even further than the traditional empiricist researcher reporting on his or her portion of the archives. The rejection by postmodernists of the metanarrative undermines the possibility of contextualizing: it is impossible to say that this or that historical event was part of this or that wider movement. Thus, the postmodernist enthusiasm for local history, for micro-history. The historical project under a postmodernist regime, it is claimed, can only be to 'gather the leaves that have blown away and study them independently of their origins'. Social historians, of course, have been particularly guilty of looking for the trunk of the tree – although they also have been the foremost practitioners of localist history – in the mistaken belief that it was possible to explain the 'essence' of a particular movement, of what it was 'really' about. The postmodernist method is to reject this possibility, to put the 'historical scraps' at the centre of attention.[36]

But if there are similarities between postmodernism and the traditional view of history as possible only in fragments, there is a powerful and important difference. Postmodernism rejects the possibility that we may re-create the past by the appeal to sources which allow us to transcend the distance between the past and the present. The tendency of postmodernism is to replace a reading that puts the historian outside of historical time with one that abandons metaphors of observation and proposes to absorb the past into the self of the historical subject or even the historian. In this respect, too, postmodernism reveals its conservative implications. For if we abandon the metaphor of the observer what means do we use to 'read' the past? Few have given much attention to this question, but one of the most perceptive postmodernist thinkers has suggested 'nostalgia' as an appropriate category for such reading because it is respectful of the distance between past and present, and allows an authentic imagined past through 'dreaming' rather than through an attempted reconstruction. This is, in fact, a creative and intriguing suggestion, but whatever its virtues it is admitted to result in a very conservative view of the past. The nostalgic past is 'a silent and static past inhospitable to the clear and forceful patterns of historical evolution that the historist always likes to discover in the past'. It is a view that emphasizes stability over change, fragmentation over coherence, genealogy and micro-history over synthesis.[37]

Theorization

Zygmunt Bauman – frequently quoted as the leading postmodernist sociologist – has remarked that the usefulness of postmodernism as an intellectual construct will ultimately be judged by its ability to provide a theorizing discourse. I would add to this formulation that it should provide a framework whose persuasiveness competes with those epistemologies that it aims to displace and replace. This is particularly true if, as is the case, postmodernism is posited as a superior epistemology to an intellectual tradition that drew upon many sources of thought and over two centuries developed an extensive and elaborate theoretical bibliography. Any assessment postmodernism claims to offer useful historical insight must, therefore, ultimately rest upon an evaluation of the strength and plausibility of its theoretical framework and architecture.[38]

It is particularly difficult to know how to judge the persuasiveness of the postmodern project because, as Neville Kirk has pointed out, postmodernism is more a field of debate than anything else. Nevertheless, the crux of postmodernism's claim to distinction from other epistemologies is its notion that representation is purely a matter of language. As Hans Kellner has put it, in contrast to the modernist view of the observer peering at a knowable world, postmodernism posits the idea that 'language constitutes the knowable world, limits the ways in which we can know and represent it, and offers us as natural what is in fact conventional'. Or, in Patrick Joyce's words: 'Taking language as the model of culture ... conceives of language not as passive and reflective, but as active and constitutive. Language does not correspond to a social referent outside it'. If we are to rest large historical arguments upon this separation of the signifier from the signified, we need to see how the notion survives interrogation. Such interrogation is quite conventional; one has only to recall the problematizing of the Marxist base-superstructure concept in the days when that was a central theoretical construct.[39]

Postmodernist procedure as it has been used by historians most commonly derives its theoretical authority from the Genevan linguist Ferdinand Saussure. It was Saussure who first offered the argument that signifier and signified stood in a separate and independent relationship. But the authority of Saussure is not quite as unproblematic as it is usually and casually portrayed. Saussure's book itself, *A Course in General Linguistics*, presents us with a nice postmodern dilemma of the relationship between author(ity) and reality. For his book was not really 'his' book, but rather what two graduate students reconstructed from their lecture notes after his death. The problematic of attribution continues to plague this document. Saussure turns out to be a poor authority for the arbitrary nature of language and meaning.

Saussure was himself a modernist who sought a metanarrative of linguistics that contained ample space for social and material forces. He insisted that the uses of language could only be contextualized within material reality, that 'speech gave presence to the world'. It does not seem to have been Saussure's intention to elevate the principle of the arbitrariness of language to define all the facets of meaning, yet this is precisely the extension that has been drawn by critical theorists. Indeed, for Saussure language only assumed meaning when it drew distinctions that were widely shared and therefore were seen as describing 'things' in a way that found broad agreement between people. Thus, 'the social fact alone can create a linguistic system. The community is necessary if values that owe their existence solely to usage and general acceptance are to be set up; by himself the individual is incapable of fixing a single value'. And again, 'language is a form not a substance'. Reading Saussure does not provide clear evidence for the kind of separation of language from a social 'reality' or for an arbitrariness from social convention that is projected by postmodern theorists. In this respect, there are good reasons to suspect that those like Derrida and Barthes who define the use of language entirely around arbitrariness violently misread Saussure who always understood the parole as a material force. If this is so, then it must throw into question the seriousness with which we should regard their arguments. [40]

In addition, the status of Saussurean linguistics within the field of linguistics itself has never been unchallenged and is today regarded as being of mainly historical, but still significant, importance. Bahktin and others, for example, grounded the sign in cultural contexts; Benveniste critiqued the notion of arbitrariness in the 1950s and Kristeva added the role of psycho-social factors. Linguists have moved the basic problem of knowledge far beyond Saussure, even if it is formulated in a way that would be familiar to Plato: how can we know so much having so little experience to learn it? Linguists recognize that this is not a problem that can be solved by reference to literary tropes or metaphors, but by appealing to cognitive science. Likewise, they understand that language change – such as that between middle and modern English in the sixteenth century – is not arbitrary and can only be understood historically. In these respects it then becomes quite easy to show how limited is the postmodernist theory of representation. Thus, at a very early age children learn more about language without actually engaging in it than they ever will again. If the literal connection that postmodernists posit between language and reality were sufficient to explain 'reality' then this would be quite simply impossible.[41]

If the view of reality as the product of language is not taken seriously in linguistics, nor will it endure serious philosophical inquiry. Postmodern theory operates at an exceedingly low level of philosophical integrity. The limits of postmodern thought are soon reached and what postmodernists seem to regard as profundity turns out to be banal shallowness. Postmodernism claims to reject the idea that there is one objective reality out there which we can describe by one meaning if we are clever enough. But this is a false formulation of what modernist thought required and a specious description of what historians or others actually do. We have already alluded to the dialectical openness of modernist epistemology. Any historian who put forward his or her interpretation of the outbreak of the First World War as the complete description of how that happened would be highly unlikely to find much acceptance. Thus, to 'identify the collapse of one philosophical picture of representation with the collapse of the idea that we represent things that we did not bring into existence is, quite simply, dotty'.[42]

It is possible, therefore, to disarm the postmodern version of knowledge with an alarming simplicity. As Hilary Putnam has pointed out, the idea that reality cannot be described apart from our descriptions of it does not lead to a truth that there are only our descriptions. We may have named the stars, but our naming did not create them, anymore than naming travel in miles per hour determines the fact that light travels at a certain speed. Gravity is an identifiable and recognizable force that can be measured outside of anyone's particular perception of it. Language may decide what we call these things, but there is no meaningful extension from this to the claim that language also determines or captures fully the existence of those things. For the postmodern theory of representation to fail we only have to admit that language cannot entirely describe the existence of an event or phenomenon, that meaning is not parochial to language. As both Putnam and John Searles have argued in different ways, arbitrariness is not the way words actually attain meaning; they gain meaning because they explain a recognizable context and the more reasonable they seem within that context, the more they will be accepted. Once we accept this, the way is open not only for an external reality to exist, but also for concepts like 'class' or 'the state' to endure outside of our particular naming of them.[43]

Postmodernist theory ignores the concrete practices of communication, rests all social experience and knowledge on the domain of language alone, denies referentiality and (in some formulations) collapses the signifier and the signified. Postmodernism therefore closes off the possibility of social theory. There is no way out of this dilemma. The most intelligent of postmodernists can only offer the consolation that 'the postmodernist mind is reconciled to the idea that the messiness of the human predicament is here to stay'. But the messiness of the world is true at all levels of analysis. Postmodernism is forced to argue the superiority of a purely local analysis, either in ethics as Bauman has done – where transcendent moral issues are denied – or in terms of historical practice where only the complexity of the local and the immediate are legitimate. Those categories that reach beyond the local, like class, state and capitalism, whose complexity is of a different order, are disabled by postmodernism. Thus, two feminist scholars speaking of Lyotard remark how 'there is no place ... for critique of pervasive axes of stratification, for critique of broad-based relations of dominance and subordination along lines like gender, race and class'. It remains to be shown that we can write a better kind of history without such categories than with them; that, we might say, is the challenge facing postmodernist historical wisdom.[44]

In place of a history underpinned by various kinds of social theory, postmodernism offers a subject-centred view of the historical process. The self turns out to be the central analytical category of postmodernism. As far as the 'professional' historian is concerned, of course, this attribute is the ultimate boundary transgression, for it promises a subjectivist focus either on the subject of study or the historian her or himself. In this model notions of seeking objectivity through a distancing from the sources or the process are abandoned. Thus, Hans Kellner finds it unproblematic that historians are

> showing less reluctance to speak of what actually happens in their
> work of representation [and] are ... returning to an earlier practice
> of unashamed, interventionist, authorship. That earlier practice of

historical writing, before professionalization had established the standards of nineteenth century science as epistemology and the realist novel as literary model, has been the center of attention for many students of historical discourse.

Thus, is von Ranke dismissed and Sir Walter Scott privileged as the exemplar of the historian's discipline in a process described by LaCapra as the 'return of the repressed.[45]

The logic of eliding the social and the self has been taken furthest, perhaps, by Cornelius Castoriades who has proposed reducing the notion of society and social forces to that of the 'imaginary' of the individual. As a model for historical writing this notion has been used by Patrick Joyce in his book *Democratic Subjects* to project a history of nineteenth-century popular radicalism through the biographies of John Bright and Edwin Waugh. Joyce identifies directly with Castoriades, claiming 'in the understanding of Castoriades and of myself, society and "the social" are the outcome of [an] imaginary' which (as Castoriades describes it cited by Joyce) is 'the unceasing and essentially **undetermined** ... creation of figures/forms/images, on the basis of which alone there can ever be a question of something'.[46]

Castoriades reduces all representation to imagination and symbolism. Thus, history is a matter of individual psychological representation: 'history is essentially poiesis, not imitative poetry, but creation and ontological genesis in and through individual's doing and representing/ saying'. Institutions are not social formations, but structures of symbolism and society cannot be understood as a series of functional arrangements because this way of thinking cannot answer the question 'functional to what end?' All the key categories of society for Castoriades are the result of imagination; like Baudrillard, he sees the social world as a system of signification and nothing more. Similarly, representation cannot be separated from the subject: 'it does not belong *to* the subject, it *is* to begin with the subject ... Representation is not tracing out the spectacle of the world, it is that in and through which at a given moment a world arises'. The world and reality are in a state of constant impermanence and flux, dependent only on the passing cognitive processes of the individual.[47]

In adopting this position, Castoriades distils the final essence of postmodernism. The laws that govern the physical world are ignored. All reason is abandoned; no reciprocity between language and the external world of life is permitted and there is no room for social praxis. Most importantly, only the validity of the rhetorical statement is allowed. There is no way of testing the truth of the semantic world aside from its own statements: no place for the 'accumulation of knowledge that would affect the previous interpretation of the world and burst a given totality of meaning'. Much of this is reflected in Joyce's treatment of Waugh and Bright whose self-referential social worlds are never tested beyond their own self-referring conceptions. What reason do we have to believe this to be a superior model of historical praxis to one which started from the individual within the social context?[48]

We arrive here at the final difficulty of using postmodernism as a source for historical insight. Confusing the distinction between the self and the social, and collapsing the boundary between representation and reality, produces a depthless history and at best a weak and inferior conception of social processes. Postmodernism cannot allow profound explorations into the past because in its various iterations it ultimately reduces all experience to the constructions of discourse, power and knowledge systems, and the expression of those systems through the self alone. The practice of history thus becomes essentially an exercise in tracking the knowledge system adhered to by the historian writing about a particular event rather then the event itself or even the significance of the interpretive insight the historian brought to the particular event. Thus, it is explained,

> the story of the historical subject is inseparable from the historical knowledge being produced. Separating subjectivity from objectivity ... is an arbitrary, if not violent, act. It not only obliterates the narrator in the process, but determines the situation of the reader. The reader cannot enter the process and is reduced to a passive, dependent role'.[49]

It is a natural extension of this collapse of any distance between historian and history to reduce the concept of 'experience' to the particular ideological system that produced its categories. Such an exercise (recently proposed by Joan Scott) is especially fatal to the practice of social history where the recovery of the 'experience' of historical subjects constitutes the foundational concept. But to deny the possibility that historians can reclaim and use the evidence of experience makes impossible any kind of history other than the production of history itself. A narrowed and somewhat shrivelled kind of history would result from this prescription. It also requires a self-proclaimed subjectivity in our historical practice that refuses to admit any possibility of distance. Yet it is 'experience' in the sense of an actual encounter with an external presence that is most commonly appealed to in both everyday life and historical procedures as a form of validation that a certain position of belief is 'true'.[50]

The postmodernist approach to history rests upon a conception of history that reduces it to another form of literary fiction. For Hans Kellner, the historians tendency to categorize and periodize is an act of repression that merely evades the recognition that historical writing is just another kind of rhetorical figuration. In place of the idea of the historian gazing at a world that can be recovered and known we are confronted with the historian as the creator of that world through his or her language and authorial role. But like other attempts at post-modernist theorization, this attempt to fold history into fiction also turns out to be easily dispersed. The claim that literary models can be seen as in some way independent of and prior to history is neither sound factually or conceptually. Thus, as Ankersmit has argued, literary models themselves can be problematized as dependent on history be-cause 'fiction' as a category can only operate on the basis of a 'histori-cal' description (or imaginary) of an event. To rest a historical epistemology on literary theory is therefore to engage in a violent reversal of the evolution of different literary forms. It is only on the basis of a sense of the past, of a desire to record and to explain the past that fiction itself can exist. Indeed, if this is true, then the more common conception of history as a visual gaze on the pictures of the past may be a better way of framing historical epistemology after all.[51]

To construct history only through the arbitrary means of language and metaphor is also to deny the possibility of history as a multilayered, intertextual set of relationships between the various spheres of social experience. Postmodernism collapses the deep layers of the past; it drains the past of a multivariate complexity and disintegrates 'past reality ... into a myriad of self-sufficient fragments'. The boundaries of history contract to the history of the historian or subject and their discourses alone. History becomes the history of an interpretation and its purpose is to uncover the narratives that lie buried in the texts or the historians' own works rather than to construct new narratives. Under this regime history is narrowed to historiography and intellectual his-tory where the apparatus of literary criticism becomes the gaze of historical inquiry, and Hayden White's four metaphoric tropes become the confining prison of historical interpretation. It was one of the strengths of modernist thought to encourage deep explorations of the interconnections between the various spheres of society. The logic of dissolving the boundary between representation and reality – of accept-ing society as an imaginary or a simulacrum or a knowledge system – is precisely to surrender that procedure. As Ankersmit has pointed out, to treat history as a rhetorical discourse is to abandon the idea of actual historical data and to leave open only the possibility of history as literary trope.[52]

It is, therefore, an (ironic) consequence of the literary exemplar of historical writing to effectively deny entry into large areas of human experience. One thinks of literature as expansive in its explorations of human existence, but disguised in the cloak of critical theory this possibility is confounded. This is true both in the subjects it allows us to write about and in terms of how we understand relationships within and between those spheres and subjects. So far, it is really only 'identities' in one form or another that have been opened out for the historian by postmodernist methods. Nobody would wish to deny this gain. But there are many other spheres of history where the yields from postmodernism are less certain. If there can be no economic reality aside from a represented reality, for example, there is no point in studying patterns of international trade, or the relationship of the ice-cream industry to Mediterranean economics. Thus, from this perspective the important thing for the postmodernist about Braudel's monumental work on the Mediterranean world in the age of Philip II is how the rhetorical structure of the book makes the argument and, not, for example, the insight that the closeness of mountains and hot coasts allowed the early development of the ice-cream industry in Italy. Unlike Braudel, however, postmodernism offers no guidance on how to comprehend the historical linkages between the dry thirsts that were slaked by snow water or ice-creams in the hot Mediterranean lands and the trade and commercial networks they spawned and sponsored.[53]

As a result, postmodernist history cannot possess the scope or sophistication of the modernist history it seeks to replace. Indeed, it is a commonplace observation amongst even sympathetic commentators that to date the postmodern corpus as a whole is shallow, provisional, pockmarked with huge absences and, most of all, attached to a profoundly thin theoretical apparatus. It is precisely the exclusion of the kinds of question instanced above that comprises the conceptual superficiality of postmodernism and the impoverished model of the historical imagination that it offers. To the contrary, it was precisely the virtue of modernism to allow for the possibility of historical inquiry into the kind of complexity instanced by Braudel. Postmodernism invites historians to shift from a complexity that we inadequately order and try to grasp, to a chaos which is tautologically produced and described only by word systems.[54]

Conclusion

It may be claimed that the arguments presented here are of no force against postmodernism since they proceed from a different concept of social communication. Postmodernism rests upon a conception of the world that is poeisis, metaphor and fiction and cannot therefore be judged by criteria like logic and reason. I do not think we need to grant such an argument. Since postmodernism epistemology has imperialist claims that include not only history but also the sciences, it must be able to sustain convincingly scrutiny from various lines of inquiry. But even if we granted postmodernism an exemption from the analytical categories of modernism, we would still be obliged to ask the question: what kind of history is produced by postmodernist theory and does it provide better answers to the kinds of question historians are interested in than histories based on modernist and Enlightenment principles? This is the question I have been concerned to probe.

My answer to that question must be clear. I do not wish to be dogmatic in rejecting out of hand all postmodernist suggestions or approaches, and I remain committed to an open mind on the subject. But to be quite plain about it I have yet to be convinced that postmodernism can deliver the promise of a better kind of historical practice. I am particularly impressed with the way postmodernism would simplify and remove the kind of complexity and interconnections from the historical process that are allowed and encouraged by positivist and modernist theories of society. Any accounting of the advantages and disadvantages for historians in adopting postmodernist theories must come to terms with this balance and with the losses that will be incurred in discarding modernism. This chapter has attempted to do that: it has subjected postmodernism to the kind of critical interrogation that has always been integral to the intellectual tradition of the Enlightenment and modernism, and to the treatment of its epistemologies. It is for everyone to decide for themselves how the balance sheet shall be tallied.

Notes

*   My thanks are due to Adele Seeff and David Lightfoot for helpful readings of this piece and to John Belchem for suggesting it in the first place.
1.   Patrick Joyce, 'The end of social history?', *Social History*, 20, 1 (January 1995), pp. 73, 82, 90; James Vernon, 'Who's afraid of the linguistic turn? The politics of social history and its discontents', *Social History*, 19, 1, (January 1994), pp. 82–97. Also, Patrick Joyce, *Democratic Subjects. The Self and the Social in Nineteenth-Century England* (Cambridge, 1994), pp. 1–23; Patrick Joyce (ed.), in *Class* (Oxford, 1995), pp. 8–9 for complaints that the historical establishment has ignored postmodernism.
2.   F.R. Ankersmit, *History and Tropology. The Rise and Fall of Metaphor* (Berkeley, 1994), p. 238.
3.   The easy assumption of the superiority of postmodernist conceptual arguments runs through the 'Introduction' to Joyce, *Democratic Subjects*, for example. The quote is from Patrick Joyce, 'The imaginary discontents of social history: a note of response to Mayfield and Thorne, and Lawrence and Taylor', *Social History*, 18, 1 (January 1993), p. 84. This is part of a

fierce exchange that was opened very bravely, as it turned out, by two American graduate students David Mayfield and Susan Thorne in 'Social history and its discontents: Gareth Stedman Jones and the politics of language,' *Social History*, 17, 2 (May 1992), pp. 165–88; Jon Lawrence and Miles Taylor came to the defence of Jones in 'The poverty of protest: Gareth Stedman Jones and the politics of language – a reply', *Social History*, 18, 1 (January 1993), pp. 1–15. Mayfield and Thorne responded in 'Reply to "the poverty of protest" and "The imaginary discontents"', *Social History*, 18, 2 (1993), pp. 219–34. See also Neville Kirk, 'History and post-modernism', *Social History*, 19, 2 (May 1994), pp. 221–40; Geoff Eley and Keith Nield, 'Starting over: the present, the post-modern and the moment of social history', *Social History*, 20, 3 (October 1995), pp. 355–64. Marc Steinberg, 'Culturally speaking: finding a commons between post-structuralism and the Thompsonian perspective', *Social History*, 21, 2 (May 1996), pp. 193–214.

4. The literature on postmodernism is enormous, and I shall make no pretence to cite all relevant pieces here. But for its relationship to history from an unreconstructedly materialist viewpoint see Bryan Palmer, *Descent into Discourse* (Philadelphia, 1990). See also, Raphael Samuel, 'Reading the signs', *History Workshop Journal*, 32 (Autumn 1991) and 'Reading the signs: Part II,' *History Workshop Journal*, 33 (Spring 1992).

5. For the cultural, political and historical context of postmodernism see Hans Bertens, *The Idea of the Postmodern. A History* (London, 1995), pp. 4–35; David Harvey, *The Condition of Postmodernity. An Enquiry into the Origins of Cultural Change* (Oxford, 1989).

6. See Joyce Appleby, Lynn Hunt and Margaret Jacob, *Telling the Truth about History* (New York, 1994), pp. 200–217. We should note here that the major philosophical thinkers associated with postmodernism – Barthes, Derrida, Catoriades, Lyotard, Baudrillard – generally made a very public migration from Marxism to postmodernism throughout the 1970s and 1980s which can be traced and comprehended in their published works. But historians who have picked up the flag of postmodernism seldom provide the same kind of explanations that allow us to understand the historical and philosophical reasoning that underlay their shifts from one book to the next and one decade to the next. Nor is it obvious why Castoriades or Baudrillard, or Lyotard *et al.* provide more persuasive epistemological inspiration to these historians than von Ranke, Collingwood, Marx, Weber. Indeed, the absence of reasoned explanation from individual historians for these often very dramatic shifts in focus and epistemology is the most disturbing feature of the phenomenon, although it is not inconsistent with the postmodern privileging of the notion of 'instability'.

7. Jean-Francois Lyotard (translated by Geoff Bennington and Brian Massumi), *The Postmodern Condition: a Report on Knowledge* (Minneapolis, 1984), pp. 3–14; Jean-Francois Lyotard, *The Postmodern Explained. Correspondence 1982–1985* (Minneapolis, 1992), pp. 17–19. For a postmodernist reading of the impact of modern technology on identity, particularly gender identity, see Alluquere Rosanne Stone, *The War of Desire and Technology at the Close of the Mechanical Age* (Cambridge, MA, 1995).

8. Steven Best and Douglas Kellner, *Postmodern Theory. Cultural Interrogations* (London, 1991), pp. 21–7, 114–34. Joyce appeals to Baudrillard

with increasing frequency, from the passing reference in 'The imaginary discontents of social history', p. 84 to a fuller attribution in *Democratic Subjects*, p. 4, 5-6, 11, 16–17. Mark Poster (ed.), *Jean Baudrillard. Selected Writings* (Stanford, 1988), pp. 1–9; Mike Featherstone, 'In pursuit of the postmodern: an introduction', *Theory, Society and Culture*, 5, 2–3 (June 1988), pp. 198–203; Douglas Kellner (ed.), *Baudrillard. A Critical Reader* (Oxford, 1993), pp. 7–9; Bertens, *The Idea of the Postmodern*, pp. 147–56. I leave aside here the key question as to how accurate or meaningful is Baudrillard's description of late capitalism.

9.   Frederic Jameson, *Postmodernism, or, the Cultural Logic of Late Capitalism* (Durham, 1991), esp. pp. 1–55. Michael Ryan, 'Postmodern politics', in *Theory, Culture and Society*, 5, 2–3 (June 1988), p. 560.

10. Roy Porter has suggested how Baudrillard's definition of late twentieth-century capitalism as defined by a morbid hysteria about consumption may be paralleled exactly during the eighteenth century. Similarly, Baroque culture of the seventeenth century was obsessed with a strong sense of the fragmented nature of social life producing anxiety around the subjectivities of self and practised irony and parody as the dominant rhetorical styles. See Roy Porter and Bryan Turner in C. Rojek and B.S. Turner (eds),. *Forget Baudrillard?* (London, 1993), pp. 3–4, 83.

11. Lyotard, *The Postmodern Condition*, pp. xxiv, 34–5, 81–2, 'I define postmodern as incredulity towards metanarratives' which he takes as the Enlightenment project but which is now being detonated in clouds of narrative language elements all different. And also in Lyotard, *The Postmodern Explained*, pp. 17–19, 52–6. Appleby, Hunt and Jacob, *Telling the Truth about History*, p. 205.

12. See Ankersmit, *History and Tropology*, pp. 44–74, 184–8, 238 for the relationship between modernism and postmodernism and how much of the postmodernist critique is prefigured by modernism. Also Bertens, *The Idea of the Postmodern*, pp. 245–7 for a discussion of this issue; Jurgen Habermas, *The Philosophical Discourses of Modernity* (Cambridge, MA, 1987), pp. 4–5. On the continuities between modernist and postmodernist history see Ignacio Olabarri, '"New" new history: a longue duree structure', *History and Theory*, 34, 1, (1995), pp. 1–29.

13. For an effective critique of Lyotard's notion of metanarrative see Ankersmith, *History and Tropology*, pp. 182–8.

14. Roland Barthes, *The Rustle of Language* (Berkeley, 1989), pp. 137–40. Anne McClintock's *Imperial Leather* (New York, 1995) is a good example of this tendency to collapse the distinction between past and present.

15. Hans Kellner, *Language and Historical Representation. Getting the Story Crooked* (Madison, 1989), pp. 63, 270–91.

16. Habermas, *The Philosophical Discourses of Modernity*, pp. 190–210.

17. Alan D. Sokal, 'Transgressing the boundaries. Toward a transformative hermeneutics of quantum gravity', *Social Texts*, 46/47, 14, 1 and 2 (Spring/Summer 1996), pp. 217–43. See also, Alan D. Sokal, 'A physicist experiments with cultural studies', *Lingua Franca* (May/June 1996), pp. 62–4; Stanley Fish, 'Professor Sokal's bad joke', *The New York Times*, 21 May 1996, p. 23; Michael Albert, 'Science, post modernism, and the left', *Z Magazine* (July/August 1996), pp. 64–9.

18. Kellner, *Baudrillard. A Critical Reader*, pp. 18–19.

19. Bertens, *The Idea of the Postmodern*, p. 156; Jean Baudrillard, *Simulacra*

and Simulation (Ann Arbor, 1994), pp. 1–42; Poster, *Jean Baudrillard*, pp. 170–72; Best and Kellner, *Postmodern Theory*, pp. 112–30.

20. Rojek and Turner, *Forget Baudrillard?*, pp. ix–xv; Best and Kellner, *Postmodern Theory*, pp. 130–34; Poster, *Jean Baudrillard*, pp. 167–70, 181. For some particularly egregious examples of the postmodern style of assertion see Jean Baudrillard, *The Illusion of the End* (Palo Alto, 1994), pp. 21–7. Thus, opening an essay on the end of history, Baudrillard asserts

> What has been lost is the glory of the event, what Benjamin would term its aura. For centuries, the keynote of history was glory, a very powerful illusion and which played on the ever-lasting nature of time ... That passion seems laughable today ... what we now seek is not glory but identity.

And then again: 'the prodigious event, the event which is measured neither by its causes nor its consequences but creates its own stage and its own dramatic effect no longer exists'. This is the 'event strike' the true end of historical reasoning. But, then again, 'what is stupendous is that nothing one thought superseded by history has really disappeared. All the archaic, anachronistic forms are there ready to re-emerge, like viruses deep in the body. History has only wrenched itself from cyclical time to fall into the order of the recyclable'.

21. Hilary Putnam, *Renewing Philosophy* (Cambridge, MA, 1994), p.109. Zygmunt Bauman is an honourable exception to this tendency (which is shamefully common amongst historians) to argue by assertion rather than by presentation, see Thomas Docherty (ed.), *A Postmodern Reader* (New York, 1993), pp.128–40.

22. Joyce, *Class*, pp. 3–7, 11–13, 71–2. For an intelligent discussion of the difficulties with the notion of 'structure' see William H. Sewell, 'A theory of structure: duality, agency, and transformation', *American Journal of Sociology*, 98, 1 (July 1992), pp. 1–29.

23. Joyce, *Class*, pp. 11–12, 54.

24. Jean-Francois Lyotard (eds R. Harvey and M.S. Roberts), *Toward the Postmodern* (New Jersey, 1993), pp. 90–92.

25. Lyotard, *Toward the Postmodern*, pp. 94–111. For a critique of Joyce's treatment of Bright and Waugh as self-referential see Richard Price, 'Languages of revisionism: historians and popular politics in nineteenth century Britain', *Journal of Social History* (Summer 1996).

26. Habermas, *The Philosophical Discourses of Modernity*, pp. 85–8 for Nietzsche; Appleby, Hunt and Jacob, *Telling the Truth about History*, p. 210.

27. Francis Fukuyama, *The End of History and the Last Man* (New York, 1992), pp. 297–8; Bertens, *The Idea of the Postmodern*, pp. 113–23; Appleby, Hunt and Jacob, *Telling the Truth about History*, pp. 207–10. For a discussion of this see, David M. Rasmussen, *Reading Habermas* (Oxford, 1990), pp. 109–13.

28. Appleby, Hunt and Jacob, *Telling the Truth about History*, pp. 212–13; Terry Eagleton, *Literary Theory. An Introduction* (Minneapolis, 1983), pp. 142–3; Putnam, *Renewing Philosophy*, pp. 130–32.

29. Habermas, *The Philosophical Discourses of Modernity*, pp. 155–60;

Jacques Derrida, 'Like the sound of the sea deep within a shell: Paul de Man's war', *Critical Inquiry*, **14** (Spring 1988), pp. 590–652; Palmer, *Descent into Discourse*, pp. 45–7, 189–98; Dominick LaCapra, 'History, language and reading: waiting for Crillon', *American Historical Review*, **100**, 5 (June 1995), pp. 816–18. Derrida's own depriveleging of writing over speech must surely be relevant to this.

30.   Zygmunt Bauman, *Postmodern Ethics* (Oxford, 1993).

31.   Joyce, 'The end of social history?', p. 81. Anthony Woodiwiss, 'The passing of modernism and labour rights: lessons from Japan and the United States', *Social and Legal Studies*, **1** (1992), pp. 477–91 for an interesting consideration of how the passing of labour rights in Japan and the United States was the product of the demise of a particular kind of modernist legal discourse. Poster, *Jean Baudrillard*, pp. 1–9.

32.   Fukuyama, *The End of History*, pp. 301–4; Appleby, Hunt and Jacob, *Telling the Truth about History*, pp. 206, 217.

33.   Bertens, *The Idea of the Postmodern*, pp. 187–9; Rojek and Turner, *Forget Baudrillard?*, p. xii; Poster, *Jean Baudrillard*, pp. 209–16. Douglas Kellner, 'Postmodernism as social theory: some challenges and problems', in M. Featherstone, (ed.), *Theory, Culture and Society* (1988), pp. 245–8.

34.   Habermas, *The Philosophical Discourses of Modernity*, pp. 286–91 for an effective critique of Foucault along these lines; Patricia O'Brien, 'Michel Foucault's history of culture', in L. Hunt (ed.), *The New Cultural History* (Berkeley, 1989), pp. 25–46; Graham Burchell, Colin Gordon and Peter Miller (eds), *The Foucault Effect. Studies in Governmentality* (Chicago, 1991), pp. 1–8, 87–104.

35.   James Vernon, *Politics and the People. A Study in English Political Culture c.1815–1867* (Cambridge, 1992); Gareth Stedman Jones, '*Industrie*, pauperism and the Hanoverian state: the genesis and political context of the original debate about the "Industrial Revolution" in England and France', paper given at Johns Hopkins University, 10 October 1994; J.C.D. Clark, *English Society 1688–1832* (Cambridge, 1985), pp. 91–2. For a treatment of language that emphasizes different and contested meanings see James Epstein, 'Understanding the cap of liberty: symbolic practice and social conflict in early nineteenth century England', *Past and Present*, **122** (February 1989), pp. 75–118. Gender is one area where contested languages may be clearly and easily demonstrated, see, for example, Sonya Rose, 'Respectable men, disorderly others: the language of gender and the Lancashire weavers' strike of 1878 in Britain', *Gender and History*, 5, (1993), pp. 382–97.

36.   Ankersmit, *History and Tropology*, pp. 175–8.

37.   Ankersmit, *History and Tropology*, pp. 196–211. Such a history would also repeat the postmodernist focus on the self.

38.   Zygmunt Bauman, 'Is there a postmodern sociology', in *Theory, Culture and Society*, **5**, 2–3 (June 1988), p. 217; Docherty, *A Postmodern Reader*, p. 139.

39.   See Neville Kirk, 'History and post-modernism', pp. 221–40; Joyce, *Class*, p. 6. Hans Kellner, 'Introduction', in F. Ankersmit and H. Kellner (eds), *A New Philosophy of History* (Chicago, 1995), p. 14.

40.   Ferdinand de Saussure, (eds C. Bally and A. Sechehaye), *Course in General Linguistics*, (New York, 1966), pp. 9, 15, 69, 74, 113–15, 122; Jonathan Culler, *Saussure* (London, 1976), pp. 25, 51, 70–72, 111–13.

Best and Kellner, *Postmodern Theory*, p. 20; Kevin MacHardy, 'Crisis in history, or: Hermes unbounded', *Storia Della Storiografia*, **17** (1990), pp. 5–27 for a defence of language as a social formation. Raymond Tallis, *Not Saussure. A Critique of Post-Saussurean Literary Theory* (2nd edn, New York, 1995), pp. 65–96 for the detailed argument that Barthes and Derrida misread Saussure.

41. 'Semiotics and literature', *International Encyclopedia of Linguistics*, pp. 408–12.

42. Putnam, *Renewing Philosophy*, p. 124.

43. Putnam, *Renewing Philosophy*, pp. 109–27. John Searles, 'Literary theory and its discontents', in W. Harris, *Beyond Poststructuralism* (University Park, PA, 1996), pp. 101–35 for a particularly effective critique of Derrida. For an extensive defence of the relationship between evidence, belief and truth see Susan Haack, *Evidence and Inquiry* (Oxford, 1995). Bertens, *The Idea of the Postmodern*, pp. 240–42.

44. Bauman, *Postmodern Ethics*, p. 245. Nancy Fraser and Linda Nicholson, 'Social criticism without philosophy: an encounter between feminism and postmodernism', in Docherty (ed.), *A Postmodernism Reader*, p. 419.

45. Ankersmit and Kellner, *A New Philosophy of History*, p. 6; LaCapra, 'History, language and reading: waiting for Crillon', pp. 799–800.

46. Joyce, *Democratic Subjects*, p. 4 after which Castoriades disappears from the argument.

47. Cornelius Castoriades (trans. by K. Blaney), *The Imaginary Institution of Society* (Cambridge, 1987), p. 331. It is interesting to note that Castoriades had begun to talk about society as an imaginary as early as 1964 and that this book was originally published in 1979. But two years before he was still writing in the materialist mode and I do not see the superiority of this postmodern Castoriades over the materialist Castoriades who appealed – in the manner of Edward Thompson – to the court of historical action to know what a subject was. See 'On the history of the workers' movement', *Telos*, 30 (Winter 1976–77).

48. Habermas, *The Philosophical Discourses of Modernity*, pp. 318–30.

49. Linda Orr, 'Intimate images: subjectivity and history – Stael, Michelet and Tocqueville', in Ankersmit and Kellner, *A New Philosophy of History*, pp. 90–105. The tendency to reduce history to the intellectual genealogy and biography of the historian is nicely illustrated in a piece by Lloyd Kramer that like so much other postmodernist interventions is essentially a deliberation of the work of other historians, in this case the founders of this method of doing history, Hayden White and Dominick LaCapra. Lloyd S. Kramer, 'Literature, criticism, and historical imagination: the literary challenge of Hayden White and Dominick LaCapra', in L. Hunt (ed.), *The New Cultural History* (Berkeley, CA, 1989), pp. 102–14.

50. Joan Scott, 'The evidence of experience', *Critical Inquiry*, **17** (Summer 1991), pp. 773–97.

51. F.R. Ankersmit 'Statements, texts and pictures', in Ankersmit and Kellner, *A New Philosophy of History*, pp. 238–9.

52. Ankersmit, *History and Tropology*, pp. 66–7, 158, 192–4. Dominick LaCapra, *History and Criticism* (Ithaca, NY, 1985) for the argument that history is about uncovering the narrative of the text.

53. Hans Kellner, *Language and Historical Representation. Getting the Story*

Crooked, (Madison, 1989), pp. 7, 60–63, 270; Fernand Braudel, *The Mediterranean and the Mediterranean World in the Age of Philip II*, vol. 1, (New York, 1976), pp. 27–9. For other references to the narrowing consequences of postmodern theory for historical study see, Bertens, *The Idea of the Postmodern*, pp. 187–9, 194; Best and Kellner, *Postmodern Theory*, pp. 177, 220.

54. Douglas Kellner 'Postmodernism as social theory: some challenges and problems', *Theory, Culture and Society*, 5, 2–3 (June 1988), pp. 251–7.

CHAPTER TWO

Language and contestation: the case of 'the People', 1832 to the present

Eileen Janes Yeo

To quote Bob Hoskins, 'it's good to talk'. Words or signs (which include non-verbal messages) are the medium of social communication. Yet the social nature of the process does not always receive proper attention from those taking the linguistic turn in cultural history. Sadly the turn at times gets itself into a twist which defocuses the sociality of language, inadequately patterns the historical evidence and, most importantly perhaps, tends to immobilize human agency both in the past and, by extrapolation, in the present. This chapter will propose a way of looking at language and discourse as contested social communication which can only be understood in the context of social relations in actual historical moments. To put the theory into practice, I will subject the resonant keyword and concept, 'the People' to this approach.[1]

I should, at the outset, indicate how I am using linguistic terms which do not always have agreed meanings. By discourse, I mean systems of knowledge or meaning which are not only articulated in books but are embedded in institutions (like families, hospitals and state apparatus of various kinds) and the conduct of social relations (parents and children, doctors and patients, voters and politicians for example). By language, I refer to systematic relations (often of binary opposition) between resonant keywords or images which convey a pecking order of human value. In this chapter one important contrasting couplet will be the People in relation to the masses. Rhetoric denotes, here, not overblown empty words but the language of persuasion, which became the subject for serious study and training from classical times onward.

Approaches to language in cultural history

Two fashionable approaches to language in cultural history conveniently, for my purposes, figure in previous important work on the People. First there is the tendency of postmodernism (discussed in Chapter 1) to see human beings as the relatively passive location of discourse (meaning here world view without its institutional embodiment), or to regard men and women as the convenient vectors of cultural narrative (which creates their identity and sense of self). In the introduction to *Democratic Subjects* (1994), where the main players inhabit a discourse of 'the "people" and "nation"', Patrick Joyce recants his earlier work where 'subjects are seen as constructing meanings, whereas meanings construct subjects'.[2] The key words which Joyce uses for expressing the relation of discourse to people, like the 'emplotment' and 'narrativization' of their lives, suggest people as somewhat passive playthings of cultural processes. But this is not the whole story for, in his analysis of historical figures like John Bright, Joyce shows that they actively reworked narratives in the context of dynamic social relations (of which language formed a constituent part).

Second, there is the tendency to see defining discourses as relatively inflexible and as carrying little diversity of meaning. The language of populism, as characterized by Joyce in *Visions of the People* (1991), far from being contested, moved in a unilinear direction precisely because it tended to be inclusive and non-conflictual. He describes populism as a

> set of discourses and identities which are extra-economic in character, and inclusive and universalising in their social remit in contrast to the exclusive categories of class. ... extra-proletarian identifications such as those of 'people' and 'nation' are involved. As well as, or instead of, conflict, chiefly evident are notions combining social justice and social reconciliation. The accent on social concord and human fellowship is very strong.[3]

By contrast, Gareth Stedman Jones sees the construct of the People as being more contested, in the sense of rival social groups wanting to annex it, when he writes about the political rhetoric of radicalism from the 1770s onwards. None the less, he fences it round with certain firm limits. He argues that this language of radicalism precluded class-consciousness because it was structured around the model of an evil political system characterized by represented and non-represented groups. Thus the rhetoric had an intrinsic inflexibility about it and became inappropriate from the 1840s onward when 'the conviction of the totally evil character of the political system itself began to fade and distress became less pervasive'.[4] A more sensational notion of the rigidity of language is that of Lyotard (described in Chapter 1) who junks the concept of the People as useless because it has been used both by democrats and by fascists.

I want to explore, for the rest of the chapter, how working with a different set of assumptions about language being plastic, multivalent and contestible can lead to different insights, and can at least account for the fact that, *pace* universal suffrage, the People is still a resonant part of political rhetoric in the 1990s. Since a ritual bow to theory

seems compulsory at the moment, I draw on a tradition of cultural and
dialectical materialism which sees language, not as a reflection of some
more weighty base, but as a vital part of the production of social life. I
especially acknowledge V.N. Volosinov who published *Marxism and
the Philosophy of Language* in 1929. Arguing against two asocial schools
of linguistics, Volosinov proposed language or signs as communcation
between social beings: 'signs do not arise between any two members of
the species 'Homo Sapiens'. It is essential that the two individuals be
organized socially that they compose a group (a social unit); only then
can the medium of signs take shape between them'.[5] He further argued
that signs are capable of carrying multiple meanings especially to different classes:

> Class does not coincide with the sign community, i.e., with the
> community which is that totality of users of the same set of signs
> for ideological communication. Thus various different classes will
> use one and the same language. As a result, differently oriented
> accents intersect in every ideological sign. Sign becomes an arena
> of the class struggle.
>   This social multiaccentuality of the ideological sign is a very
> crucial aspect. By and large, it is thanks to this intersecting of
> accents that a sign maintains its vitality and dynamism and the
> capacity for further development.[6]

What is helpful here is the idea that the vitality and dynamism of
particular signs are closely linked to their 'social mutiaccentuality', a
cumbersome term which means their capacity to carry different meanings for different groups of people. It is this mutivalency which should
alert historians to the possibility of contestation. Whether the key con-
tests are between social classes or not, seems to me to be a matter for
historical study rather than an a priori assumption or a foregone conclusion.

   Legitimating social and political discourses in any historical era offer
particularly glittering prizes. We should expect them to be contested,
extended, subverted and reworked in every possible way. Indeed the
more the discourses stress the universal attributes and rights of humanity, the more the instances of fracture between universal promise and
limited practice or application can be exposed and exploited in order to
push the discourse, language and rhetoric further down the road of its
democratic, universalizing and inclusive logic. But long before the advent of Enlightenment rhetoric about the rights of man, the concept of
the People was being contested. The People has been a central concept
indeed the legitimating authority in British political and religious thought
since the English Revolution. Even King Charles I, before he lost his
head, presented himself as the authentic voice of the People, in a contest

with a Parliament which insisted that it had this role. During the same decades different churches and sects were vying for the mantle of the chosen People whose voice was the voice of God.

Episodes in the history of 'the People': Chartism

Although there has been a continuous tussle about who should be included in or excluded out of the People, certain episodes in the nineteenth and twentieth centuries will preoccupy me here. The prelude to, then the agitations and the aftermath of, the Chartist period will be one focus of attention. I will go on to highlight patterns of usage which were previewed just after Chartism, which then developed more fully and which have become conspicuous again in the Thatcherite period of Tory government. Taking this longer chronological view can help to identify patterns of continuity and change and examine the flexibility or rigidity of certain languages as historical situations change.

During the agitation which delivered the 1832 Reform Act, the issue of who were the People was high on the political agenda. Conservatives clung to the doctrine of virtual representation, identifying the owners of landed property as the People to whom political rights and powers belonged and who would 'virtually' represent the rest. Reformers insisted that the People were the middle and working classes who together constituted the industrious or the productive classes, the favoured names. Obviously another type of virtual representation was at work here because one section of the people, the middle classes, would get the vote and represent the other which would remain disenfranchised; but at this point in time the issue was not as contentious as it would become.

How this changed is registered in the changing language of a reformer who later became a West-Riding Chartist, Abraham Hanson of Elland, a shoemaker and mechanic-preacher in the seventeenth-century mould, a local healer whose medical skill had been learned in the 'college of nature', and a keen thespian whose career culminated with the part of Last, the political cobbler, in William Cobbett's play, *Surplus Population*. In 1830, he made a speech which directly addressed the issue of the composition of the People:

> The only rational hope of restoring to the people their legitimate rights is a union of the people. For by a co-operation between the middle and lower classes of society a full, free and equal representation of the people may be obtained ... What constitutes a people or nation? According to my opinion, it is composed of that class of inhabitants who, by their moral and intellectual qualities, and

> active pursuits, form, as it were, the kernel of the population. It is
> this class that furnishes the standard of manners, intelligence, and
> all the useful arts that are necessary for man; – it is from this class
> that an opinion ought to be founded – it is in this that the national
> character centres. – (cheers, and cries of hear.) Then, I say, neither
> the highest nor the lowest class ought to be taken as a standard; for
> we cannot judge of a nation by its extreme luxury on one hand, or
> its indigent wretchedness on the other (hear, hear) and so it follows
> that it is not the extremes but the middle class, united with honest
> industrious labour, that constitutes a nation. Then I ask, is this
> body of the people fairly represented (no, no). I say 'No!' ... We do
> not wish to destroy one particle of the Constitution, but to restore
> it to its pristine vigour.[7]

An exemplary political speech of the period, it locates itself within
constitutional thinking, although on the radical wing which wants to
restore the constitution to its pristine purity (corroded by the Norman
Yoke). It points to the People as the middle and working classes, who
have pre-eminent moral and social value, furnishing the optimal standards of behaviour and qualities of character as well as providing, 'all
the useful arts that are necessary for man'.

By the Chartist years, Hanson had changed his tune. Like other active
Chartists he was probably disillusioned with the outcomes of the 1832
Reform which were experienced as an attack on the religious and
constitutional rights of labour and the poor: the Anatomy Act (1832)
which allowed medical mutilation of poor peoples' corpses, the New
Poor Law (1834) which separated families in the workhouse (thus
putting asunder those whom God had joined) and which punished
poverty as a crime and denied God's law to 'dwell in the land and verily
thou shalt be fed'. As oppressive was the transportation of trade unionists – the Tolpuddle martyrs and the Glasgow cotton spinners – and the
passing of the 1835 Muncipal Corporations Act which actually deprived many working people of local political rights and powers.

Chartists tended to evict both middle and upper classes from the
People, unless these groups showed a willingness to commit themselves
to the Charter, in which case they became 'friends of the People'. At a
large Peep Green demonstration in 1838, at which delegates to the
General Convention or People's Parliament were elected, Hanson now
made clear that only the labouring classes constituted the People, by the
will of God:

> 'Twas said that labourers could do nothing; and yet they were
> continually doing everything. (Cheers) ... They were everything to
> the higher orders of society – let them now try and be something to
> themselves. Their labour was the source of all property – they
> performed that labour by the physical power of their bodies – they
> derived that power from none but God, and therefore, they were

the unlimited proprietors of their own industry, and no one had a
right to tax that industry without their consent, or that of their
deputies. ... But the time was now come when the force of the
people was irresistible.[8]

This labour-value theology coincided nicely with radical constitutional-
ism which democratized the meaning of property into labour power
and juxtaposed the productive classes to the parasites.[9]

By 1842, as Dorothy Thompson has recently argued, the Chartist
understanding, which equated the People with the working classes, had
become common currency and was used in this way by Queen, Parliament and middle-class friends of the People.[10] The Chartist challenge
had extended the meaning of the People, indicating how contest insures,
in Volosinov's words, that 'the sign maintains its vitality and dynamism
and the capacity for further development'. However, the issue cannot be
left there. What now needs to be explored are the very different forms
of power relation embodied within rival constructs of this usage of the
People which have ramified ever since.

Whether it was the Queen in 1842 referring to 'my people' or parliamentary sympathizers depicting the suffering people, both constructed
the People as dependent and, in the latter case, ground down into a
state of misery which could foster either passivity or desperation. In
either case they needed leaders – from above. This stance was taken
most consistently and revealingly by the Birmingham Political Union
(BPU), spearhead of the Reform agitation in 1832 and coadjutor in
Chartism until the middle-class defection in April 1839. Clive Behagg
has perceptively analysed the language of banker Thomas Attwood, the
key leader in the BPU, showing that 'in Attwood's own nomenclature
the working class were always the "masses", but with the addition of
the productive element of the middle class they became the "people"'.[11]
Attwood could support universal suffrage as the only way to win 'the
hearts of the masses' but he was clear that the real task was to elect 'a
majority of men of business who understood the true interest of the
people, instead of lordlings and scions of nobility'.[12]

Repeatedly Attwood insisted, in different ways, that self-governing
popular movements could not succeed: 'there is no instance in history
in which political movements have been successful without leaders
and in almost every instance those leaders have been men of wealth
and influence'.[13] This same middle-class attempt at virtual representation within the People again proved a stumbling block when the BPU
stalwarts tried to launch a Complete Suffrage Union in 1843. When
Attwood was told that only an endorsement of 'those great and invio-
lable principles of political justice embodied in the People's Charter'
would win Chartist support, he responded: 'if I interfered at all in any

public movement it would be my duty to teach and guide, and not be taught and guided'.[14]

One large fracture in the understanding of the People was the split over whether working people would represent themselves and have the determining power in the social and political state or whether they would be led (or guided) by others. For working-class radicals of the period the issue of power relations ramified far more widely than formal politics, indeed arose in every area of social life – even in shopping. To patronize supportive shopkeepers and Chartist co-operatives became a test of political commitment, together with the attack on the truck system and the boycott of hostile traders.[15]

Chartists boasted of self-government within their movement, 'we have no rich men leading or driving us but, in the true democratic spirit, manage our own affairs'.[16] Their attempts to find democratic forms of internal organization showed their continual attention to the almost insoluble paradox of ensuring effective self-determination by working people who had little time and money to devote to democratic participation.[17] What they called their public (not mass) meetings democratized the county meetings of the eighteenth century and provided the occasion where the legitimate People could express their public opinion in a public (both visible and constitutional) setting.

In education, 'making every man his own lecturer' would prevent the emergence of 'a mere system of lectureship'[18] which, doubtless, would have pleased Attwood better. In religion, Chartists also challenged outside authority and substituted self-activity instead: 'The principles of social benevolence and justice, of civil equality and of political right, though recognised by the Bible, are denounced by the priesthood; and hence their determination to erect their own temples, and offer their own worship, to the God of Justice, whom they serve.'[19] The complex interplay between understandings of the People in terms of control from above or self-determination from below developed further in three key areas in the nineteenth and twentieth centuries in the post-Chartist period.

The People and the masses

The juxtaposition of the People to the masses, detectable in the language of the BPU, became increasingly salient in formal political discussion as working people slowly, incrementally, fought for and gained universal suffrage. As the next section will show, the relation between the two also became conspicuous in statements from the emerging leisure industries from the 1850s onwards. Most of the meanings of 'the masses' have been less than complimentary. Raymond Williams hit the nail on the head when he wrote, 'there are no such things as "masses", there are only ways of seeing people as masses'[20] and added that we never see ourselves as one of the masses but rather reserve that tag for others.

These others have usually been depicted as less than human, either as apathetic, inert and idle or else as aggressive and violent.[21] At moments of high Chartist excitement, activists repudiated the term 'the masses'. Reverend J.R. Stephens 'never said one thing to "the masses", as they (the Whigs) chose to call the people and another to the myrmidons of power'. But in later years, disappointed leaders started blaming the failure of Chartism, in reality its defeat, on the supposed character defects of their followers. George White reflected in prison in 1849, 'on the cold indifference of the masses – their willing slavery – their apathy and downright dishonesty. I next began to excuse them with that sublime and truly holy saying imputed to Christ: "They know not what they do"'.[22]

It was during the 1867 Reform Bill agitation that conservatives most consistently mobilized the language of the masses to demote the People. Reformers repudiated the term 'masses' but tried to dignify the People by now promoting them linguistically to 'citizens'. Thomas Carlyle, in 'Shooting Niagara', made the most spectacular use of denigrating imagery when he distinguished between 'a *wise* minority of *good citizens* and the masses', and characterized the latter as a stuporous species of low animal life, who 'lie torpid, sluggishly gurgling and mumbling, spiritually soaking in "the Devils Pickle"'.[23] Two years later, Matthew Arnold identified the violent potential of the 'populace' or 'vast residuum' as an awakening, beast: 'marching where it likes, meeting where it likes, bawling as it likes'.[24]

By contrast, the *Bee-Hive*, the voice of the organized labour movement, conflated the People and the citizenry by mobilizing the old arguments about the working classes being the source of national prosperity and insisting that they were 'entitled to the rank of citizens and to have the rights of citizenship conferred upon them' and in this way bring about 'democratic government by the whole people, for the whole people, the only way to prevent class ascendancy and produce general security and satisfaction'.[25] Populist Liberals like John Bright allied with the working class, indeed led the suffrage campaign, drawing on a rhetoric of the People which stressed its inclusivity. Yet, at the same time, the Liberal Party was increasingly building a political practice which gave the controlling role to the male middle class, in the running of local associations, in the planning of 'mass' meetings in or out of doors and in the spatial arrangement of the audience: largely middle-class ticket holders at the front, all-comers (working men) at the back and women in the gallery.[26]

The political and linguistic co-operation which delivered the 1867 Reform proved unstable, particularly as observers from above began to feel that the experience of party politics and of trying to 'educate our new masters' was supposedly revealing a large mass of recalcitrant people uninterested in becoming active citizens. Even some of the most democratic of the New Liberals in the decade before the First World War, especially after the Mafeking victory celebrations, became disenchanted with the People and linguistically transfigured them once again into 'the masses' or else stretched even farther back and reached for the concept of a 'mob-mind'. C.F.G. Masterman, in *The Condition of England* (1909), saw only the blurring of individuality in the city crowd:

> immediately the mass of separate persons has become welded into the aggregate, this note of distinction vanishes. Humanity has become the Mob, pitifully ineffective before the organised resistance of police and military, and almost indecently naked of discipline or volition in the comparison; gaping open-mouthed, jeering at devotions which it cannot understand, like some uncouth monster which can be cajoled and flattered, into imprisonment or ignoble action.[27]

The new discipline of social psychology, which developed from 1908 onward, scientificized the idea of the mob, arguing that the crowd had a 'herd instinct' or collective characteristics different from those of its individual members and that the crowd manifested animal behaviour like marked irrationality and potential for violence.[28]

It is worth pulling back from the historical material for a moment to notice a number of themes. First, that the masses or the crowd or the mob is always characterized in ways that make it less than fully human and therefore unable to think or act on its own behalf. Imagery to demote the masses includes depicting them as childlike, gaping, gurgling and mumbling rather than adult, rational and articulate; passive to the point of torpor and inertia almost like mindless physical matter; vegetating and usually rotting (especially in city slums), or at the opposite extreme, violent like an uncontrolled wild animal or supernatural monster. Obvious prey for demagogues ('the crowd remains, to-day as yesterday', according to Masterman, 'an instrument which the strong man has always used and always despised in the using') the real need was, as Attwood had earlier insisted, for proper outside leadership. Significantly within the view from above, even the concept of the People, now being juxtaposed to the citizen, was being rendered more passive and mute, again in need of outsiders to articulate its will and act on its behalf. 'The Multitude is the People of England', explained Masterman, 'that eighty per cent. (say) of the present inhabitants of these islands who never express their own grievances, who rarely become articulate, who can only be observed from outside and very far away'.[29]

Yet, within the socialist revival during the same decades, the language of the People as the useful producers and active makers of social and political life was still alive and well, although women had to remind male comrades that such rhetoric applied to them too (see pp. 69–70 below). Robert Blatchford, editor of *The Clarion*, and author of pamphlets which sold in their millions explained,

> Socialism says that England shall be owned and managed by the people for the people.
> Non-Socialism says England shall be owned and managed by some persons for some persons.
> Under Socialism you would have all the people working together for the good of all.
> Under non-Socialism you have all the persons working separately (and mostly against each other), each for the good of himself.
> So we find Socialism means co-operation and non-Socialism means Competition.[30]

The People and commercialized leisure

Another key feature of the masses or the crowd was their annoying preference for affluence, leisure (especially sport) and pleasure over work, improvement and politics. Thus Thomas Cooper the Chartist made his famous reference to post-Chartist working men as 'idiots leading small greyhound dogs'. Fifty years later, Masterman identified football as the quintessence of joy: 'see it in concentrated form when a selection of all the Saturday football crowds has poured into London for the "final contest" at the Crystal Palace for the "Cup," which is the goal of all earthly ambition'. Given the real choices for working people in capitalism, this might have been a very sensible set of preferences but it is also important to point out that, in an accelerated way from the 1850s onward, commerical entrepreneurs were developing leisure activities for profit and had a vested interest in mobilizing such propensities, even in creating them.

Commercial entrepreneurs now targeted a working-class market which had, to some extent, been revealed by preceding radical activity, and mobilized the language of the People as part of the project.[31] These commercial populists, particularly the new wave of publican-entrepreneurs called themselves 'caterers' in the double sense that they supplied food and also catered for the taste of the People. Billy Holland, the London music hall owner, named himself 'the People's caterer'. To begin with, their establishments were populist as well as commercial. Thus William Shaples refurbished the Star in Bolton on the model of a working-class cultural centre in 1843, adding to the standard concert room for music and dancing, a picture gallery, museum and menagerie, together with lectures on the exhibits and topical subjects. Similarly Charles Morton rebuilt the Canterbury Lambeth, usually seen as the first London music-hall, on the same pattern in 1854 with a hall, a library and reading-room and a picture gallery. The Sunday press, in the case of papers like *Reynolds News* and *Lloyds*, offered a rich mixture of radicalism and salesmanship.

However, as the leisure and communications industries grew, their fundamental logic began to conform more closely to the tendencies of other business enterprises. As ownership of music-halls became more concentrated and local music-halls developed into national chains of theatres of variety often called Empires, the formula for success became more tailored to protecting large capital investment, by standardizing the entertainment formula, by rendering its content inoffensive (so as to safeguard the licence), by making the audience more sedate in fixed seating, by establishing more control over the performers.[32]

What went along with the desire for a mass audience was the attempt to characterize the mass People – and then the invidious slippage, to say that the qualities assigned really exist and that the product supplied is a full measure of what is demanded and even an indication of what people are really like. One owner of a music-hall chain, Leweson, would supervise the performances from the wings while 'contemplating his patrons with an air of undisguised contempt'; another, Stoll, would watch audience reaction with his back to *his* performers and then stand outside Charing Cross Station with a notebook 'calculating the common denominator of a reformed popular taste'.

A staff writer described how the baron of the new cheap daily press, the owner of the *Evening News* (1894), the *Daily Mail* (1896), the *Daily Mirror* (1903), *The Times* (1908), Lord Northcliffe, saw the public as,

> A creature that slobbered over its bib and cooed with contentment over the results of races which it didn't bet on, and pictures of the underclothes of actresses in another continent, and the details of the weddings of royalties it had never seen. ... He felt that the public was like a great ape begging you to scratch it. ... Sometimes when he walked north of Regent's Park, towards Highgate, he looked at the rows of villas that were just running up, and told

himself that all those houses were alike, all those gardens alike; thus they must be let to people whose tastes were alike. If one could discover that taste one would be able to sell the same newspaper, all along the row, just as one sold the same quality of tea.[33]

This passage gives a clear picture of the hardening assumption of the clonelike quality of mass humanity and the possibility of hitting the commercial jackpot by supplying a standardized product to suit the identikit masses. Vice versa, it illustrates the commercial fantasy about there being a perfect fit between supply and demand and about how what is produced on the supply side can be taken to be a true pointer to human nature and desire: the standardized product reveals homogenized humanity. Or another elision, this time typical of high culture, or of élite cultural critics, is to assume that the media have the power to shape a supinely passive mass audience. This attitude was as conspicuous at the turn of the twentieth century as it is now in Baudrillard's postmodern contempt for 'the masses' supremely manipulated by media who define their values, choices and available identities (pp. 20–21 above).

The making of the English consuming masses from the last quarter of the nineteenth century onward is as important a subject for historical work as the making of the English working class. And a good deal of the shaping would have come from above. 'Giving the people what they want' has been a leitmotif of commercial rhetoric. But leaving it to the supplier to investigate, in characteristic ways, and decide what the People want has also become a key feature of the process. Market research of more sophisticated varieties than standing and watching outside a railway station developed in the twentieth century. Starting first in the United States, by the 1930s manufacturers in Britain were also commissioning surveys on the consumption of food, entertainment, media and glamour products, and they redoubled their efforts after the Second World War.[34] Since the suppliers (of commodities or politics) usually commission the inquiry, it is their agenda of questions being asked to people who are assumed to have no other way of registering their views. There have been other historical possibilities. In the working-class co-operative movement, before it succumbed to dominant commercial logic in the 1960s, the consumer-shareholders could express their views on what they wanted the store to stock at the quarterly members' meetings. Mutual forms made theoretically possible the production and marketing of commodities and services for self-articulated need and desire.

Twentieth-century patterns: the abstract People

By the early twentieth century some characteristic patterns had formed around the People and a connected cluster of terms. At one extreme, the People had become an abstraction, a way of depicting numbers unlimited of people and citizens but in a passive pose so that they were unable to speak for themselves or act on their own behalf. This inability has immediately created the need for very concrete groups of outsiders to decipher their will and carry it out. Characteristic twentieth-century élites, who have defined the People in this way, and then have to step in and represent them, have included sections of the state (government, bureaucrats, political parties), newspaper magnates, consumer kings, and social science experts.

Paradoxically, the public opinion polls came into existence to counteract this trend but ended up helping to accelerate it. Thus George Gallup and Saul Forbes Rae, in 1940, called attention to nationwide political parties and mass media and observed that,

> inevitably, these new agencies of communication gave those who controlled them the power to influence as well as to express public opinion. More and more voices claimed they spoke for the people. Powerful newspapers called themselves the true *vox populi*. Glib party leaders declared that their policies were inscribed in the hearts of the American working man. Motion-picture and radio executives asserted their belief that at last 'the public was getting what it wanted'. As the old equality of participation gradually disappeared, the voice of the common man grew faint in the din and clatter of other voices speaking in his name.[35]

Gallup and his associate argued that true democracy was not simply about voting but involved a 'process of constant thought and action on the part of the citizen' which called for

> participation, information, the capacity to make up one's own mind. 'The people', it has been truly said 'must understand and participate in the basic ideas of democracy if these ideals are to be defended against attack. They must learn that it is not shibboleth but a vital truth that the state is their own, that they are free citizens with rights and responsibilities'.[36]

Yet the form of democratic participation being proposed was the exact opposite of what had been developed by working people one hundred years before when they fought their way into and extended existing political forms. Public opinion, once considered to be the views of the active People expressed in a visible setting, usually a large public meeting or a smaller quarterly meeting, was becoming the view elicited from a representative but passive cross-section of the People interviewed

behind closed doors in their own privatized homes by the employees of
a commercial organization which framed the questionnaire. Opinion
polling, in the longer historical perspective, appears a decidedly trun-
cated way of enabling 'the American people to speak for themselves'.

Moreover, the view which sees as the healthy social state pollsters
and others mediating the inarticulateness of the People also redefines
older modes of public self-representation as disorder. The idea of the
People as the British nation who became most responsible and legitimate when they remained the silent majority and allowed their will to
be articulated by their prime politician was put clearly by Brighton MP
Sir Julian Amery when he boasted of how 'the British people are regain-
ing confidence in themselves. It is the people who have done this. What
Margaret Thatcher's Government has done has been to show them the
way, and to put their basic instincts into words'.[37]

This view erects the People as an overriding tribunal of appeal to
discredit militant sectional activity of any kind: by class, gender, race or
region. Visible during the turbulent years preceding the First World War
with their explosive cocktail of labour, suffragette and Irish militancy,
this movement of language received enormous impetus from 1917 when
Bolshevism did not seem to be safely contained in one country. Government ministries and owners of the tabloid press (the two coalescing in
Lord Beaverbrook) deliberately created a discourse to bring militancy
into disrepute. To convey an interest more legitimate and comprehensive than labour's they used a barrage of roughly synonymous words
which have done service ever since: the (great) British People (public),
the general public, the community as a whole or at large and the nation.
In fact so pressing was the threat of labour militancy that by 1919
women were being moved over linguistically into the camp of true
public opinion because 'they steadied public life in this country and
stemmed the tide of socialism, Bolshevism and unrest'.[38]

The most aggressive uses of 'the People' to discredit labour have
continuously targeted striking miners. During the General Strike of
1926, for example, the Government's *British Gazette*, run by Winston
Churchill, presented itself as relying 'on reason, public opinion, and the
will of the people', and presented the strike leaders as a body of men
who 'represent only a section of the public and have derived no authority from the people comparable to that of the House of Commons'.[39]
Prime Minister Stanley Baldwin spoke of 'the Government' as the custo-
dian of liberty: 'The laws of England are the people's birthright. The
laws are in your keeping and you have made Parliament their guardian.
The General Strike is a challenge to Parliament and is the road to
anarchy and ruin.' Lord Balfour spoke of methods 'to dispossess the
people of their Parliamentary liberties and to hand over our national

heritage to be squandered amid incalculable suffering by violent and irresponsible doctrinaires'.[40] More extreme still, the *Daily Mail* mobilized the old bogey of outside, indeed nearly foreign, agitators when it celebrated the routing of 'extremist leaders with heads stuffed with theories which emanated from half-witted Germans and Russians such as Marx and Lenin' and two days later when it boasted in one breath of the defeat of Germany in the World War and of the destruction of 'the internal cancer introduced by aliens'.[41]

In a famous remark of July 1984, Margaret Thatcher drew a parallel between the Falklands War and the miners' dispute and, like the *Daily Mail* in 1926, talked of having 'had to fight the enemy without; but the enemy within much more difficult to fight was just as dangerous to liberty'. This enemy within were not only violent Marxist extremists different from 'the best of British' (the working miners and their housewives), Thatcher told the Conservative Party Conference in October, but, as in Balfour's rhetoric, they were out to destroy the 'framework of the law ... the common law (enforced?) by fearless judges and passed down across the centuries. It was legislation scrutinized and enacted by the Parliament of a free people ... No government owned the law. It was the law of the land, the heritage of the people'.[42] Not only were trade unionists different from the People in the present but they were repudiating the whole history of the People from time immemorial! Chartists would have made short shrift of this equation of judges (as well as the police) and Parliament with the People throughout history. Thatcher (and Peter Walker, Minister of Power, and MacGregor the 'geriatric American' brought in to head the National Coal Board) also linguistically smudged any dividing line between the miners and the criminal fraternity by calling them 'thugs', 'bully boys', 'mobsters'.[43]

Stuart Hall, in 1982, shrewdly observed that Thatcher's populism constructs a political identity in which divisions count for less 'than the undifferentiated, unclassed, unsexed, unraced unity of "the people"' and then projects this identity back so far into the past as to make it seem like eternal and therefore quintessential Englishness.

> This ideological construct – 'the people' – has been much in evidence since 1975. It was in evidence during the 'winter of discontent', when the discourse of the radical Right successfully counterposed the working class against the people. Within this ideological framework the politicised sectors of the working class are represented as nothing more than a narrow interest group, while, out there, are the people – who may well, of course, be the sectional group 'holding the nation up to ransom' in some other dispute. Nevertheless, they come to see themselves, to position themselves, as simple, uninvolved, depoliticised commuters: 'the people' who can't get home, who can't bury their dead, who can't

shop, can't catch any trains or can't get hospital treatment. Who is causing all this? The workers. The unions. The leadership. Or the Left. The Marxists. The Trots. Somebody. Some other, tiny group of politically-motivated militants is standing in the way of 'what the people want'.[44]

It is important and rather painful to remember that Thatcher hijacked or displaced a lively rhetoric of the People which people like me were using extensively in the neighbourhood and community politics of self-representation which also characterized the 1970s. When we fought a prolonged campaign to get a derelict building in our local park made into a nursery school and park centre rather than a luxury casino and restaurant, our slogan was: 'for people not profit'. When we challenged the plans of the huge leisure conglomerate EMI for imposing a marina and luxury flats on to our local seafront, we presented an alternative blueprint for 'the People's Marina'. We sometimes dropped the definite article in order to make the People less abstract and more recognizable as local neighbours. But we were again trying to mobilize the meaning of the People which stressed the vast majority of working people (of hand or brain) as active shapers of our own social, political and cultural lives, encapsulated in the slogan, popular at that time 'power to the people'. It was then that I became interested in the cultural politics of the Chartist movement and learned much as an activist from Chartist language and rhetoric.

Stuart Hall chided labour and the Left in the 1980s, and his rebuke still applies in the 1990s, for ceding history to the Right and proposing 'no alternative vision of what or who the people *are*'. He reminds us that 'freedom of speech, of assembly, the franchise etc., the things we took to the high seas to defend have only been won in our society as a result of the prolonged struggle of working people. That is what democracy actually is'.[45] Whether the understanding of the People from below has been permanently closed down by the Thatcherite linguistic turn, is impossible to say. We can certainly try, as historians, to spotlight the amount of struggle and contest that has been involved in the development of this resonant idea over time. But we must not become word fetishists after all. William Morris got to the heart of the matter, despite his gendered language in *A Dream of John Ball*, when he, 'pondered all these things and how men fight and lose the battle, and the thing they fought for comes in spite of their defeat, and when it comes turns out not to be what they meant, and other men have to fight for what they meant under another name'.[46]

Notes

1. This chapter draws on work in an MA course on Keywords and Concepts
    in History, which I developed with Stephen Yeo at the University of
    Sussex, exploring the history of categories for analysing groups of human
    beings such as People, Public, Class, Masses, Community, Family and
    Nation.
2. P. Joyce, *Democratic Subjects. The Self and the Social in Nineteenth-
    Century England* (Cambridge, Cambridge University Press, 1994), p. 11.
3. P. Joyce, *Visions of the People. Industrial England and the Question of
    Class, 1848–1914* (Cambridge, Cambridge University Press, 1991), p. 11.
4. G. Stedman Jones, 'Rethinking Chartism', in his *Languages of Class.
    Studies in English Working-Class History, 1832–1982,* (Cambridge, Cam-
    bridge University Press, 1983), pp. 107, 176 ff. For contestation over the
    People, see too, G. Crossick, 'From gentlemen to the residuum: languages
    of social description in Victorian Britain', in P. Corfield, *Language, His-
    tory and Class* (Oxford, Basil Blackwell, 1991), pp. 157–8.
5. V.N. Volosinov, *Marxism and the Philosophy of Language,* 1929 trans L.
    Matejka and I. Titunik (Cambridge, MA, Harvard University Press, 1986),
    p. 12.
6. Ibid., p. 23.
7. *Halifax Commercial Chronicle,* 5 June 1830. For Hanson's life, see a
    cutting from the *Boot and Shoemaker,* n.d., in a file compiled by J.
    Horsfall Turner, Halifax Central Library. For popular constitutionalism,
    see J. Epstein, *Radical Expression: Political Language, Ritual and Symbol
    in England, 1790–1850* (New York, Oxford University Press, 1994).
8. *Northern Star,* 16 October 1838; Stedman Jones, 'Rethinking Chartism',
    p. 104 notes the working-class appropriation.
9. See Mrs Hanson, *Northern Star,* 21 April 1839, on parasites; see E. Yeo,
    'Christianity and Chartist struggle, 1838–42', *Past and Present,* 91 (1981),
    pp. 112–13, for convergence of radical religion and constitutionalism; for
    earlier views of property in labour, see C.B. Macpherson, *The Political
    Theory of Possessive Individualism: Hobbes to Locke* (Oxford, Clarendon
    Press, 1962).
10. D. Thompson, 'Who were "the People" in 1842?', in M. Chase and I.
    Dyck (eds), *Living and Learning. Essays in Honour of J.F.C. Harrison*
    (Aldershot, Scolar Press, 1996), pp. 118–32.
11. Quoted in C. Behagg, 'An alliance with the middle class: the Birmingham
    Political Union and early Chartism', in J. Epstein and D. Thompson (eds),
    The Chartist Experience, (London, Macmillan, 1982), p. 75.
12. Ibid., pp. 73–4.
13. Ibid., p. 75.
14. Quoted in Behagg, 'An alliance with the middle class', typescript version,
    p. 26.
15. Robert Lowery of Newcastle insisted that 'the man that will not go to the
    length of the street to spend his money in the shop of a friend or a store
    the profits of which he may be sure, will never walk ten miles with the
    musket on his shoulder to fight for freedom': *Northern Star,* 5 October
    1839. I have argued that the Chartist concern with democracy and repre-
    sentation extended throughout social life in several places, including E.
    Yeo, 'Some practices and problems of Chartist democracy', in Epstein and

Thompson, *The Chartist Experience*, (London, Macmillan, 1982), pp. 346–9.

16. *Northern Star*, 22 December 1838.
17. Yeo, 'Chartist democracy', pp. 345–60, esp. 353 ff. for ways of ensuring accountability of officers and paid officials.
18. William Thornton at a delegate meeting, *Northern Star*, 28 August 1841.
19. Revd William Hill (ed.), ibid., 3 April 1841; see Yeo, 'Christianity'.
20. R. Williams, *Culture and Society* (Penguin, Harmondsworth, 1963), p. 289.
21. S. Yeo, 'On the uses of "apathy"', *European Journal of Sociology*, **14** (1974), pp. 305 ff. perceptively analyses some patterns of thinking in relation to 'masses'.
22. G. White to M. Norman, 2 October 1849, in Black, F. and Black, R. (eds), *The Harney Papers* (Assem, Van Gorcum, 1969), p. 86.
23. T. Carlyle, 'Shooting Niagara: and after?', 1867, in *Critical and Miscellaneous Essays*, vol. 6 (London, Chapman and Hall, 1869), pp. 354, 353.
24. M. Arnold, *Culture and Anarchy*, 1869 (Cambridge, Cambridge University Press, 1963), p. 105.
25. *Bee-Hive*, 5 January, 16 March 1867, 7 April 1866. Thanks to Sarah Cooper for drawing my attention to this material.
26. H. Matthew, 'Rhetoric and politics in Britain, 1860–1950', in P. Waller (ed.), *Politics and Social Change in Modern Britain. Essays Presented to A.F. Thompson* (Brighton, Harvester, 1987), pp. 42–3. I am grateful to J. Belchem and J. Epstein for sight of their MS 'Argument. The nineteenth-century gentleman leader revisited' which analyses the mid-century platform.
27. C.F.G. Masterman, *The Condition of England* (London, Methuen, 1909), pp. 121–2; also L.T. Hobhouse, *Democracy and Reaction*, 1904 (Harvester, Brighton, 1972), p. 279.
28. R. Soffer, *Ethics and Society in England: the Revolution in the Social Sciences, 1870–1914* (Berkeley, University of California Press, 1978), pp. 217 ff. discusses McDougall, Trotter and other students of crowd psychology.
29. Masterman, *Condition*, p. 96.
30. R. Blatchford, *Real Socialism, What Socialism is and What Socialism is Not*, Clarion Pamphlet (1898). See L. Barrow and I. Bullock, *Democratic Ideas and the British Labour Movement, 1880–1914* (Cambridge, Cambridge University Press, 1996) for quotes from many socialist and trade union factions about the People in relation to democratic government.
31. For a fuller discussion of the themes in this paragraph, see E. Yeo, 'Culture and constraint in working-class movements', in E. Yeo and S. Yeo (eds), *Popular Culture and Class Conflict, 1590–1914* (Brighton, Harvester, 1981), pp. 179 ff., also 290 ff.
32. P. Summerfield, 'The Effingham Arms and the Empire: deliberate selection in the evolution of music hall in London', in E. Yeo and S. Yeo (eds), *Popular Culture and Class Conflict, 1590–1914* (Brighton, Harvester, 1981), pp. 222–31.
33. W. George, *Caliban* (London, 1920) quoted by P. Ferris, *Observer*, 16 May 1971.
34. M. Abrams, *Social Surveys and Social Action* (London, William Heinemann, 1951), pp. 61–2.

35. G. Gallup and S. Forbes Rae, *The Pulse of Democracy. The Public-Opinion Poll and How It Works* (New York, Simon and Schuster, 1940), p. 13.
36. E. Lederer, 'Public opinion', in M. Ascoli and F. Lehmann (eds), *Political and Economic Democracy* (New York, 1937), p. 291 quoted in Gallup and Forbes Rae, *The Pulse of Democracy*, pp. 4, 12.
37. Julian Amery's Election Address for the Brighton Pavilion Constituency, 1983.
38. W. Coote, 4 April 1919, *Parliamentary Debates. Official Report. House of Commons*, vol. 114, col. 1585. For language to discredit labour, see E. and S. Yeo, 'On the uses of "community" from the Owenites to the present', in S. Yeo (ed.), *New Views of Co-operation* (London, Routledge, 1988), pp. 246–8; R. McKibbin, *The Ideologies of Class. Social Relations in Britain 1880–1950* (Oxford, Clarendon Press, 1994), pp. 284–6.
39. *British Gazette*, 5 May 1926; 13 May gives a history of the *Gazette*. The *British Worker. Official Strike News Bulletin. Published by the TUC*, 5 May 1926 tried to position itself as the patriots by declaring it was 'not making war on the people. It is anxious that the ordinary members of the public shall not be penalised for the unpatriotic conduct of the mineowners and the government'.
40. Baldwin and Balfour, *British Gazette*, 6 May, 10 May 1926; see K. Martin, *The British Public and the General Strike* (London, Hogarth Press, 1926), ch. 2 for a useful account of 'Newspapers and the general strike'.
41. *Daily Mail*, 13 May, 15 May 1926.
42. *The Times*, 20 July, 28 July, 13 October 1984; see R. Samuel (ed.), *The Enemy Within. Pit Villages and the Miners' Strike of 1984–5* (London, Routledge and Kegan Paul, 1986), 'Introduction' for a good discussion of the archetypal images used by both sides in the struggle; also B. Schwarz, 'Let them eat coal: the Conservative Party and the strike' in H. Beynon (ed.), *Digging Deeper. Issues in the Miners' Strike* (London, Verso, 1985), pp. 57 ff.
43. *The Times*, 20 July 1984 for Walker; 28 July 1984 for MacGregor; also I. MacGregor with R. Turner, *The Enemies Within. The Story of the Miners' Strike, 1984–5* (London, Collins, 1986).
44. S. Hall, 'The battle for socialist ideas in the 1980s', *Socialist Register* (1982), pp. 15–16.
45. Ibid., p. 16. It is no surprise that the History part of the National Curriculum was the most sensitive with Thatcher intervening directly in its development.
46. W. Morris, *A Dream of John Ball (1886–7) and a King's Lesson* (London, Longmans Green, 1918), pp. 39–40.

PART TWO
Gender

CHAPTER THREE

Fractured universality: the language of British socialism before the First World War

Karen Hunt

Socialism is usually understood as both a universal and an emancipatory ideology – hence part of its appeal is its apparent inclusiveness. This chapter explores some of the ways in which that universality was, and indeed is, fractured by a range of fault lines, particularly those of gender and race. These fractures have not necessarily led to exclusions but rather to equally damaging equivocations, typified by a sense of not belonging, of marginality. In order to explore this I want to consider a phrase, 'the language of socialism,'[1] and the extent to which the apparently universalistic socialist project is flawed by the uncritical use of a deeply gendered language. My examples are drawn from Britain in the period from the 1880s to the First World War, principally, although not exclusively, from Britain's first Marxist party, the Social Democratic Federation (SDF).

To contextualize what follows I want to consider the socialist construction of the woman question[2] – that is, how socialists of this period understood women's oppression and women's place within the socialist project. Based upon the work of Engels and Bebel,[3] the socialist construction of the woman question paradoxically marginalized women within contemporary socialist concerns while also drawing them more firmly into the socialist arena. The duty of women who wanted emancipation was to join in the class struggle, in order to achieve a socialist society in which the woman question, so it was promised, would be addressed. In a sense, there was no sex question under capitalism, only one of class, and to engage in sex issues, that is feminism, would only delay the achievement of socialism and thus the resolution of the woman question. In this way women's issues were marginalized by socialists. Merely by engaging in the class struggle in capitalist society, women were doing as much as was necessary at that historical juncture to gain their freedom in the long term.

The legacy of the founding fathers, Engels and Bebel, was an ambiguous one. They appeared to collapse sex into class oppression, and built

the rest of their arguments on this assumption: yet the sex/class analogy[4] was never fully explored or justified. This ambiguity provided grist
to the mill for the very different practical interpretations of the relevance of the woman question to socialists. Women were to be integrated into the heart of socialism, its class analysis, through the sex/
class analogy; yet that analogy precluded the emergence within socialist
thinking of any developed understanding of women's oppression. All
too often, the woman question found a socialist 'answer' by disappear-
ing into the class, or 'social', question. There was no clear theoretical
space to develop an understanding of patriarchy, as either a separate or
a related system to capitalism.

The invisibility of sexual oppression was not total. For in order for
this sleight of hand to occur, the concept had first to be recognized.
Ironically, the fact that Bebel accepted the existence of sex oppression,[5] if
only to then dissolve it into class oppression, gave a status and recognition to the experiences of women and ensured the acceptance of the
woman question as an issue for socialists.

For the SDF, and most of its contemporary Second International
parties, the crucial divide in society was economic, essentially, one of
class, and everything else was secondary.[6] This premise led to a narrow
definition of the issues which were regarded as crucial to socialist
politics. In contrast, a wide variety of other debates, such as those over
religion, teetotalism and feminism, were defined as peripheral, as matters of personal conscience. The most important implication of the
SDF's construction of the woman question was that it made a virtue out
of the political vacuum it created around women. As a conscience issue,
the woman question provided no measure for socialist practice in relation to women. As a consequence, it allowed all sorts of assumptions
about women to gain credibility. This was to be important for any
language of socialism. Nevertheless, it is important to recognize that
this was not purely the result of individual prejudice and misogynism; it
was rooted in the ambiguities of the theory itself. If these prejudices and
assumptions had remained the dark secrets of individuals, then the
woman question would not have been as significant an issue for socialists as it undoubtedly was. The fact that men predominated within the
party hierarchy, and within the pages of the SDF press, gave individual
men the opportunity repeatedly to express their private views on women.
Moreover, the party's analysis of the woman question ensured that they
were beyond official criticism or sanction. It therefore became possible
for a relatively small group of opinionated men to dominate internal
discussion within the SDF on the substance of the woman question and,
perhaps even more importantly, to appear to be the voice of the whole
party on these matters. The fact that there was no party position on this

question of individual conscience became obscured to those outside the party, and even to some within it, when persistent and loud voices proclaimed woman's inferiority, her privilege and her limitations.

However, the party was officially committed to sexual equality in its programme[7] and needed to recruit women to the socialist cause if the battle to end class society was ever to succeed. In that sense the woman question could not be shelved, and in reality it rarely remained merely a matter of private conscience. There were always members of the SDF who recognized woman's oppression and argued for her emancipation as an essential part of socialism.[8] However, without a party position on the woman question, they had few weapons other than argument against the persistence of sexist assumptions about women, their capacities and potential. This was to be important for women's engagement with the language of socialism.

So what do I mean by a language of socialism? A 'language' of socialism can be understood in a number of different ways. It includes, apparently straightforwardly, the words people use in speech, in writing and therefore in thought. It also includes the broader cultural framework in which these words sit, including the extent to which a particular language goes against the grain of its immediate environment and/or of the dominant culture. A language also employs conceptual frameworks to give it order. It is in these ways that I want to consider the language of socialism in a specific historical context.

There are day-to-day struggles over language, particularly in trying to develop a language which is inclusive. This is not just an obsession of the 'politically correct' 1980s and 1990s – and all those tiresome jokes about Personchester – but was an issue which was raised in relation to British socialism before the First World War. Sometimes, the lack of an appropriate language revealed then, as it often does now, an underlying sense of unease at the changes that the requirement for a new or revised language represents. For example, in an 1893 report from Salford, it was observed:

> Do we want the women? Cease your silly tattle. Don't you know we have got the women – in Lancashire. In some of the branches the men are at home mending the stockings and nursing the baby – the best place for them – whilst the women are out in the squares and at the street corners. The lady members are taking the chair so often now that our speakers are finding some difficulty in beginning their addresses. 'Mrs Chairman' won't do; 'Comradess' won't do; and one of the dear, darling creatures was offended the other Sunday because the speaker addressed her as 'Madam'![9]

Here was a warning to other men of the danger of reversed sexual roles which could be associated with women taking a more assertive role.

The quibble about nomenclature suggested that there was no name, and therefore no acknowledged tradition, for this form of women's activism. The writer also engaged with the dominant stereotype of woman by suggesting that women have no sense of humour. Any suggestion of bending gender roles clearly made male activists very uncomfortable and this could be reflected in uncertainties over language.

Socialism can really only be understood by exploring the assumptions that underlay the apparently neutral language employed at a day-to-day and at a conceptual level. One example is the word 'socialist'. This could be defined in terms of a commitment to socialist theory and was often seen as synonymous with party membership. There is much that could be said about what was understood by the term 'socialist' and I have discussed this in my work on politicization.[10] In this context it is worth noting that across the socialist organizations of the time, as June Hannam notes of the Independent Labour Party (ILP), conscious and unconscious appeals for members were couched in male language, for example Keir Hardie addressed his propaganda to 'Young Men in a Hurry!'[11] But a linked phrase, often used in SDFers' discussions of the woman question, is even more revealing. This was the term, the 'socialist's wife' usually to be found prefaced with the words 'the problem of … '. The whole conception of 'the problem of socialists' wives' was, of course, redolent with assumptions. Socialists were generally assumed to be men, and women SDFers were noted in terms that suggested they were exceptions.[12] Moreover, there was no equivalent notion of, or indeed discussion of, the 'socialist's husband' – whether problematic or not!

The SDF, like other parties of the Second International, sought to mobilize the family as an area of support and reinforcement for its membership. Female members of the (presumed male) SDFer's family were expected to extend their caring and supportive role to sustain practically and psychologically the party member against a hostile world. On this assumption, the 'want of sympathy shown by the wives of socialists for the work we have in hand'[13] presented a pressing practical problem to the SDF for 'members are often lost because their wives are prejudiced'.[14]

By discussing one small part of the language of socialism, the 'socialist's wife', the assumptions that underpinned it can be exposed. The problem was not exclusive to the SDF, for Julia Dawson highlighted a similar situation in the woman's column of *Clarion*.[15] As a result of her support for the socialist's wife and criticism of socialist husbands, she reported that some of her readers had unsuccessfully tried to keep that particular edition of *Clarion* from their wives, while others complained that if they did as she had asked, they would be tied to their wife's apron strings and there would be no work done for socialism at all.[16] Here was some indication of the power of 'naming' when it was thought necessary to hide a discussion of the socialist's wife from socialists' wives.

More important for the language of socialism was the context in which that language was used. Women complained about the male atmosphere of SDF branches.[17] This was not on the whole acknowledged or understood within the party. Yet without a sense of the culture created by those who were committed to this universalist ideology, then the way in which the language of socialism could exclude or marginalize can be easily overlooked. For example, Ellen Batten felt that women socialists were regarded as a nuisance or as mild enthusiasts who must be tolerated but who would be better off at home engaged in gossip, tea-drinking and other feminine frivolities.[18] Complaints were made in *Clarion* that ILP and SDF branches gave a cold reception to those women who ventured to attend them and that neither gave any indication that they actually welcomed women.[19] Although all women's experience was not the same, some women spoke of them 'like a fish out of water, or a stranger listening to a foreign tongue'[20] when attending an SDF meeting. Apparently they were not familiar with nor felt included within the day-to-day language of socialism. On the other hand, Nellie Bloodworth, a long-time member of the SDF, disagreed that women were contemptuously brushed aside in meetings or treated as camp-followers.[21] The conduct of meetings, which one woman described as 'stiff, formal and gloomy',[22] could have a crucial impact on women who were isolated within and outside the party. Tentative political commitment could be crushed in a hostile environment, particularly when women's political activity was vulnerable to social pressures beyond those experienced by men.[23]

Women SDFers commented on the male image of the party and since there was little belief that other socialist organizations differed, this easily became criticism of socialism itself. 'Hopeful', a correspondent to *Justice*, pointed out that the language used by most socialists reflected the assumption that socialists were necessarily male. She warned, 'all speakers must be very careful to avoid speaking of "working men" and omitting the women. We women feel repelled at the continual sole use of the masculine nouns and pronouns'.[24] Here was a keen awareness of women's absence from the collective language of socialism. As she said, 'the chief thing is to awaken interest. Now this will never be done if men call us frivolous'.[25] Ellen Batten shared this concern and commented on male socialists' behaviour towards women: 'When one sees the half-contemptuous smile, or hears the slighting remark when women are mentioned as workers or speakers one cannot help feeling that those socialists are not as advanced or as true to their principles as they ought to be.' She warned that such behaviour would repulse potential women socialists and would eventually drive existing women members to abandon socialism.[26] It seemed that the gulf between socialist men's theory and practice was symbolized by the ease with which patronizing and excluding assumptions about women surfaced in the day-to-day language of socialism. This constituted a real barrier to women's participation in the party.

Women's expectations of socialist men's practice were based on the identification of socialism with a commitment to sexual equality. Some were disillusioned when their own experiences of socialist parties failed to include any measure of prefigurative practice and little respect for women. Dora Montefiore quoted from one woman who had been an active socialist:

> Honestly I have little hope of making any impression on the mind of the ordinary male Socialist, who I believe, notwithstanding all his professed theories of equality, etc, has little or no sympathy with the women's movement. That fact chiefly led to my complete withdrawal from the Socialist movement. I would rather be associated with the ordinary 'mere male man', whose ignorance and inherited prejudices are not so closely bound up with exalted notions or theories.[27]

Disappointment could turn to cynicism, when socialist men turned out to be little different from their non-socialist brothers.

This complaint was one made against socialism generally rather than merely against the SDF.[28] For example, Elizabeth Wolstenholme Elmy argued in *Justice* that a large number of women were sympathetic to socialism but were driven away from socialist parties 'by the all but universal failure of male Socialists to recognise *practically* in women the other half of humanity, with rights absolutely equal to those of the male half'.[29] Hannah Mitchell, as a member of the ILP, had been similarly disappointed by the gap between the anticipated and actual behaviour of socialist men, which was generally undifferentiated from male attitudes within the wider society. She remembered that 'A lot of the Socialist talk about freedom was only talk and these Socialist young men expected Sunday dinners and huge teas with home made cakes, potted meats and pies, exactly like their reactionary fellows'.[30]

The SDF did not escape criticism. Hannah Taylor pointed out that the rules of the SDF included working for equality between the sexes, yet 'We do not see the spirit of this object carried out in our branches to any great extent'.[31] John Spargo, an ex-member of the SDF who had emigrated to the United States, was willing to acknowledge 'that we have consistently and deliberately ignored the women's side of our programme'. This had blinded socialists to 'the fact that "Workers of the World Unite!" means the woman in the factory as well as the man who works by her side; the woman toiling at home with the babies as well as her husband in the workshop or mine'.[32] This was a statement which many male socialists seemed unwilling to endorse. However, even this was an impersonal acknowledgement of the particular experiences that women faced within the SDF and other socialist parties. For them the gulf between the theory and practice of the woman question was not an abstract or a rhetorical issue but one that affected their daily lives and their choices of becoming or remaining socialists. The SDF's understanding of the woman question permitted the voicing of such criticisms, doubts and disillusionment but it provided no impetus for action at an organizational level. This reinforced the isolation of individual women socialists, and indeed socialists' wives, and made it all too easy to dismiss their experiences as either unfortunate but not typical, or as demonstrating the problem that women posed for socialism.

One of the most important ways in which women were marginalized from the SDF was the manner in which they were represented within the party's press. There were objections to the way in which women were stereotyped. Marion Coates demanded of *Justice* that they 'Stop putting flippant silly pictures in front of us women. Treat us with the reverence and respect that you wish for yourself'.[33] Mary Boyd was one of the women who warned against the 'vulgar abuse' and 'insidious innuendoes' which appeared in *Justice*: 'It is not calculated to induce women to join the organisation and may alienate some who belong to it already'.[34]

There was a particularly strong reaction when blatant misogynism was printed within *Justice* and *Social Democrat*. Critics suggested that not only was this unacceptable in itself but also that it would damage the SDF in the eyes of actual and potential women members. After a particularly virulent piece by Belfort Bax, Catherine Davidson asked angrily whether the party would castigate Bax or would choose to remain silent and, in effect, endorse his views. She argued:

> If this view be upheld by the SDF then women's place is outside; let our members take their courage in both hands if they believe it and say so. Self-respecting women members will then resign. If this view be not upheld, then the columns of *Justice* ought to be closed to anyone who wishes to insult either sex.[35]

In an organization in which propaganda was central to its existence, the form and content of the language used was a crucial part of the message. Many women recognized this and yet the party could not.

Having explored the ways in which explicitly and implicitly the day-to-day language of socialism stereotyped women and marginalized them from the heart of the socialist project, I now want to look at the way in which another part of the language of socialism was gendered. The example I will use is the SDF's understanding of unemployment. The specific nature of women's unemployment in this period and the campaigns around it have not been seriously addressed by historians.[36] Yet unemployment was a particularly important issue for the SDF, both in their theory and in their practice. Indeed the organization of the unemployed in periods of recession was one of the SDF's major political activities throughout its lifetime. This in itself raises the question of the relationship between unemployment as a general campaigning issue for the SDF and the assumptions about women's nature and role that formed their understanding of the woman question. Was the party's approach to unemployment gender-specific? Indeed, was the term 'unemployment' itself deeply gendered?

I want to look at the SDF's argument concerning unemployment and specifically the party's commitment to the right to work. Was this a right seen as extending unproblematically to all people or did some groups in society have less of a right, or indeed no right, to work?

In the SDF's writings on unemployment, and in particular in their reports on agitational work, the assumed gender of the unemployed was male. The language the SDF used made this assumption clear: its aim was 'that every man who is willing to work shall be afforded the opportunity to maintain himself and his family in decency and comfort by productive labour'.[37] The references made to unemployed women were rare and indicated that they were not part of the general term 'unemployed' but formed a separate category. Unemployed women tended to be referred to in specific contexts which, again, emphasized their difference. There was a tendency to see unemployment's effect on women as a composite one. This allowed the SDF's theoreticians to unproblematically bring together women who would usually be engaged in paid work with the wives of unemployed men. Thus, for example, the unemployed women's deputation to the Prime Minister, Arthur Balfour, which was organized through the SDF-dominated Central Workers Committee, consisted of both these groups of women.[38] The testimony of this delegation shows that women were seen as representing the deleterious effect of unemployment on the family rather than on women as individuals. It was hard to hear in the general campaign for the right to work the voices of those who spoke up for the particular experience of the women unemployed and who offered solutions which might relieve their distress. Official attitudes, particularly those to be found within the operation of the Poor Law, coupled with the SDF's own ambivalence about women's work – particularly married women's work – made it much easier for the party to overlook women's unemployment and to concentrate on the more emotive subject of the effect of unemployment on the family.[39]

Gender differentiation in relation to unemployment was also reinforced by the tactics used by the SDF in unemployed agitation. The form of the 1880s unemployed protests, particularly when organized by socialists, had been seen as threatening. There had been a potential for violence even if it was not often realized. Therefore although these tactics were thought by the party to be successful, the SDF did not think that they were appropriate for women's direct involvement. Thus most of the marches and demonstrations organized by the SDF or by groups in which they played a leading part, such as the London and District Right to Work Council, were for the male unemployed.[40] Women's events were organized separately. This difference is underlined by the comments made in *Justice* after the women's delegation to Balfour in 1905:

> On Monday, had only the word been given, when the women were safely settled indoors, the scenes of 1886 might have been repeated. Whether it is necessary to repeat that history remains to be seen, but the workers should organise, should prepare for the next great march – this time not of weak though brave women, but of men who, with what strength semi-starvation has left in them, will demonstrate in such fashion that neither Balfour nor any other shall say them nay.[41]

Although women SDFers spoke at meetings of the unemployed and took part in the general campaign, for example through sitting on Distress Committees, unemployed women were not encouraged to attend public marches. This party attitude made women's experience of unemployment seem marginal to the SDF's unemployed agitation. It seemed that once again women were being called upon to support an essentially male campaign by working quietly in the background. Women's activities were to be confined to reinforcing the overall campaign by demonstrating the effect of male unemployment on wives and children. Did SDF women aquiesce in this? Were women not to make their own demand for the right to work?

SDF women did use the language of rights and extended the concept of a right to work beyond a purely male right to include women as well. Thus although the 1905 March of the Women included banners demanding 'Work for our men', there were also banners which read 'We demand the right to labour in order that we and ours might live'.[42] At a Right to Work meeting in 1906 Margaret Bondfield, at that time an SDFer, made a strong demand for 'woman's right to work – not to drudgery'.[43] Margaretta Hicks was driven to ask, during the 1907 SDF Conference's debate on unemployment, 'This resolution speaks of "men". I take it that

it refers to women also ... I should like women to be put in'.[44] But this
was one of only two references to women in Conference debates on
unemployment.[45] By contrast, the SDF Women's Annual Conference in
1911 discussed a much clearer resolution which recognized that 'unemployment affects women, both as wage earners and housekeepers'.[46]
Clearly, therefore, SDF women did make an explicit commitment to
women's right to work. But this demand was also implicit in the practical
action for which they argued and, indeed, took. Most of the SDF wom-
en's energy went into the women's workrooms: calling for them to be set
up; stopping them being closed; assisting in running them; and trying to
ensure that the women who attended the workrooms had useful work to
do which would help them to get a job.[47]

It was women SDFers who recognized and promoted women's right
to work within their own party. But despite making interventions within
the SDF and publicizing their own work they had little impact on the
primary campaign for the right to work. This was stubbornly focused
almost exclusively on the male unemployed. SDF women were able to
argue for women's right to work and engage in practical campaigns to
help unemployed women without meeting criticism from the party. Yet
they were unable to change the fundamental assumptions on women
and work to which many party members clung. This is further evidence
of the practical implications of the SDF's theoretical formulation of the
woman question. There was space for women to set their own priorities
provided they did not threaten the party itself. Anything which smacked
of feminism was thought to do just this. The price that women paid for
even this limited freedom was that no party decision was ever made on
subjects that were deemed part of the woman question. It was also very
hard to change the terms of the debate on issues already regarded as
important, such as unemployment. This was particularly the case when
both the general context and assumptions within the party were unsym-
pathetic to the principle of a woman's right to work. Thus the language
of socialism once again proved to have concepts and slogans within its
lexicon which were deeply gendered – not only the term unemployment
but also the central demand of a right to work.

Finally, I want to consider one of the other ways in which the process
of marginalization and exclusion worked in the language of British
socialism. This is the issue of race which was addressed in this period
most frequently in relation to the Jewish question.[48] Studies by Cohen
and others reveal the pervasiveness of anti-semitism amongst British
socialists of this period, including the SDF.[49] The SDF's anti-semitism
provides another way of illustrating the similarities and differences
between the party's treatment of sex and race and the implications this
had for an apparently universalistic language of socialism.

Like the woman question, the Jewish question was seen by many SDFers as an economic issue. A distinction was made between rich and poor Jews. Often, the Jewish capitalist was identified as 'par excellence the personification of international capitalism'.[50] Jews, like women, were stereotyped by the SDF. Jews were either 'imperialist financiers' or 'lumpen scabs', and this was reinforced by the campaigning and often virulent debates which led to the Aliens Act of 1905. There was a significant strand amongst SDFers – and socialists in general – which held that attacking capitalism and attacking Jewry were interchangeable parts of the economic analysis of socialism. Bebel called this the 'socialism of fools'.[51] Both Hyndman and Quelch, however, displayed these prejudices but denied that they were anti-semitic. For them, attacking capitalist Jews, or bourgeois women, was only about class and not about race or gender.

A comparison of reactions to displays of anti-semitism or misogynism by SDFers reveals both parallels and some significant differences. Anti-semitism attracted strong reactions from members, particularly but not exclusively Jewish SDFers, who argued firmly that the equation of international capitalism with Jewry was unequivocally anti-semitic. Anti-semitism, they pointed out, should be anathema to socialism. This issue came to a head during the Boer War, when SDF opposition to the war provided Hyndman with the space to argue that it was the product of an international Jewish conspiracy.[52] In response J.B. Askew argued that the editorials of *Justice* should not be used to propagate members' 'individual fads and fancies – much less to make remarks which can hardly fail to be offensive to a large section of our comrades'. He warned against 'substituting futile racial bickering for the class war'.[53] For some weeks, the only correspondence published was highly critical of the identification of the SDF with anti-semitism. As M. Shayer wrote, '*Justice* is on the high road to real anti-semitism ... We accept your assurance of your good sentiments, but *Justice* cannot be judged by that; it must be judged by what you write in it'.[54]

Hyndman and Quelch's response to this criticism shared many of the characteristics of the discussions over the woman question. There was, for instance, the claim that rather than being anti-semitic, the article or comment in question was merely 'a statement of facts'.[55] Then there was the disingenuous denial of anti-semitism followed by a repeated avowal of the offending sentiments. Hyndman even resorted to claims of personal friendship with Jews in his own defence. All these strategies find their parallel in responses within *Justice* to criticism over the patronizing attitude of some SDF men towards women.

Other attitudes expressed towards critics of anti-semitism within *Justice* also have a familiar ring. One was the rehearsal of the detail of the prejudiced stereotype, followed by a denial that the writer actually believed this. Most space was thus given to the repetition of the prejudice, rather than to the denial. This tactic was often linked with the assumption that there was some truth in the stereotype, and that the oppressed group in some way brought vilification upon themselves.[56] There was even the suggestion that Jews, like women, were too sensitive to these matters; they were urged 'not to be so thin-skinned over such a trifle, or so narrow'.[57] Once again the victim was to blame.

It was not just the tone and attitudes reflected in the response to criticism of anti-semitism which bore a strong likeness to those marshalled against the proponents of the woman question. Some of the arguments used by the critics also show a strong similarity. It was argued, for instance, that senior members of the party abused their positions of influence so that their personal views were printed. These could then be mistaken for party policy.[58] Once again it was not just a question of what kind of language was being used, but who had greatest access not only to that language but also through it to the socialist audience. But here there was a difference between the woman question and the Jewish question, explained by the different degrees of access enjoyed by the principal opponents in each question. Those who opposed anti-semitism within *Justice* included Theodore Rothstein and Belfort Bax, who were both influential in the party. Although their letters appeared alongside equally vehement ones from rank and file SDFers, their undoubted influence with the SDF leadership gave a greater force to their intervention. With the woman question, where the marginality of women within the organization minimized their access to the centres of decision-making, women's opposition in the press appeared to be much more muted.

There were parallels too, between the arguments made by the critics of anti-semitism within *Justice* and those made by feminists. Speaking from their own experience, opponents challenged the economic analysis that some SDFers made of Jewry, pointing out that race prejudice affected all Jews, rich or poor. The effect of campaigns against capitalist Jews would only rebound on poor Jews, whom the SDF maintained they supported. Therefore the SDF would have to choose whether it was for international social democracy or for race prejudice; the two were mutually exclusive.[59] Rothstein spoke for all the critics when he said that anti-semitism constituted 'an indelible stain on English Socialism'.[60] Nor was claiming merely to reflect the commonly held assumptions of the time any defence, for the critics argued that to claim to be socialists, SDFers had 'to rid themselves of the race prejudice they have imbibed with their mother's milk'.[61] Such opposition to the anti-semitic tone of *Justice* appears effectively to have curtailed further excesses from being published; there were few anti-semitic letters in *Justice* after 1899.[62] Anti-semitism became far less publicly acceptable than mere misogynism. But this is not to argue that both were not part of the fundamental assumptions of many SDFers. It merely implies that the opponents of anti-semitism had more of an effect on limiting the public utterances of the SDF's more anti-semitic members.

The 1900 SDF Annual Conference resolved that at an organizational level anti-semitism was a problem with which socialists had to deal.[63] This was a sharp contrast to the policy on the woman question. There was little comparable recognition at a party level of the damage that the pervasive attitude to women expressed in SDF publications had on women, or on their perception of the SDF and of socialism.

In summary, there were many similarities between the tone and the type of response made by the SDF to the problems of race and sex. The similarities consisted of the hold enjoyed by a few individuals over the party press, and their use of it to parade their own prejudices. The anti-semites and sexists also share similar reactions when criticized for positions which, theoretically at least, were recognized as incompatible with socialism. The principal difference is demonstrated by the coherence and vehemence of the opposition to anti-semitism in the Boer War period, contrasted to the more muted, but long-lived complaint, that the party's theory and practice on the woman question were out of alignment. In the wider society of the time, it would have been futile to speculate on the relative power of Jews as against women, for the two groups were fractured by race, sex and class, and were not comparable. Yet within the SDF, anti-racist[64] members were more successful in making their case heard than the anti-sexists. This reflected the relative power of the particular SDFers involved. Anti-semitism remained something which the majority of socialists did not want to be openly associated with, despite the anti-semitic feelings of many. There was, by comparison, no critical mass of the membership which felt that the party's attitude to women might equally undermine its socialist credentials. At its crudest, it was felt that anti-semitism might deter more potential members than it recruited. Misogynism was not regarded so seriously, partly because those who might be alienated were already perceived as problems for socialism.

So, to conclude, within the language of socialism the socialist construction of the woman question meant that sex was marginalized by class in the continual debate over what was crucial to a woman's political identity: her sex or her class. This was reinforced by the SDF's inability to do anything other than equivocate on the woman question because of its positioning as a conscience issue. Socialist women may have observed that too often the language of socialism uncritically presumed 'the socialist' to be male, that the broader socialist culture did not feel woman-friendly and that important political campaigns such as that around unemployment and the right to work appeared to exclude women from that right – but these women were in an invidious position. The socialist construction of the woman question gave women the space to note the sexist language and practices which could all too easily prevail despite the party's commitment to sexual equality but it gave women no power to remake the language of socialism. This was not an exclusion but neither was it an inclusion – the language of socialism appeared to be universalistic but at root it was fractured. At its heart was a theory which overstamped class interests on to any other identities so that the apparently gender-neutral terms and concepts of the language of socialism always turned out to reflect the experiences of white, working-class males.

Notes

1. Karen Hunt, *Equivocal Feminists. The Social Democratic Federation and the Woman Question 1884–1911*, (Cambridge, 1996), pp. 195–6.
2. For further discussion of the socialist construction of the woman question, see Hunt, *Equivocal Feminists*, chs 1–2.
3. Frederick Engels, *The Origin of the Family, Private Property and the State*, (London, 1973); August Bebel (tran. Daniel De Leon), *Woman Under Socialism*, (New York, 1971).
4. See Engels, *Origin*, p. 129; Bebel, *Woman*, p. 9; Hunt, *Equivocal Feminists*, pp. 25–6.
5. For example, Bebel, *Woman*, p. 1.
6. See G.D.H. Cole, *History of Socialist Thought, vol. 2: Marxism and Anarchism, 1850–1890*, (London, 1954), p. 410; Willard Wolfe, *From Radicalism to Socialism: Men and Ideas in the Formation of Fabian Socialist Doctrines, 1881–9*, (New Haven, 1975), pp. 98–100.
7. *Programme and Rules of the SDF*, (London, 1894), p. 1.
8. See, for example, *Justice*, 28 November 1896; Dora B. Montefiore, *The Position of Women in the Socialist Movement*, (London, 1909), p. 8.
9. *Justice*, 23 September 1893.
10. See Hunt, *Equivocal Feminists*, pp. 197–203: Karen Hunt, 'Making socialist woman: politicisation, gender and the Social Democratic Federation, 1884–1911'. Paper given to Ninth Berkshire Conference on the History of Women, Vassar College, 1993.
11. June Hannam, 'Women and the ILP, 1890–1914', in D. James, T. Jowitt and K. Laybourn (eds), *The Centennial History of the Independent Labour Party*, (Halifax, 1992), p. 213.
12. The most obvious way in which women were noted as exceptions to the male membership was the self-congratulatory branch reports which announced the branch's first woman secretary (*Justice*, 18 April 1896); a woman 'very pluckily taking the chair' (*Justice*, 16 July 1898); or even their first women members (*Justice*, 16 December 1905; 23 January 1909).

13. *Justice*, 15 May 1886.
14. *Justice*, 28 September 1907.
15. *Clarion*, 27 March 1897.
16. *Clarion*, 17 April 1897.
17. For example, *Justice*, 10 October 1896.
18. *Justice*, 2 September 1893; also 22 May 1909.
19. *Clarion*, 25 January 1896; 24 July 1897.
20. *Justice*, 22 May 1909.
21. *Justice*, 8 May 1909.
22. *Justice*, 9 September 1893.
23. See, for example, Margaret McCarthy, *Generation in Revolt*, (London, 1953), p. 37.
24. *Justice*, 23 September 1893. See also *Clarion*, 14 September 1906.
25. *Justice*, 23 September 1893.
26. *Justice*, 2 September 1893; 30 September 1893.
27. *Justice*, 11 October 1902; also 4 October 1902, 18 October 1902.
28. This was a complaint made by socialist women throughout the Second International. For example, in the Socialist Party of America (Bruce Dancis, 'Socialism and women in the United States, 1900–17', *Socialist Revolution*, 27 (1976), p. 86) and in the SPD (Karen Honeycutt, 'Clara Zetkin: a left-wing socialist and feminist in Wilhelmian Germany', PhD dissertation, Columbia University, (1975), p. 338).
29. *Justice*, 25 October 1902.
30. Hannah Mitchell, *The Hard Way Up*, (London, 1977), p. 96.
31. *Social Democrat*, December 1901, p. 369.
32. *Justice*, 25 April 1908.
33. *Justice*, 30 June 1894.
34. *Justice*, 18 April 1896. Also see her letter in *Justice*, 9 May 1896.
35. *Justice*, 9 April 1910.
36. See Bentley B. Gilbert, *The Evolution of National Insurance in Great Britain: the Origins of the Welfare State*, (London, 1966), ch. 5; Jose Harris, *Unemployment and Politics: a Study in English Social Policy*, (London, 1972). Mary Langan does have one paragraph on the female unemployed in her article 'Reorganizing the labour market: unemployment, the state and the labour market, 1880–1914', in Mary Langan and Bill Schwarz (eds), *Crises in the British State 1880–1930*, (London, 1985), pp. 120–21.
37. *Justice*, 21 February 1903.
38. *Deputation of Unemployed to the Rt. Hon. A.J. Balfour MP*, (London, 1905). See also *Justice*, 11 November 1905, 22 July 1905.
39. Pat Thane, 'Women and the Poor Law in Victorian and Edwardian England', *History Workshop Journal*, 6 (1978); Hunt, *Equivocal Feminists*, ch. 5.
40. See Kenneth D. Brown, *Labour and Unemployment 1900–14*, (Newton Abbot, 1971).
41. *Justice*, 11 November 1905.
42. Ibid.
43. *Justice*, 3 March 1906.
44. *SDF Conference Report*, 1907, p. 19.
45. The other was in the *SDF Conference Report*, 1905, p. 25.
46. *Justice*, 1 April 1911.

47. *Justice*, 30 September 1905; 26 September 1908; 12 December 1908.
48. For an exploration of the contemporary labour movement's attitudes to race, see Kenneth Lunn, 'Race relations or industrial relations? Race and labour in Britain, 1880–1950', in Kenneth Lunn (ed.), *Race and Labour in Twentieth Century Britain*, (London, 1985).
49. Steve Cohen, *That's Funny You Don't Look Anti-Semitic: an Anti-Racist Analysis of Left Anti-Semitism* (Leeds, 1984), esp. pp. 19–36; P.D. Colbenson, 'British socialism and anti-semitism, 1884–1914', PhD dissertation, Georgia State University (1977).
50. *Justice*, 9 September 1899.
51. Quoted in Cohen, *That's Funny You Don't Look Anti-Semitic*, p. 9.
52. For example, 'The Jews war on the Transvaal', *Justice*, 7 October 1899.
53. *Justice*, 9 September 1899.
54. *Justice*, 7 October 1899.
55. See the editorial comment in *Justice*, 9 September 1899.
56. For example, *Justice*, 26 August 1899; 28 October 1899.
57. *Justice*, 4 November 1899.
58. For example, *Justice*, 14 October 1899.
59. See *Justice*, 7 October 1899; 14 October 1899.
60. *Justice*, 28 October 1899.
61. *Justice*, 7 October 1899.
62. See, for example, *Justice*, 4 November, 11 November 1899.
63. *Justice*, 11 August 1900.
64. In this case anti-racist is understood as those who fought anti-semitism for there was no real consciousness of black racism within the SDF, or beyond. The question of anti-Irish chauvinism was viewed as a separate matter. Geoffrey Bell notes that Hyndman may have been anti-German and anti-Jewish but he was not a chauvinist on Ireland (Geoffrey Bell, *Troublesome Business: the Labour Party and the Irish Question*, (London, 1982), pp. 2–3. It seems that among socialists at this period only those who were committed to opposing anti-semitism perceived their fight as one against racial prejudice.

CHAPTER FOUR

'A bit of mellifluous phraseology': the 1922 railroad shopcraft strike and the living wage

Susan Levine

In thinking about the 'linguistic turn' in labour history is it important to consider the context in which language was used and the different, often conflicting, groups that used the language. Recently, for example, there has been a renewed debate in the United States about the minimum wage. Connected with this debate is a discussion of the 'living wage'. What constitutes a living wage at the end of the twentieth century is clearly different than what constituted a living wage at its beginning. But, more important even than the dollar figure attached to the idea of a 'living wage' is its contextual meaning. We, in the late twentieth century, consider certain consumer items (a refrigerator, a car, a television and Nikes, not to mention central heating, running water, and indoor plumbing, for example) to be essential to a decent standard of living. During the 1920s a living wage could be imagined in quite different terms. But in the 1920s, as in the present era, the term 'living wage' was much contested. Employers posed a definition of the living wage that workers often challenged. Men and women might consider different domestic components essential to a living wage. In every case, the definition of the term 'living wage' was not simply a scientific fact, but was rather a question of political power and social conflict. It is the language of conflict that we will address here.

In the summer's heat of July 1922, shopcraft workers on almost every American railroad line walked off their jobs. The nation's transportation lifeline came to a halt. For the next three months railroad workers and their employers engaged in a classic confrontation. Throughout the country, opinion was divided between those who supported the workers and those who condemned their actions. In railroad towns across the nation fights broke out between scabs and union men, women stoned strikebreakers, roundhouses were bombed, lives were lost, and in several states the national guard was call out to maintain 'public order'. President Harding declared a national emergency and sent federal troops in to protect the flow of mail and the property of railroad companies.

The issues in the strike were not unusual. Wages, seniority, working conditions, and the status of the unions defined the centre of the conflict. Since 1920 the railroads had been regulated by the Railroad Labour Board (RLB) which included representatives from employers, unions, and something known as 'the public'. In January 1922 the RLB agreed to employer requests to suspend provisions for Sunday and holiday overtime pay and to contract out repair work (often to non-union shops). Soon afterwards the Board also approved a wage cut for railroad shop workers. The shopcraft unions protested, appealed and, finally, went on strike to resist the cutbacks.[1] The railroad shopcraft strike proved to be a bitter, sometimes bloody confrontation. Employers imported scab labour provoking dramatic, often violent incidents. In the South, employers brought in black workers, thus fuelling racial tensions in the region. The women's auxiliaries of the railroad unions served hot meals to the men, raised thousands of dollars in strike funds, and walked picket lines in railroad towns throughout the country. Finally, the federal courts issued one of their most sweeping injunctions restricting strike leaders from picketing, speaking, or even writing leaflets.[2]

So far, the story is a familiar one for labour history. Working men valiantly struggle to maintain their rights on the job, resist employer encroachments on their livelihood, and insist that the Government protect all citizens, not just the wealthy business class. Unions battle over jurisdiction, skilled workers resist challenges to their prerogatives, women appear in militant yet subordinate roles, and the problem of racial prejudice clouds the workers' universal claims to justice. Although at the time, Samuel Gompers considered the strike 'a test for the AFL as a whole', and other labour leaders deemed the conflict 'a crucial indicator of future relations with capital', the 1922 railroad shopcraft strike has, in fact, generally been given short shrift in US labour history. Largely because the railroad workers went down to a 'devastating defeat', the strike has usually been seen as the last gasp of the First World War industrial militance before the labour movement's somnolence of the 1920s.[3]

Embedded in the strikers' demands, however, was an issue that suggested a new turn for labour in the twentieth century. One of the central points of conflict between the striking shopcraft workers and their employers was the notion of a 'living wage'. The unions insisted that the 'only duty of the board was to fix wages on a scale that would provide for the lowest paid employee a living wage'. To establish anything lower, they insisted 'makes that Board, not merely a lawless body violating the act of Congress, which created it, but makes it an enemy of the public welfare and a menace to the present health and the future stability and prosperity of the United States'.[4] The living wage, the employers countered, was simply 'a bit of mellifluous phraseology' which, 'if carried to its legitimate conclusion, would wreck every railroad in the United States, and, if extended to other industries, would carry them into communistic ruin'.[5]

During the RLB deliberations and the ensuing shopcraft strike three dimensions of the idea of a living wage became clear. First, both sides measured the value of the wage – whether the shopcraft unions' living wage, or the employers' profit-level wage – according to criteria firmly located in the domestic sphere and the emerging consumer market. If employers and workers disagreed about the principle of the living wage as a standard in labour negotiations, they agreed that the wife's domestic skill combined with the local cost of living determined the meaning of the husband's wage. Indeed, they also agreed that the only realistic way to measure the value of the wage was to explore its domestic and consumer implications. Thus, while presenting 'objective' evidence such as the price of meat or the cost of housing, both sides in fact admitted that workers' living standards depended in important ways upon the work and skills of the housewife, reflecting the family's relationship to the consumer market-place rather than the individual worker's relationship to the means of production.[6]

If employers and unions agreed that wages bore a critical relationship to the domestic sphere, they seriously diverged in their evaluation of family contributions. Labour asserted that a living wage ought to support the 'average' working-class family – a worker, his wife, and three children. Management rejected the notion that one man's wage ought to provide security for such a family. Rather, the railroad owners contended, most workers' families in fact, included more than one wage-earner and thus as employers they had no need to consider the entire family's income in their wage calculations. Indeed, the objective level of wages approved by the RLB was based upon criteria that had earlier been established to determine the minimum wage for (single) women.

The final aspect of a living wage that concerns us here is the connection that railroad shopcraft workers made between high wages and citizenship. Only with a living wage, the unions contended, could working-class people fully participate in American democracy. For unions, the living wage constituted a fundamental pillar of citizenship without which workers as well as their wives and children were simply downtrodden victims of unscrupulous employers or corrupt politicians. With a living wage, however, workers' families would have the dignity and self-respect (as well as security for the future and the prospect of educating their children) required to be responsible citizens. What is more, in the shopcraft strike, railroad workers demanded that the State guar-

antee their wage levels thereby regulating employer profits and legitimizing trade union organizations.

The living wage dispute hinged on the perceived value of railroad
men's wages. For both sides in the railroad strike, evidence for the value
of workers' wages could be found in household budgets and cost of
living studies. If railroad workers and their employers disagreed about
the principle of the living wage, both sides accepted the 'science' of
household budgets and cost of living studies, although each claimed
their own studies to be more objective and true. The shopcraft strike
marked the first national labour confrontation in which both sides
amassed budgets and cost of living studies to present to a presumed
impartial government commission, the RLB. Workers had used household budgets to defend their wage claims during earlier street railroad
and coal strikes but these had been directed toward employers and to a
certain extent public opinion (rather than to a government board).
During the First World War, government agencies increasingly used cost
of living studies but considered them temporary, wartime factors. During the railroad strike the RLB agreed to consider consumer status as a
criteria for wage considerations, thus legitimizing the use of factors
outside the workplace to define the meaning of the wage.[7] In particular,
family consumer behaviour (rather than the wage itself) became a critical factor in assessing living standards.

Embedded within the household budget studies were explicit assumptions about the value of the husband's wage and the role of the wife in
maintaining family living standards. In pressing for a living wage, for
example, the shopcraft unions insisted that a man's earning should be
sufficient to support a family. The family, in union and employer budgets alike, consisted of a male wage earner, his wife, and three children
under the age of fourteen. This particular family was considered almost
universally to be 'normal' and 'necessary for the race to perpetuate
itself'.[8] The well-known labour economist, W. Jett Lauck, who presented evidence on behalf of the railroad unions, declared, 'unmarried
men are less desirable than married men, individually, socially, physically and morally'.[9] A final, practical, consideration also influenced the
use of this particular family. Lauck admitted, 'federal and state experts
do not make out budgets for less than families of five, thus neither
public nor expert opinion sanctions a smaller standard'.[10]

Having agreed on the 'normal' family, workers and owners proceeded to chronicle with great detail both the items necessary for such a
family to live in 'health and decency' and the cost of such items in
various parts of the country. The entire debate over the living wage
hinged on intimately detailed examples of family expenditures and
lengthy compilations of the month-by-month cost of living in different

communities. It was, needless to say, a futile effort. As one trainman observed, 'the cost of living is not necessarily a fixed money cost'. Rather, he admitted, it depends upon the worker's stage in life, his years in marriage, and his relationship with other family members as well as neighbours, and his particular job, skills, and whether he belonged to a union.[11]

Most importantly, both owners and workers agreed that the value of the wage depended upon the skills of the wife and her ability to negotiate an uncertain consumer market. The workers' budgets submitted as evidence in the RLB wage hearings carefully specified in great detail just what resources a wife would have to work with – how many pounds of steak, roast, stew, pork chops, turkey, hens, and ham she could cook, how many pounds of flour, corn meal, corn flakes and rolled oats she could expect to cook, how many hats, undershirts, nightgowns, and shoes she could hope to purchase, and how many times in her life she might expect to buy a new winter coat for herself, undershirts for her husband, or mittens for her children. The consumer market did not yet, however, entirely define the wife's contribution to the family's living standards. The budgets routinely included entries such as the following under 'Year Round Clothing: Dresses, cotton suits, rompers, overalls, etc., (*to be made at home*)'.[12]

The clear assumption in workers' family budgets and in community cost of living studies was that the wife's skills gave substance to the husband's wages. By accepting the strategy of listing household items and estimating cost of living from family budgets, workers acknowledged that their own wages actually accounted for only a part of the family's living standards. Despite the workers' attempts to present detailed family budgets as evidence of their own poor pay, they admitted that individual ingenuity, in particular women's skills 'in cooking, tailoring, shopping, and in many other skilled trades which she must practice' made it difficult to measure the wages in any precise manner.[13] A budget submitted by the Order of Railroad Trainmen, for example, admitted that 'the average housewife is not a perfect cook, a perfect seamstress, or a perfect "shopper" (*sic*), nor does she have time even if she has the ability to attain 100% efficiency', still, it asserted, 'almost every housewife does possess certain abilities along one or more lines and by the exercise thereof is able to reduce expenditures along these lines to below the average'.[14]

Even the most skilled housewife, however, could not extend inadequate wages without employing other resources. Putting it charitably, the trainmen's budget pointed out that 'no housewife can reasonably be expected to perform more than one miracle of domestic economy each day'. Many families thus depended upon the contributions of other family members as well. Often, the trainmen pointed out, 'the husband and even the children are able to contribute certain services' which reduce the need for 'actual money expenditures'.[15] Taken together, the contributions of family members, including wives and children, clearly could extend the husband's wages.[16] In fact, these contributions could substantially reduce market prices for many items in the family budget. The husband's wage could thus be substantially extended 'by a family which is thrifty ... which is fortunate in escaping unexpected expenses and avoiding bad bargains, and in which the housewife is physically strong and is highly intelligent in purchasing supplies and in the management of a home'.[17] The railroad men, in admitting their wives' skills as evidence in their own wage hearings, were giving subtle credence to a new definition of wages, one which encompassed the consumer market and the family as active agents as much as the men on the shop floor.

Having acknowledged the housewife's contribution to the family budget, the railroad unions pressed for wages high enough to enable their wives to avoid having to make cash contributions to the family income. Railroad workers insisted that justice as well as good economic theory required employers to pay them wages sufficient to allow a man 'to live and exist and bring up his family and educate his children and live up to the American standard of living'.[18] The railroad unions and their expert spokesmen argued that a living wage meant a wage high enough to support a family 'in health and decency'. For labour, in other words, a living wage constituted what has, in historical circles, come to be known as the family wage.[19]

In fact, at the time, as used in the RLB hearings, the term 'family wage' actually connoted wages so low that the husband's earnings alone could not support the family. Jett Lauck asserted, 'the prevailing wage in American industry ... is a family wage. The energies of all the members of the family capable of working are required in order to secure an income sufficient for average needs'.[20] Lauck and the union representatives refused to give up the idea that a man should earn enough to provide for his family. Lauck told the Board, 'you must make the wage the head of the family wage, and liberate the wife and children from work'.[21] The railroad workers' living wage was, as Martha May has described the family wage, tied to the idea of an improving living standard.[22]

Before the era of state-sponsored welfare supports, (whether in the form of labour laws protecting union benefits, medical assistance or welfare as we now define it) railroad workers' wives clearly saw their husbands' unions as insurance against the 'family wage'. Mrs G.H. Gotthart, a Sacramento California machinist's wife fully supported her husband's strike efforts. 'We know you are fighting our battle,' she told the strikers, 'that it is with the ultimate hope of being able to fully and properly provide for us and our children that you are still putting up such a noble fight.'[23] Another union wife observed, 'It is the (union) pay check that determines what kind of a house they shall live in, its locality, and how often they shall have new clothes ... when workers go on strike ... they are striking on behalf of the welfare of the women and the children'.[24] Railroad workers' wives saw the union's efforts to maintain high wages not only as insurance against wage work for other family members, but also as a guarantee of a more secure and stable family life. A machinist's wife commented, 'unions mean a lot to the woman'. She elaborated,

> they mean that far less often than in the days before the union the men came home injured and crippled from industry ... men have more time to spend in the home as the result of unionism ... Women have the union to thank that their husbands leave home for work later in the morning and return earlier at night. It is unions that have given them the pleasure of more of their men folks' time.[25]

The railroad workers and their wives did not advocate a 'head of the family wage' simply out of a romantic notion of domesticity or female subordination. Both shopmen and their wives feared that in the absence of such a moral or ethical principle, employers would stick to the bare minimum. Indeed, the same fear had motivated Progressive Era women to suggest state welfare policies to protect working women.[26] In 1922, the low wages of women, unskilled, immigrant, and black workers loomed as the most potent threat during discussions of the living wage. In fact, a key element in labour's objection to the wage rates suggested by the RLB was the fact that the minimum wage set for certain railroad men, $11.40 per week, was the same amount established as the minimum wage for women. That minimum, the railroad workers protested, was clearly not sufficient to support a family. It is obviously unjust, the shopcraft spokesmen claimed, 'to expect railroad employees who should be responsible for the maintenance of families to endure wages at a level designed as the minimum for the support of single women'.[27] In dissenting from the decision to reduce railroad wages, Board member A.O. Wharton noted, 'a wage which does not allow of the matrimonial condition and the maintenance of about five persons in a home, would not be treated as a living wage'.[28] The living wage held within it the assumption that a male worker would be part of a family unit and that the female members would (or should) not be required to enter the labour market in order to maintain the family's welfare.[29]

Withholding women's labour from the wage market was thus both a bow to masculine pride and patriarchal family structures and a calculated response to declining wage levels. Without the later state-sponsored safety net of unemployment insurance, social security for old age, and other insurance benefits, the union high-wage strategy also spoke to long-run family welfare. Shopcraft workers and their wives essentially appropriated the tactics of Progressive Era welfare reformers like Florence Kelley who argued that the protection of women and children would be a first step toward state protection of workers' rights. In this case, a living wage for railroad shopcraft men would not only ensure protection against a low 'family wage' but would ultimately ensure an American standard of living for workers generally.[30]

In 1922, railroad owners rejected the shopmen's assertion that a living wage should provide enough for a man and his family. Rather than seeing wages as linked to family units, the employers preferred to see employees, whether male or female, simply as potentially self-sufficient individuals. Wages could not, they insisted, be based upon any assumption of family responsibility nor were employers obligated to consider family ties when determining wage rates. The employers' argument drew on a logic previously reserved for single working women. Earlier discussion of a minimum wage for women assumed that female wage earners 'had only the responsibility for supporting herself'. In fact, women had 'no legal responsibility for the family at all', and once in the labour market essentially became 'one who supports herself by her own exertions'.[31] By 1922, employers and an increasing number of policy-makers as well, came to define the male wage-earner in a like manner.

To justify the assumption that wage-earners were economic individuals, railroad owners challenged the unions' descriptions of working-class families. Railroad owners defended the 1922 wage cut not only on the basis of economic necessity, but on their perception of the realities of working-class family life. The employers argued that few working-class families actually depended entirely upon the male breadwinner to maintain their living standards and readily acknowledged that most working-class families contained more than one wage-earner. This fact, the owners maintained, was a matter of choice, not necessity. Workers, in order to participate in the consumer market, sent multiple members into the workforce. The owners doubted, in fact, that workers would settle simply for a 'head of the family wage' but rather expected and promoted the economic contributions of other family members. One railroad executive suggested that even if husbands earned a high wage, they 'might want to do even a little better, and say, "it won't hurt John to have his little job, and it will not hurt Bill to do this ..."' in fact, 'they might count on getting just that little bit more in order to live a little bit better'. This, concluded the owner, would not be practical for the employers.[32] Even liberal economists such as Paul Douglas had on occasion expressed doubt about the feasibility of employers providing wages sufficient to support a family. Douglas mused,

> I believe we shall have to abandon this (the living wage) as a uniform minimum standard for two reasons: first because it would probably absorb too large a share of the national income for industry to stand the strain, and second, because such a family is not typical of actual workingmen's families.[33]

Thus, while the workers praised their wives for shaping their meagre wages into a decent standard of living, employers pointed to the contributions of wives and other family members as justification for paying the men less. It was not up to the employers to ensure workers a minimum living standard, the owners asserted, only to ensure that their business ran efficiently and profitably enough to provide employment. W.E. Williams, assistant to the Chief Operations Officer of the Missouri, Kansas, and Texas Railroad Lines told the RLB the railroad owners could not determine a living wage for their workers but could only guard against 'being required to pay more for wages than he (the railroad man) can afford under the earnings he receives'.[34] United Brotherhood of Maintenance of Way Employees president, E.F. Grable, countered, 'the opponents of the living wage principle have now centered their opposition chiefly in the contention that ... there is not enough to go around, and that, consequently, a certain portion of the working population must go without some of the essentials and most of the comforts of existence'. These contentions, he argued, 'have never been supported by any sound reasoning'. He argued that industry could well afford to pay workers a living wage by increasing efficiency and, if necessary 'a part of the increase might be taken from the present return to capital'.[35] While Grable's suggestion was dismissed as a rhetorical flourish, he did pose an alternative basis upon which to determine wages.

Workers and their wives did not expect employers on their own volition to willingly ensure high living standards. Protecting wage levels had been, after all, one of the major responsibilities of trade unions. In 1922, however, railroad workers began to suggest as well that the Government had a role to play in protecting their rights as citizens. The Government, they argued, had a duty to protect citizens' right to living wages just as it protected employers' profits. Grable told the RLB that the railroad wage decrease was 'contrary to public policy and to our self-governing institutions'. The wages set by the RLB, he declared,

> are a denial of the fundamental charters of our rights and liberties. The Declaration of Independence asserts that all men are entitled

to 'life, liberty, and the pursuit of happiness.' Under the rulings of
this Board, however, I regret to say ... our members are barely
permitted even physically to live and are entirely debarred from the
pursuit of happiness.[36]

Railroad telegrapher, O.E. Hoyte from Iron Ridge, Wisconsin challenged the RLB members to imagine an equivalent cut in their own
wages. 'Can you imagine yourselves supporting a family of our size on
$118 per month', he asked. Another told the Board that society had no
more right to fix a wage 'below the point of living ... than it is to fix a
return on capital below a reasonable point'. Some way, he pleaded,
must be found 'to enable the Government to determine what is a "living
wage" just as the Government is enabled to determine what is a fair
return on capital invested'.[37]

The unions' ladies auxiliaries similarly demanded that the Government recognize the needs of all citizens. Indeed, as I have argued elsewhere, the wives of skilled workers were perhaps more ready than their
husbands to look to the State to protect those citizens unable to fend for
themselves.[38] As producers, the women argued, workers contributed to
the nation's well-being, and as citizens they were entitled to its protections. Machinists' Ladies' Auxiliary President, May Peake, insisted that
the workers had exhibited their patriotism during the war and now
expected the Government to defend their right to a living wage. She
particularly singled out the RLB as having abdicated the worker's interests. 'After all this heroic service and sacrifice for "democracy",' she
said, 'we find an autocratic board (the RLB) working against their
interests.'[39] The shopmen, she told her members, were striking 'that
their children may have nourishing food, a comfortable home and
opportunities for education. This is something every American citizen is
entitled to'.[40] Another auxiliary leader, Mrs Singer, added that workers'
wages ensured the next generation of responsible citizens. A living
wage, she asserted, would 'protect our homes and families and ... keep
the dinner pail full that our children may develop into strong, robust
men and women. Furthermore, we want our children educated to be
equipped to take their place in the world with the children of our
employers'.[41]

The relationship between the living wage and workers' status as
citizens rested on the notion of an American standard of living. Shopman
E.M. Wilson was appalled when one railroad owner admitted he could
not discuss what constitutes a living wage 'because it is a question on
which there seems to be a difference of opinion and every man settles
that largely to his own view'. Wilson could not believe that this employer was so far removed from the lives of his workers. 'You practically admit,' Wilson said, 'that you do not know what it would take for

the employees and their families to live on.' Eager to inform the owner, Wilson declared, 'your proposition would reduce your employees below an American standard of living and we further contend that your employees are entitled to more than a mere minimum upon which life can be sustained'.[42]

The 'American Standard of Living', like the term 'living wage' was a much contested concept. On the one hand, the American standard has worked to exclude certain groups (including women, blacks, and immigrant workers) from labour's gains.[43] On the other hand, the notion of an American standard of living has also been used to include newcomers and to insist on the promise of American democratic abundance for all.[44] During the shopcraft strike the union spokesmen focused more on the potential of the American standard of living achieved through a living wage, to raise all workers' standards. In his testimony before the RLB, for example, Jett Lauck asserted a 'labour standard' which assumed that all groups of workers would want to attain it. 'It is not questioned ...' he said, 'that Mexican and even Negro labour in the South and Southwest, with low standards of living, could be employed by the railroads at rates lower than those appropriate to the living standards of the American white labourer.' None the less, he said, 'this Board cannot possibly consider such conditions as a guide in fixing the rates of pay of railroad labour'. No worker, he argued, would settle for low standards if given a choice:

> The recent Hungarian immigrant in New York or a Mexican peon in El Passo will gladly accept wages less than those required by the native American worker. But surely the Railroad Labour Board cannot accept the argument that, because of this fact, the Mexican or Hungarian railroad employee should receive less than the American worker.

Unlike some critics Lauck blamed low standards on low wages, not the worker's race or cultural background. The basic minimum wage sufficient to permit every citizen a good life, he said, 'is just as applicable in a town in Arizona as it is in Boston or Chicago'.[45] As one reporter observed, 'there is no such thing as the "American Standard of Living." Poorhouses and millionaires, both are equally American'.[46]

Railroad workers argued that the entire nation's well-being ultimately depended upon workers' living standards. The effect of low wages on citizenship, however, carried vastly different implications for women than for men. Most significantly, low wages would render men dependent. E.F. Grable, for example, argued that for husbands, low wages implied far more than hunger and debt, but threatened 'the constant fear of dependency'.[47] For women, on the other hand, the low wage threat to citizenship meant being forced into the labour market. Wom-

en's citizenship rights included the right to be supported by her husband
and thus his right to a living wage.

Finally, low wages threatened the very fabric of American communities. Grable argued that 'for the community it means child labour and
the harmful forms of woman labour. In all of these ways it saps the
strength of the nation itself, and undermines the vitality of democratic
institutions'.[48] Chicago's *Union Leader* put it bluntly:

> The railroad employees who refuse to submit themselves and their
> families to the degradation of living which they would suffer by
> accepting ... such wage standards, are fighting not just a selfish
> struggle for a decent livelihood, but a battle to preserve the health
> and energy of the manhood and womanhood of the nation and to
> perpetuate American institutions.[49]

The 1922 shopcraft strike may thus be seen as a turning-point in
organized labour's definition of citizenship. Until the 1920s, skilled
trade unions only reluctantly endorsed state-sponsored welfare measures, preferring instead to rely on the strength of the trade unions to
protect workers' welfare. While unions had previously supported state-
sponsored protective legislation only for dependent classes, namely working women, in 1922 they began to extend their view of state responsibility.
The 1922 strike may be thus be viewed as the first step toward what,
during the 1930s, became labour's wholesale embrace of state protections for workers' welfare (as well as state protections of unions themselves).[50]

Ultimately, the railroad workers lost their attempt to establish the
living wage as a principle for negotiations. The shopcraft strike lasted
into late 1923 and early 1924 ending in what Colin Davis has termed a
'devastating defeat'.[51] While the shopcraft strike might with a certain
lens be viewed as the last struggle of an older, skilled order, the surrounding debate over the living wage revealed workers efforts to define
labour's place in a new, state-oriented, consumer culture. By 1922
labour was on its way from a traditional defence of skill – a fair day's
pay for a fair day's work – to a consumer-oriented living wage. If, as
Kathryn Kish Sklar points out, 'perhaps the most fundamental characteristic of the emerging welfare state was the effort to provide minimum
standards for living and working conditions', railroad workers in 1922
had entered the debate over what the welfare state ought to look like.[52]

In labour's transition, domestic categories and family work strategies
played a critical role. The male enclave of the shop floor, perhaps never
as remote from community and family concerns as once thought, by
1922 encompassed much wider concerns. The debate over the living
wage in 1922 in many respects anticipates union strategies during the
1940s and 1950s. Certainly the detailed accounts of cost of living

anticipate an essential part of labour's collective bargaining strategy after the Second World War. However, while railroad workers and their wives conceded a role for state protections, they did not abandon their older faith in trade union protections as well. As one machinist's wife put it, 'We have often heard that old adage, "the world owes us a living," but we have also found from experience that it is up to us to collect'.[53]

Notes

1. New York *Times* (hereafter NYT) 6 June 1922, 'Expect strike votes to follow wage cuts'. Six shopcraft unions struck: machinists, boilermakers, blacksmiths, carmen, electricians and sheet metal workers. They were joined within two weeks by clerks, signal men, telegraphers, maintenance of way, and stationary firemen and oilers. See NYT, 15 July 1922, 'More vote to join rail strike'. The 'Big Four' railroad Brotherhoods and the switchmen were not affected.
2. The strike has been carefully documented and studied in Colin J. Davis, 'Bitter storm: the 1922 national railroad shopmen's strike'. PhD dissertation, SUNY Binghamton (1983). Also see accounts in Mark Perlman, *The Machinists: a New Study in American Trade Unionism*, (Cambridge, MA, Harvard University Press, 1961) esp. pp. 58–60, and Robert Zieger, 'From hostility to moderation: railroad labour policy in the 1920s', *Labor History*, 9, 1 (Winter 1968), pp. 23–38.
3. Davis, 'Bitter storm', p. 371.
4. 'Statement of the case for the railway shop employees', Chicago *Union Leader*, 29 July 1922.
5. 'Labor Board holds "the living wage" theory untenable', *NYT*, 30 October 1922, and 'Labor Board brands "living wage" theory baseless delusion', Atlanta *Constitution*, 30 October 1922.
6. For a discussion of consumerism and working class culture see Lizabeth Cohen, *Making a New Deal: Industrial Workers in Chicago, 1919–1939*, (Cambridge, Cambridge University Press, 1990). Also see Susan Levine, 'Workers' wives: gender, class and consumerism in the 1920s United States', *Gender and History*, 3, 1 (Spring 1991), pp. 45–64.
7. For information on previous use of family budgets see *Family Budgets of American Wage Earners: a Critical Analysis*, National Industrial Conference Board Research Report 241, September 1921, (New York, The Century Company, 1921), pp. 81–2.
8. Testimony of W. Jett Lauck, United States Railroad Labour Board (RLB), transcript, 30 August 1922, docket 2500, v. III pp. 444–5. In US National Archives Record Group (NARG) 13, entry 58, box 765 (hereafter cited as Lauck Testimony).
9. Ibid. Also see Davis, 'Bitter storm', pp. 127–8.
10. Lauck Testimony, pp. 444–5.
11. Order of Railroad Telegraphers, System Division no. 23, v. The Chicago, Milwaukee, and St. Paul Railway Company, Supplemental Brief. In Correspondence and Documents Relating to various points of Docketed Case

1300 and the Order of Railroad Telegraphers. NARG 13, entry 60, box no. 1176, sheet no. 2.

12. 'Summary of expenses for family of five', Federal Shopcrafts of Toledo, Peoria and Western Railway Company. Correspondence and Documents Relating to Various Aspects of Docketed Case 1300, NARG 13, entry 59, box 1175 (emphasis added).

13. Order of Railroad Trainmen, System Division No. 23, The Chicago, Milwaukee and St. Paul Railway Co., Supplemental Brief. Correspondence and Documents relating to the various points of Docketed Case 1300 and the Order of Railroad Trainmen, NARG 13, entry 60, box 1176, sheet no. 2.

14. Ibid.

15. Ibid.

16. Ibid.

17. Ibid.

18. Testimony of Joseph Sweeney, General Chairman, United Brotherhood of Maintenance of Way and Railroad Labourers, Portland, Maine, 5 August 1922. RLB Docketed Cases Files 1920–26, NARG 13, entry 56, box 761. folder: docket 2500–95B, 'Joint Submission for Decision'.

19. See Lawrence B. Glickman, 'A living wage: political economy, gender, and consumerism in American culture, 1880–1925', PhD dissertation, University of California at Berkeley, (1992). Also, Martha May, 'The historical problem of the family wage: the Ford Motor Company and the five dollar days', *Feminist Studies*, 8, 2 (Summer 1982), pp. 399–424; Jane Humphries, 'The working class family, women's liberation, and class struggle: the case of nineteenth century British history', *The Review of Radical Political Economics*, 9, 3 (Fall 1977), pp. 25–41 and *idem*, 'Class struggle and the persistence of the working-class family', *Cambridge Journal of Economics*, 1, 3 (September 1977), pp. 241–58.

20. *Decisions of the United States Railroad Labour Board with Addenda and Interpretations, 1922*, v. III, (Washington, DC, Government Printing Office, 1923), p. 781 (hereafter, *Decisions*).

21. RLB Proceedings and Stenographic Transcript, 30 August 1922, Maintenance of Way and Railroad Shop Labourers and Brotherhood of Railroad Station Employees, docket No. 2500, v. iii, p. 326. NARG 13, box 765, folder: docket 2500.

22. Martha May, 'The historical problem of the family wage'.

23. *Machinists' Monthly Journal* (March 1923), pp. 144, 172 (hereafter *MMJ*).

24. *MMJ* (August 1923), p. 323.

25. Ibid.

26. See Kathryn Kish Sklar, 'The historical foundation of women's power in the creation of the American welfare state, 1830–1930', in Seth Koven and Sonya Michel (eds), *Mothers of a New World: Maternalist Policies and the Origins of Welfare States* (New York, Routledge, 1993).

27. Quoted from Justice Henry Bourne Higgins in *Harvard Law Review*, 29, 1, in *Decisions*, p. 405.

28. Ibid.

29. See debate on the family wage, May, 'The historical problem of the family wage', and Humphries, 'The working class family'.

30. See Sklar, 'The historical foundation of women's power', p. 73.

31. *Decisions*, p. 405.

32. *Decisions*, p. 781.
33. 'Cost of living in relation to wage adjustment: a standard measure', *Monthly Labor Review*, 24 January 1920.
34. Testimony of W.E. Williams, 'Exhibit A', Missouri, Kansas, and Texas Lines v. Order of Railroad Carmen and Brotherhood of Railway Trainmen, 28 December 1921, Part 1 or 2, p. 6. NARG 13, entry 59, box 1172, folder: M, K, and TX Lines, 1300–13H, 13G.
35. Brief on Behalf of E.F. Grable, Grand President, and J.C. Smock, Assistant President, United Brotherhood of Maintenance of Way Employees and Railway Shop Labourers, docket 2500, p. 11. NARG 13, entry 56, box 754, folder, 2498 through 2500 – extra copies.
36. Opening Statement by E.F. Grable, 30 October 1922, pp. 2–3. NARG 13, entry 56, box 754, folder, United Brotherhood of Maintenance of Way Employees and Railway Shop Labourers versus Various Carriers (hereafter, Grable Statement).
37. *Decisions*, p. 779.
38. See Levine, 'Workers' wives'.
39. *MMJ* (August 1922), p. 38–9.
40. *MMJ* (August 1922), p. 539.
41. *MMJ* (March 1921), p. 218.
42. Testimony of E.M. Wilson, 'Exhibit C'. NARG 13, entry 59, box 1172, folder, Missouri, Kansas, and Texas Lines, 1300–13H, 13G Part 1 of 2.
43. See Dana Frank, *Purchasing Power: Consumer Organizing, Gender, and the Seattle Labour Movement, 1919–1929*, (Cambridge, Cambridge University Press, 1994).
44. See for example, Glickman, 'A living wage', and James R. Barrett, 'Americanization from the bottom up: immigration and the remaking of the working class in the United States, 1880–1930', *Journal of American History*, 79:3 (December 1991), pp. 996–1020.
45. Lauck Testimony, p. 339.
46. *Monthly Labour Review* (February 1921), p. 263.
47. Grable Statement, p. 15.
48. Ibid., p. 16.
49. Chicago, *Union Leader*, 29 July 1922, p. 1.
50. See Kathryn Kish Sklar, *Florence Kelley and the Nation's Work: The Rise of Women's Political Culture, 1830–1900*, (New Haven, Yale University Press, 1995).
51. Davis, 'Bitter storm', p. 362.
52. Sklar, *Florence Kelley*, p. 73.
53. *MMJ*, January 1921, p. 813.

PART THREE
Community and workplace

CHAPTER FIVE

'An accent exceedingly rare': scouse and the inflexion of class*

John Belchem

Although a rash undertaking for a relative newcomer to Merseyside, this attempt to decode 'scouse', to analyze not just a pattern of speech but a micro-culture in historical formation, has an important historiographical purpose. This chapter seeks to expose some limitations of the fashionable 'linguistic turn' in historical studies and to raise questions about Liverpool's proverbial exceptionalism, its incompatibility with the main narrative frameworks of modern British history.[1] As a social historian, my purpose is not to engage with the complexities of semiotics and linguistic theory. I intend simply to offer some historical commentary on linguistic studies of Liverpool's vernacular speech, the unmistakable accent upon which the various cultural representations of the 'scouser' have been constructed. Although instantly recognizable today, the Liverpudlian accent and identity pose considerable problems of historical reconstruction, exposing the ambivalence and tension between cultural representation and socio-economic materialism.

While now exalting its importance, historians still tend to view language in narrow and restricted manner. For all its pretensions, the linguistic turn has brought little engagement with semiotics or with the forms as well as the content of social communication. The ideas and idioms of public language – rhetoric, discourse and text – retain pre-eminence.[2] Demotic or vernacular speech is seldom considered, even though it is speech patterns which tend to express and encode critical differences of power and status in modern Britain.[3] Concentrated for the most part on public political language – on the means by which political formations deploy rhetoric, narrative and other discursive practices to construct identities and create constituencies of support – the linguistic turn has marked a backward step, reaffirming the traditional historical agenda. In practice, linguistic deconstruction of social reality and the 'social' has proved less radical and innovative than the theortical assertion of fragmentation, dissonance and postmodernist aporia. Analysis of the 'representational' is restricted to a narrow and often readily accessible range of public 'texts'.[4]

An accent not a dialect, 'scouse' does not lend itself to such textual deconstruction. In the virtual absence of a distinctive grammar or extensive vocabulary, the peculiarities of scouse are almost entirely phonological, comprising (as detailed linguistic study has shown) the preferred position of speech organs, the way plosives and nasals are produced, and the distribution of prominence in diphthongs and pitch patterns.[5] Velarization, the accompaniment of other articulations by the raising of the back of the tongue towards the soft palate, produces the famous Merseyside sound which suggests to outsiders some congestion in the upper respiratory tract. Scousers articulate a constant stream of prosodic patterns and segmental features which distinguish them unmistakably as Liverpudlians.[6] Their identity is constructed, indeed it is immediately established, by how they speak rather than by what they say. Instantly recognizable, the accent is the essential medium for the projection and representation of the local micro-culture, the 'scouse' blend of truculent defiance, collective solidarity, scallywaggery and fatalist humour which sets Liverpool and its inhabitants apart.

The scouse accent announces a cherished otherness which not all visitors appreciate. 'There is a rising inflection in it, particularly at the end of a sentence that gives even the most formal exchange a built-in air of grievance', Alan Bennett noted in his recent critical account of Liverpudlian self-dramatization: 'They all have the chat, and it laces every casual encounter ... They are more like Cockneys than Lancashire people and it gets me down.'[7] Unlike cockney, however, scouse lacks a long and changing history: there is no 'sequence of representations' to reconstruct.[8] As an accent (and much more), scouse is a recently invented tradition, a cultural response to the city's decline.

As accent and/or identity label, scouse does not figure in nineteenth-century accounts of Liverpool. Until the late 1880s, indeed, serious phonetic studies made no distinction between the town and the surrounding countryside: apparently Liverpool spoke like the rest of south Lancashire.[9] Liverpudlians – or Liverpolitans to use the genteel inflexion which remained in fashionable use throughout the nineteenth century and beyond – deployed a variety of names to identify themselves, but scouse did not feature among them. One common practice in the early nineteenth century was to add some forename (usually Dick) to that of the town's emblem, the mythical liver bird,[10] guardian of 'shipping and sailors, commerce and counting-houses, mud and merchandise, tar and traffic, pitch and prosperity, and all other ingredients that contribute to the filling up of his "pool"'.[11] For reasons which remain obscure (but hint at the growing importance of American influences in the town), Dick Liver was replaced by Dick(e)y Sam, the preferred nomenclature throughout the nineteenth century.[12] 'I am myself a Liverpool man, or Dicky Sam, as we love to call our native-born inhabitants', J.A. Picton, the distinguished architect and local historian, introduced himself when drawn into the controversy in *Notes and Queries* in 1888, 'Does Mr Gladstone speak with a provincial accent?' Where previous contributors had detected a 'northern' or 'Lancashire' edge to the grand old man's accent, Picton, a fellow-Liverpudlian, insisted that Gladstone's 'tones and mode of utterance are decidedly of Liverpool origin. We bring out our words "ore rotundo", without the mincing word-clipping of the cockney, and equally distant from the rough Tim Bobbin Lancashire dialect'. Picton offered no further elucidation of the Liverpool accent, other than to insist on its distinct difference from nearby Manchester urban dialect.[13]

Dicky Sam gradually fell out of use, leaving Liverpudlians without an eponym until the advent of radio when various local characters were introduced to a national audience by a succession of Merseyside comedians. 'Frisby Dyke', named after the town's leading drapers and outfitters, was probably the most memorable, a 'truly Scouse character' according to Frank Shaw, pioneer revivalist of Liverpool's cultural heritage.[14] By this time, however, whacker or wacker – probably derived from army slang – was the emerging generic term for Liverpudlians and was the common form of address within the town (hence its prominence in the first volume of *Lern Yerself Scouse* published by the newly established Scouse Press in 1966). After a brief period of interchangeability – during which Liverpudlians were known as scousers to outsiders but continued to converse with each other as wackers[15] – scouse has now firmly established its supremacy. Frank Shaw's *My Liverpool* (1971), a celebration of 'Scousetown', stands as the foundation text. The totemic slogan, 'Scouse Power' adorns the football supporter's coat in the exhibit in the Liverpool Life Museum commemorating the Hillsborough disaster. As memories prompted by the recent fiftieth anniversary of VE-day have recently confirmed – in letters sent to the local press from around the world – 'Scousers: They're the "salt of the earth"'.[16]

In its origins, scouse refers to a type of cheap food, to the sailor's dish of stewed meat, biscuits and vegetables similar to Scandinavian lobscouse.[17] Food, of course, is often an essential ingredient of identity: along with dress and religion, diet is the main badge of ethnicity, hence the proliferation of 'ethnic' restaurants. It figures prominently too in the construction of regional cultural stereotypes – black pudding is to the industrial north what scouse is to Liverpool. Few groups, however, choose to name themselves after a particular (and humble) dish. The first recorded use of the term was in 1837 by the cost-conscious Chadwickian surgeon of the Liverpool workhouse who reported on the successful application of the 'evaporating process' to 'Meat Scouse', leaving 'a solid mass of nutritious food'.[18] Despite its continued association with pauperism,[19] scouse became a popular local dish, always eaten with red cabbage pickled in vinegar – the presence of meat depended on economic circumstance, being absent from 'Blind Scouse'. Trade was brisk late on Saturday nights at the 'scouseboat', a steaming cauldron of stew strategically located on the junction of Wellington Street and Scotland Road. 'Scouse Alley' ran underneath Paddy's Market in St Martin's Hall, offering scouse for a 1*d* a plate and wet nellies, another local speciality, at a halfpenny each.[20] A sense of pride and identity with the dish seems to have developed: to the consternation of middle-class Fabian women who ran the socialist Cinderella club in Falkner Street in the 1890s, the local children rejected cocoa and cake and insisted on being treated to scouse;[21] on arrival in Wales, wartime evacuees from Liverpool schools were greeted with scouse.[22] However, scouse was not the culinary highpoint for humble Liverpudlians: for the true Scottie Road scouser, as a spate of recent autobiographies attest, the real joy of the past was salt fish on Sundays (known in the Park Lane area as bacalhao).[23]

As the brief etymology suggests, there are historical gaps to fill and important historiographical questions to ask. Given its provincial pre-eminence, why did nineteenth-century Liverpool not acquire a distinctive linguistic identity? What are the historical foundations for the 'scouseology' which now enlivens contemporary representations of 'heritage' Liverpool. How does the 'vile catarrhal accent' (to use Frank Shaw's description)[24] relate to the current image and perception of Liverpool as working-class, distressed and different?

From the construction of its innovatory wet-docks system in the early eighteenth century, Liverpool, the 'western emporium of Albion', identified its prosperity with commerce, not with manufacture.[25] 'The History of a place which chiefly subsists by foreign Commerce, cannot be expected to furnish many materials on the head of Manufactures', William Enfield attested in 1774 in his pioneer *An Essay towards the History of Liverpool*.[26] When 'surfeited with capital', John Gladstone, one of the migrant Scottish mercantile community and father of the future Prime Minister, followed the Liverpool tradition, studiously avoiding any form of industrial investment.[27] Guidebooks duly welcomed the absence of industry, noting with relief that the curse of the factory system stopped short of Liverpool and its independent workers.[28] Having overhauled Bristol, Liverpool was proud of its commercial image and provincial pre-eminence. Acknowledged in Moss's *Guide* of 1796 as 'the first town in the kingdom in point of size and importance, the Metropolis excepted',[29] Liverpool sought to rival London in its commercial infrastructure, to establish itself as a 'self-dependent financial centre'.[30] Vaunting its status as 'second metropolis',[31] nineteenth-century Liverpool, the 'modern Tyre', aspired to combine commerce, culture and civilization. A kind of city-state, it craved recognition as 'the Florence of the north', a fitting tribute to William Roscoe, self-made role model and icon for the mercantile élite.[32] Picton's civic improvement proposals encouraged its citizens to 'render the external appearance of their town worthy the exalted role she seems destined to fill in the commerce of the world'.[33] Subscription societies attended to the promotion of literature and the arts, supplemented by a number of voluntary associations specifically geared to the education and recreation of young clerks, 'Liverpool gentlemen' – not 'Manchester men' – in the making.[34] Through the hasty invention of tradition, Liverpool acquired a number of 'old families' to attest to the nobility of commerce.[35] The ethos was to endure, preventing a wider (and much needed) industrial diversification.

A northern outpost of gentlemanly capitalism with a flourishing extra-European trade, Liverpool defined itself against industrial Manchester and in rivalry with commercial London. Thomas Baines's *History of the Commerce and Town of Liverpool* (1852) provided the requisite historical perspective to confirm the port's commercial pre-eminence:

> the commerce of Liverpool extends to every port of any importance in every quarter of the globe. In this respect it far surpasses the commerce of any city of which we have a record from past times, as Tyre, Venice, Genoa, Amsterdam, or Antwerp, and fully equals, if it does not surpass, that of London and New York, the one the avowed capital of the first commercial state in the world, the other the real capital of the second.[36]

For all its concern with image and identity, however, Victorian Liverpool failed to establish a distinctive voice of its own a deficiency which Picton, the 'annalist' of the town, sought to redress.[37] Outside the dialect culture and 'old codgers' speech of the industrial north, Liverpool was unable to match the rhyming-slang and pearlie dress of the late-Victorian music-hall cockney.

An early form of commercial culture, mid-Victorian dialect literature built upon the ballad tradition and oral culture that preceded it. In a spirit of self-conscious promotion, dialect 'texts' were recited in the home and spoken or sung in the various venues of working-class associational culture throughout the industrial districts of Lancashire and the West Riding. Parallel to the process of economic change in these manufacturing districts, dialect literature developed through symbiotic interaction of the familiar and the progressive. Language, Patrick Joyce insists, was the 'central symbol' of the culture of the working people, the medium through which they handled change and created new identities. Although phrased in linguistic post-structuralism, Joyce's study of dialect and the making of social identity draws heavily on recent research in economic and social history stressing continuity and adaptation in the Industrial Revolution: the phased movement to larger towns, the cellular growth of towns around earlier settlements, the similarity of environment between different urban-industrial situations, and the role of the family in mediating the transition to urban factory life.[38] However, these revisionist perspectives – which no longer equate industrialization with the breakdown of previous patterns of community and family life – may not apply outside the emblematic (and much studied) northern heartlands. A short distance away, economic and social change – and ultimately the pattern of speech – differed markedly. As the emergence of scouse confirmed, Liverpool was in the north of England but not of it.[39]

Liverpool sits awkwardly outside the main narrative frameworks of economic history (just as it was excluded from the Victorian social novel).[40] Accounts of the Industrial Revolution, revisionist and otherwise, privilege the manufacturing north, (the setting of the 'industrial' novel). Alternative studies of economic history which recognize Victorian England more as the clearing-house than the workshop of the world, have a restricted vision that tends not to extend beyond London, (the city which preoccupied the urban novelist).[41] Liverpool's commercial and mercantile significance is thus overlooked. As a great seaport and commercial centre, Liverpool underwent exponential growth, attracting long-distance migrants, primarily the Irish, but also significant numbers of Welsh and Scots, to its various labour markets. Beneath the skilled city trades and the booming commercial services sector, the casualism of the docks – 'the mecca of all British jetsam'[42] – facilitated ready ease of entry. Here indeed the swelling numbers of long-distance migrants (most pressing, of course, at the time of the Irish famine) may have exercised a 'crowding out' effect, limiting the extent of in-migration by poor labourers in agricultural areas adjacent to Liverpool. Then there were the unsettled transient poor, caught in a 'curious middle place'. Disoriented by the lack of funds for further travel, they found themselves unexpectedly stuck in Liverpool, the human entrepôt for transcontinental emigration. In its pattern of growth and in-migration Liverpool differed significantly from other northern conurbations (and, as a recent comparative study has emphasized, from other European 'grandes villes').[43]

Industrial conurbations usually grew out of conglomerations of small towns and villages, augmented by short-distance rural in-migration which tended to reinforce their culture, character and status as regional centres. The urban speech of Manchester–Salford and Leeds–Bradford differed from that of the surrounding countryside, but it remained speech of the same kind. Long distance in-migration – the multi-ethnic, mainly Celtic inflow – transformed Liverpool, setting it apart from its environs. When Liverpool eventually acquired its own voice – by general consent, John Kerrigan notes, 'a mixture of Welsh, Irish and catarrh'[44] – it contrasted sharply with the surrounding dialects of Lancashire and Cheshire.[45]

As it grew from the central waterfront, Liverpool expanded outwards in a cultural vacuum, as it were, urbanizing an area largely without previous geographical and occupational identities. An isolated port, Liverpool was transformed into 'the supreme transportation node of the North West' by infrastructural development in the late eighteenth century, prompting an 'industrial efflorescence' which, Langton notes, was 'as brief as it was spectacular'. By 1800, Liverpool was 'set fair on the course which led to the status of entrepôt'. Dock development was accompanied by deindustrialization: waterfront craft industry was driven far away, to be followed by heavy industry as Liverpool chose not to exploit its near monopoly hold of raw materials, particularly coal, from the 'inner ring' of its hinterland. Unable to challenge the dominance of the Atlantic shipping trades and commerce, industry relocated in specialist fashion well out in the hinterland itself, distinct and apart from Liverpool.[46] In the absence of surrounding (and/or single industry) out-townships, Liverpool – an urban island superimposed on a landscape of good husbandry[47] – lacked the autochthonous cultural legacies and 'structural' foundations upon which northern industrial dialect was readily constructed.[48] The obscure Dicky Sam apart, there was no Liverpudlian equivalent of such long-established identity figures and subsequent dialect heroes as Tim Bobbin, the Lancashire weaver, or Bob Cranky, the Geordie pitman.[49] Nor, as will be shown later, was there anything to match the London cockney for whom consumption and display, not occupation or craft skill, was the defining motif.

Liverpool, one of the publications in 1907 commemorating the seven hundredth anniversary of the granting of its first charter observed, was 'a city without ancestors':

> Its people are people who have been precipitately gathered together from north, from south, from overseas by a sudden impetuous call. Its houses are houses, not merely of recent birth, but pioneer houses, planted instantly upon what, so brief a while ago, was unflawed meadow-land and marsh.[50]

This remarkable pattern of in-migration, 'the precipitancy of her uprising', also accounts for another distinctive feature: spatial segregation. As historical geographers have shown, Victorian Liverpool emerged in precocious manner as the prototype of the modern twentieth-century city with distinct social areas. The 'collar gap' widened as clerical workers took advantage of by-law housing and transport improvements to move out to new suburbs. Within the working class, residential location was a similar compromise between proximity to work and a suitable residential area in terms of cost (often linked to position in the family life cycle), social status and ethnic affiliation. The inner residential suburbs were favoured by skilled workers and by Welsh and Scottish minority groups. A large proportion of the unskilled and semi-skilled working class clustered close to casual labour markets of the city centre and the waterfront, areas associated with the Irish.[51] These spatial variations, however, did not prevent the emergence of a common accent: only the trained local ear could appreciate micro-cultural nuance.

Little has been recorded of the development of scouse, but what seems to have happened, Gerry Knowles maintains, was an initial linguistic polarization, followed by a remarkable two-way flow across the boundaries of social segregation. On its emergence, some time after the famine influx, the Anglo-Irish vernacular of the central area became the non-prestige form, opposed by those who upheld traditional north-western English (as modified by other in-migrants) as the local standard. Throughout the next hundred years, Knowles suggests, prestige grammar, vocabulary and phonological structure percolated downwards to impose considerable uniformity on working-class speech, while the phonetic forms and tonetic features of Anglo-Irish – linguistically the defining characteristic of scouse – spread upwards and outwards.[52] Unfortunately, Knowles produces little evidence to substantiate his thesis. Viewing 'non-prestige' scouse as an Irish implant, he attributes its influence to a process not dissimilar to the 'contamination' observed by Dr Duncan, Liverpool's pioneer medical officer of health:

> the native inhabitants are exposed to the inroads of numerous hordes of uneducated Irish, spreading physical and moral contamination around them ... By their example and intercourse with others they are rapidly lowering the standard of comfort among their English neighbours, communicating their own vicious and apathetic habits, and fast extinguishing all sense of moral dignity, independence and self-respect.[53]

In-migration undoubtedly accentuated Liverpool's notorious public health problems, but the linguistic impact of new arrivals is much more difficult to assess. The Irish contribution to the making of scouse may well have been more complex and protracted than Knowles implies. Comprising both transients and settlers, the famine Irish were by no means as discrete, linguistically and otherwise, as other migrants, most notably the Liverpool Welsh. Being dispersed throughout the conurbation, the Welsh contributed little to the pattern of urban speech on

Merseyside. They kept their own language for themselves: families travelled long distances to worship together in Welsh-speaking Calvinist chapels; Welsh newspapers circulated in the city; and the National Eisteddfod was held there on several occasions.[54] While the Irish lacked such cultural insulation – Irish gaelic was seldom heard in Liverpool – oral history casts doubt on the speed and extent of their 'contaminating' linguistic impact on others. At first, they were curiosity figures whose dialect, demeanour and appearance caused much amusement, prompting the *Picturesque Hand-Book to Liverpool* to recommend a visit to the Clarence Dock when the Irish packets docked: 'At the stern will be seen, as usual, a freight of bipeds, old and young, holding converse in a jargon that it would be difficult to interpret; whilst the rest of the deck will be crowded with a medley of sheep, pigs, and oxen.'[55] Literary and journalistic sources continue to suggest a sense of vernacular apartness, as in Dickens's night out on the Liverpool waterfront – where Irish and 'negro' characters are distinguished by phonetic spelling[56] – and in Hugh Shimmin's delight in encountering the 'rich smack of the true Milesian brogue'.[57] Furthermore, oral historians attest that many working-class Liverpudlians failed to exhibit any 'scouse' characteristics (Irish or otherwise) in their speech until well into the twentieth century.[58]

Although problematic in its immediate post-Famine origins, Knowles's account of the subsequent diffusion of scouse accords well with Liverpool's distinctive socio-economic and topographical structure. Once established as the vernacular of the central areas, 'slummy' scouse flourished in a nodal position at the heart of the Merseyside communications network and the main labour market. While residential distance from the centre was increasingly possible and desirable, everyday working contact with scouse was unavoidable. Unlike London, there were no boundaries for *flaneurs* to transgress:[59] commerce, the waterfront and the 'secondary economy' of the slums were coterminous in central Liverpool. The central landing-stage, 'the half-mile raft, moored to the City's gates', encouraged social intermingling: 'Half of Liverpool uses it as a matter of business, the other half as a matter of health and pleasure, and it presents all day long the appearance of a democratic promenade'.[60]

Casualism too facilitated the diffusion of a distinctive vernacular. There was considerable mobility and cultural interaction throughout the dockside labour market despite the sectarian geography of a Catholic north and a Protestant south, and increasing job specialism according to type of cargo, dock, vessel or employer.[61] Whatever their ethnic origin or sectarian affiliation, dockers cherished the variety and sociability of their itinerant work culture as they moved along the 'seven-mile sequence of granite-lipped lagoons',[62] relying on scouse, the vernacular of the central waterfront, as a lingua franca. In establishing credentials and comradeship along the waterfront, casual workers – prototype 'stage scousers' – accentuated the phonetics and the humour:

> We went wherever a ship was, all along the docks, meetin' 'undreds of different characters, both bosses an' men. Like der Music Halls, hundreds of different turns, all travellin' der country, usin' one act, an' bringin' down der 'ouse, but we only seen it once. Same on der docks; yer travelled all over, meetin' perhaps once every six weeks or maybe more. So yer see, yer'll soon get fed wid Wally tellin' 'is same stories, even though 'e's great when 'e tells 'em.[63]

This is to suggest that the pronounced adenoidal quality of scouse was a form of linguistic bonding, an assertion of group identity, rather than a symptom of the notorious problems of public health which made Victorian Liverpudlians prone to adenoids and respiratory disease. The wit and humour, it seems, soon spread from the waterfront to the commercial offices. Ron Garnett's autobiography revels in the author's 'junior clerical work-experience as a series of send-ups and shambles in true Liverpool tradition'.[64]

Once scouse emerged as a distinctive voice, Liverpudlians took exaggerated delight in their divergence from the industrial north – 'strange places like Wigan and St Helens, never mind the dark interior called Manchester'[65] – and its dialect culture. *Scouse Wars*, one of the more humorous publications of the current nostalgia boom, revels in cultural stereotypes as it celebrates the 'ancient conflicts of Woollybacks and Wackers':

> Woollybacks come from Woollydom, in the North of England. Woollydom is a land of cobbled streets, mills, pits and flat caps, where men are fed on pie and mushy peas, black-pudding and tripe; a land where men prize their pigeons, worship their whippets and fondle their ferrets; a land where men are bred not merely born. Wackers are the inhabitants of the city of Liverpool – famed for their humour, football, dockers and judies. Wackers eat scouse and wet nellies. Wackers and Woollybacks are tough yet warm breeds. Although both are Northerners, they are different in many ways; culture and traditions and even language divides them.[66]

The sub-text here hints at a common antipathy to London and the south. Forced by jealous rivalry of London into conditional alignment with the north, Liverpool brought a special angle to the north/south divide. Throughout the nineteenth century, London was much resented for its monopolistic privileges and practices, anachronistic obstacles in the path of Liverpool's rise to commercial pre-eminence:

> Whilst Liverpool yields to London in the extent of its trade with the continent of Europe, it surpasses the capital in its trade with America, and already rivals it in the trade with the East, although

it was not allowed to have any commerce with India previous to the renewal of the company's charter in 1813, nor with China previous to the subsequent arrangement of the Indian Government in 1833.[67]

To Liverpudlians, unfair commercial privileges and practices were personified in the character of the arrogant cockney. When James Morris, a director of the Bank of England, came up from London as Ewart's running mate in the 1835 parliamentary election, he was immediately stigmatized as a 'cockney' by local Tories envious of metropolitan monopoly and chartered commercial privilege. In the posting-bill advertising two hacks for sale, Ewart was offered as 'Lot 1: NONENTITY', while Morris was paraded as

> Lot 2: COCKNEY: a South Country Horse, 11 1/2 hands high, sent here with a *false pedigree*; Sire stated to be *Free Trade*, but though *quite unknown* here, he is ascertained to have been got by *Monopoly*, trained in Threadneedle-street, where he has been used by an *Old Lady*, who has got a Patent, for making Rags into Money, and who prosecutes with the utmost rigour anyone else that attempts to follow the same trade. Though not vicious in other respects, 'COCKNEY' like all *London*-bred Horses, is very *jealous* of those bred in the *North*, particularly *Liverpool*.[68]

Commercial rivalry was compounded by matters of style and taste. While Liverpool aspired to 'second metropolis' status, it was adjudged provincial by cultured Londoners, by those who spurned the designation 'cockney'.[69]

In early nineteenth-century London, as Gareth Stedman Jones has shown, use of the term 'cockney' mediated between the aesthetic and the political, distinguishing the cant of the vulgar from the refined language of the educated. The distinction, Stedman Jones notes, 'referred to a difference not between middle and lower, yet alone working, class, but between the citizen and the courtier, the plebeian and the patrician, the vulgar and the genteel'.[70] With the metropolitan arrogance which offended the Liverpolitan mercantile élite, refined Londoners refused to extend these distinctions beyond the capital: provincial culture was assumed to be vulgar. John Walker epitomized the attitude in his *Critical Pronouncing Dictionary* of 1791:

> The grand difference between the metropolis and the provinces is that the people of education in London are free from all the vices of the vulgar; but the best educated people in the provinces, if constantly resident there, are sure to be tinctured with the dialect of the country in which they live.[71]

On a visit to Allerton Hall in 1813 Maria Edgworth was impressed by Roscoe's learning but repelled by his 'strong provincial accent which at once destroys all idea of elegance'.[72] Others described the great renaissance scholar's accent as that of a 'barbarian',[73] while later in the century, as noted above, the residual provincial tones of another Liverpudlian scholar-politician, W.E. Gladstone, were cause for comment. What prompted the correspondence in *Notes and Queries* was the question of whether Gladstone had a 'provincial' accent.[74] It was not 'scouse' which betrayed Victorian Liverpudlians, but a basic provincialism.

While a distinctive 'scouse' accent had yet to be identified in the age of Gladstone, a new populist 'cockney' culture was celebrated nationwide. In the superdromes of late-Victorian commercial music-hall, where polite, Bohemian and popular culture intersected, 'cockney' underwent rapid social descent. The solid burgher was replaced first by the sham-genteel swell, hero of the 'Arry-stockracy' of office clerks, and then by the costermonger pearlie, immortalized on stage by Albert Chevalier.[75] These new representations were to resonate with Liverpool audiences. From the time of the short-lived Roscoe Club, the pretensions of junior young office clerks featured prominently in local satirical publications.[76] Costermongers and hawkers – trades dominated by Irish women, or 'Mary Ellens' as they were known on Scotland Road – were a pervasive presence. Along with bookies, pawnbrokers, common lodging-house keepers and prostitutes, they serviced Liverpool's thriving 'secondary economy' of the streets. Constantly moved on from respectable areas, this boisterous arena catered for the needs of the city's poorest inhabitants and least wary visitors.[77] While responding to new representations of the cockney, Liverpudlians still lacked their own stage identity: scouse humour had yet to transfer from the docks and the streets to the boards of the national music-hall circuit.

Having been adopted by the poor on the streets, Chevalier's cockney enjoyed considerable longevity. The speech patterns, dress, gestures and milieu, offered a culture for populist celebration. By the end of the First World War, however, the cockney was an increasingly elusive figure on the streets. Until reincarnated in air raid shelters as the spirit of the nation, cockney pride was marginalized in Baldwin's middle England: 'safety first' policies drew upon the culture of the shires.

As the pearlie cockney ossified into a nostalgia figure – 'an intermittently renewed metaphor for the corrosive character of modernity'[78] – a succession of Liverpool-raised (and 'slightly touched') comedians (Arthur Askey, Tommy Handley, Derek Guyler, Ted Ray, Bill Danvers, Harry Angers, Billy Bennett, Robb Wilton, Billy Matchett, Beryl Orde, Norman Evans, and on to Ken Dodd, et al.) acquired national celebrity for their humour. Although at the time there was little emphasis on Liverpudlianism, this comic efflorescence appears as a defining moment for scouse, an early instance of the Merseyside symbiosis of economic decline and cultural assertion. As a major export port, Liverpool was hit disproportionately hard by world-wide depression as trade declined more rapidly than production. Throughout the 1930s the local unemployment rates remained resolutely above 18 per cent, double the national average.[79] Even so, Merseyside was not designated as a depressed area in the legislation of 1934. Liverpool found itself disabled within inter-war discourse of unemployment and economic policy. Priority was accorded to the problems of the industrial north and other distressed manufacturing areas, while efforts to regain comparative advantage as the world's clearing house were exclusively centred on the city of London. Having to come to terms with its distinctive and accentuated structural problems, Liverpool of the depression made itself heard through humour. When asked why Merseyside produced so many comedians, Arthur Askey replied: 'You've got to be a comic to live in Liverpool'.[80]

Radio was the medium which brought scouse comedians national recognition. In the transition from music-hall to radio comedy, Tommy Handley was probably the most innovative figure, pointing the way forward to the zaniness of the *Goons*. Where other Liverpool comics like Askey and Ray tried (not always successfully) to conceal their vernacular nasality by adopting north country or standard stage accents, Handley – ably assisted by Deryck Guyler's Frisby Dyke – was unashamedly scouse (although his repertoire was by no means exclusively Liverpudlian). Through Handley's contribution to the writing and performance of *Itma*, the Liverpool accent became synonymous with verbal wit, holding its own against Mona Lott, the cockney char.[81] During the war, the pronounced scouse humour of *Itma* offered an alternative to the 'carry-on spirit' cockney revival. For local inhabitants – who celebrated Handley as 'one of ours' – it served as some recompense for news broadcasts which failed to recognize Liverpool's special plight:

> On the radio, Liverpool was never specially mentioned for being bombed; you heard only of 'the north-west'. This was a propaganda exercise because Liverpool was a strategic target for enemy bombers, but it demoralized the people of the city because they felt – as they feel today for different reasons – that they were ignored and perceived to be of no consequence.[82]

By the end of the Second World War, humour was firmly established as Liverpool's response to its psychological, economic and structural problems. Verbal wit – a cultural form which, like football, seemingly extended across sectarian boundaries[83] – spread beyond the bonding rituals of workplace and local pub to become the defining characteristic of the scouser. Surreal wordplay was highly prized, distinguishing scouse humour from the slow-building, anecdotal, character-based northern monologue and the fast patter of cockney dialogue.[84] Young men in particular prided themselves on their wit, mouthiness and verbal invention, attributes which set the real scouser apart from other lads or 'bucks':

> The difference between a buck and an everyday scouse is this: The buck is aggressive. He says, 'Warra yew luken at?' The scouse replies, 'I dunno, the labels fell off'. The buck threatens to hit you with a brick; the scouse says, 'Gowome, yermum's got cake!' A stranger on asking a buck a simple question like, 'Where's the urinal?' would be given a surly look and the words, 'Fuck off, wack!' The scouse would reply to the same question, 'How many funnels has she got?' Verbal badinage comes natural to the scouse but one gets only abuse from the buck.[85]

This is not to suggest the absence of violence in the scouse mentality. Besides humour, the macho world of the docks produced a proud boxing tradition and a shamefully high incidence of domestic violence directed against females.[86]

Just as Chevalier's cockney had been to the London poor, so the scouse comedian – as projected first on the radio and then in innumerable television soap operas – has offered humble locals an attractive and attainable role model. 'Every Liverpudlian', Alan Bennett rued, 'seems a comedian, fitted out with smart answers, ready with the chat and anxious to do his little verbal dance.'[87] Aided by broadcasters like Billy Butler and Brian Jacques on local radio, nostalgia and the heritage industry have fortified the cultural inheritance: there are collections of children's rhymes[88] and multivolume thesauri – or 'cacologies' of 'scouseology' – produced by Scouse Press, 'Liverpool's first publisher of local humour and local history'.[89] Somewhat belatedly, Liverpool has acquired its dialect literature, works of reference and reverence in which native wit is accentuated by such devices as circumlocution, an Irish-like preference for the long-winded picturesque and aphoristic phrase; 'diddymization', a seemingly contradictory liking for short forms and pet names formed by adding a 'y' to the first syllable (much favoured in 'Brookside', the soap opera which relies on 'professional' scouse); and the comic malapropism, verbal 'near misses' known locally as Malapudlianisms or Merseypropisms. It is an unfortunate irony that while lovingly preserving the wit and wisdom of yesteryear, 'heritage' publications have perpetuated some of the unflattering myths and misconceptions about contemporary Liverpool.

As with cockney, scouse has acquired metaphoric force in hostility to modernity. Prefaces to individual volumes of 'The Great Scouse Tetralogy' splenetically chart the baleful and irresistible influence of television and drug-related inner-city crime, developments which have fractured the unity and decency of scouse culture. 'While the good, old-fashioned Scouse people have lost none of their charm, wit and friendliness, those disposed to evil-doing have, alas, got worse', Fritz Spiegl rues in his 'Serious Foreword' to *Scally Scouse*. Through the curse of television, adolescents (or rather, 'the aggressive, unthinking young') have become 'prey to every pressure: greed fed by TV advertising, cops-and-robbers violence and the grubby life-styles of "soap" heroes'. In seeking a return to a golden age, Spiegl and other contributors to the Scouse Press look back beyond the early 1960s when the Beatles – four lads who shook the world – brought Liverpool global attention. In conservative nostalgia, there is no place for the 'amphetamine-boosted talents' of the Fab Four. As hero-worshipped drug-abusers, they stand condemned along with other exponents of the Mersey sound, and the accompanying (but soon southern-based) 'professional scousers', the novelists, poets and playwrights of the 1960s Mersey boom: 'The swinging, pop-crazed 60s led directly to the present drugs scourge, to narcotics-related crime and junkie-spread AIDS ... Liverpool could have done without such heroes'.[90] Viewed through this jaundiced perspective, the cultural efflorescence of the 1960s – a remarkable accompaniment to adverse structural change as the port adjusted to the end of Empire, containerization and eventual entry into the European Union – marked a sorry turning-point. Abandoning the standards of the past, Liverpool set itself on course to become the 'shock city' of post-industrial Britain. 'Suicidal' industrial militancy and 'toy town' political extremism were symptoms of cultural collapse as decent honest scouse was transmogrified into 'whingeing scouser': even the accent lost appeal, becoming associated 'more with militant shop-stewards on television than comedians as of old'.[91] Heritage 'scouse' has thus reinforced external perceptions of 'self-inflicted' decline in Liverpool, now the country's most working-class and deprived city.

In the early 1980s the *Daily Mirror* advised Liverpudlians to build a fence around their city and charge admission: 'For sadly, it has become a "showcase" of everything that has gone wrong in Britain's major cities'.[92] In media and popular perception, Liverpool has paid the price for its cherished but self-defeating 'otherness', its refusal to comply with the economic 'realities' of enterprise Britain. Media images of the 'militant' 1980s have endured, undermining the prospect of rebirth as the nation's 'city of architecture':[93]

> The long lens view of the heroic towers of the Liver Building, with the Pierhead in the foreground apparently swamped by mountains of rubbish left by striking municipal workers, but actually separated from it by the Mersey, still seems the personification of civic

squalor. And Giles Gilbert Scott's masterpiece, the Anglican cathedral, Britain's largest, marooned in an urban free-fire zone more like the South Bronx than anything in an English city, was witness to decay on a frightening scale.[94]

As shock city – Britain's Beirut[95] – Liverpool (and its inhabitants) have been accorded a crucial role in dominant political discourse. Where cockney had been evoked as the essential spirit of the nation, an emblematic figure of wartime and Butskellite consensus, the whingeing militant scouser has come to personify the 'other' against whom the respectable, responsible and 'realistic' define and align themselves. United in rejection of the Liverpool spectre of self-destructive working-class militancy, diverse social groups are brought together in a conventional wisdom of economic and political 'realism'.[96] Liverpool's recalcitrance, its undue reluctance to accept market realities, is given an ethno-cultural explanation which emphasizes its class 'otherness'. Scouse militancy is not only irrational but also unEnglish, deriving its impetus from celtic truculence, from the city's Irish heritage.

The Liverpool-Irish (of whom Heathcliff, the great other/outsider of Victorian literature, brought starving and houseless from the streets of Liverpool, may well have been one)[97] have always suffered the prejudice and negative reputation which now blight the city itself. Condemned by Dr Duncan as a contaminating presence, they have yet to be rehabilitated. They have no place in the revisionist narrative of the Irish in Britain, a celebration of widespread distribution, successful integration and 'ethnic fade'. Labelled as 'the dregs' by Father Nugent (an Irish-Liverpudlian himself), those who remained in the port of entry have been dismissed as the *caput mortuum*, a kind of underclass, as it were, unable, unwilling or unsuited to take advantage of opportunities elsewhere in Britain or the new world.[98] An enduring cultural legacy of immobility, inadequacy and irresponsibility, this 'Irishness' has purportedly set Liverpool apart. Immune from the enterprise culture, their descendants have sunk further into economic depression and (ungrateful) welfare dependency, remaining working class when all around have moved onwards and upwards. An anachronism elsewhere in Thatcherite Britain, the term 'working class' retained a residual pejorative relevance – a form of linguistic devaluation – when applied to Liverpool and its 'celtic' lumpenproletariat.

Unfortunately, this crude but effective ahistorical ethnocultural stereotyping has not been challenged from within. In Liverpudlian popular history and working-class autobiography, the unadulterated image of the lowly Irish 'slummy', reckless and feckless, has been adopted as the foundation character, a symbolic figure of inverse snobbery and pride in the evolution of the true Scottie Road scouser.[99] Furthermore, the dialect-heritage industry has traced the perceived slovenliness of the local accent back to the assumed laziness and casualism of its Irish originators. The fugitives from the Potato Famine, Spiegl contends, 'gave the Liverpudlian (whose speech was formerly Lancastrian rustic) not only his accent but also his celtic belligerence'.[100]

While these images, myths, and stereotypes await historical deconstruction, linguistic studies have begun to point the way forward, undermining preconceptions and prejudice about the nature of scouse. Without denying the substantial Irish input, application of Labovian and other forms of socio-linguistic analysis has underlined the systemic nature of Merseyside vernacular speech. By no means unpatterned and slovenly, the vernacular discipline extends across local micro-cultural variations of scouse. Furthermore, aesthetic prejudice against the accent seems inconsistent: although more open to innovation than the dialect of many northern towns, it has kept closer to the standard of grammar, vocabulary and pronunciation. In phonological evolution, indeed, scouse has undergone sound changes similar to those which occurred in the ancestor of received pronunciation some centuries ago, developments then considered high-status and prestigious.[101]

While still stigmatized as slovenly and working class, even by some native speakers, scouse is not considered as unattractive as the accents of the West Midlands in general and Birmingham in particular.[102] Scouse, indeed, has proved a cultural force of growth, extending both its geographical and social field of force.[103] In Knowles's study, middle-class informants in Aigburth studiously avoided the shibboleths of scouse, but even when using 'prestige' forms, they were still recognizably Liverpudlian.[104] As Carla Lane, Jim Hitchmough and other writers have appreciated, the external ear can readily distinguish between 'posh' and 'popular' in Liverpudlian vernacular, an essential juxtaposition for the comedy of manners. Through a process of historical inversion, snobbish pretension, the original hallmark of the Liverpool gentleman, is now the butt of humour in which 'dead' scousers, true working-class Liverpudlians, have all the best lines (suitably domesticated of course for a mass television audience).[105] Furthermore, the new climate of populism has brought a fashionable edge to certain non-standard accents in middle-class professional circles, accompanied by a new-generation nostalgia beyond the limits of conventional heritage. The Merseybeat of the 1960s has become retro-chic, celebrating a 'scouse style' linked with 'the birth of the original Britpop and the lairy humour of TV series like *The Liver Birds*'.[106] A fashionable accessory, scouse is now accentuated and cultivated, no longer concealed.

The cultural spread of scouse stands in marked contrast to Liverpool's continuing economic and demographic decline, its spiralling descent into 'Objective One' European funding status. The media myth and political rhetoric of militant Merseyside aside, scouse 'otherness' has a wide appeal, prompting some to emulate (and thereby fragment) its accent. A series of writers and dramatists, including Alun Owen, Neville Smith and Jim Allen, brought Liverpool to national attention, enabling the next generation of playwrights (often ex-schoolteachers) – Willy Russell, Alan Bleasdale, Jimmy McGovern et al. – to probe more deeply into scouse surrealism (from wacker to wacky?) and Merseyside exceptionalism. Humour and black market ingenuity – a natural extension of the traditional 'secondary economy' of the streets – are now privileged in cultural celebration of the 'scally' scouser. Incorporated into comedy series and soap operas, scallies are distinctly less laudable and heroic than wartime cockneys, but they evince their own form of 'carry on spirit'. Their dubious tricks, ploys and survival techniques[107] – what might be called a liminal form of British endurance – offer much amusement to nation-wide television audiences. In true Liverpool fashion, scallies exemplify what Matt Simpson describes as 'a come-day-go-day attitude to life born out of the seafaring traditions of months at sea followed by a few days back home "blowing" pay as if it were an embarrassment'.[108] A counterbalance to the militant Merseysider, the scally scouser of popular cultural representation acts as a roguish saturnalian safety-valve, providing humour out of economic adversity.[109]

The 'scally' is the latest product of a scouse culture that is reactive to rather than causative of economic decline.[110] Admittedly, cultural factors may have hindered Liverpool's belated industrial diversification.[111] Workers in the new industrial plants of the Merseyside Development Area soon gained a reputation for antipathy to factory discipline and managerial prerogatives, prompting some observers to trace a cultural continuity back to the old traditions of waterside casualism and seafaring independence, the legacy of dockers who offered themselves for employment when they wished and of seamen who were able to pick and choose the ships.[112] Many of the plants were abruptly closed once development aid and other short-term advantages were exhausted, the alleged 'militancy' of the local workforce serving to justify a boardroom decision taken far away from Liverpool. In the continuing tendency towards rationalization, giant combines, as P.J. Waller has noted, seem always to single out the Liverpool limb for amputation.[113] Decline and disinvestment have reduced the local resource base, but 'scally' scouse resilience seems replenished.

Always vibrant in response to adverse structural change, scouse has periodically revitalized itself, taking a variety of cultural forms (such as the dramatic renaissance briefly noted above) since the radio comedy of the inter-war depression.[114] Although he never visited the city, Jung captured its ambivalence in a famous dream, a 'pool of life' amid squalor and decay.[115] One new arrival in the economic blight of the early 1980s was immediately struck by the 'new Liverpool rock scene', the latest 'Scouse Phenomenon':

> Amidst all the well-documented problems that face Liverpudlians day in and day out, some things have never changed. The people remain confident, amusing and resourceful; the football teams beat everybody, and the music is as fresh, interesting and influential as ever. It's the music that grabbed me and made me stay![116]

Music offers perhaps the best insight into Liverpool's distinctiveness or 'otherness': significantly, tongue-in-cheek lyrics are the hallmark of the latest fashion, 'Scalpop'.[117] As with dialect, there is no indigenous 'folk' tradition in Liverpool – other than the sea-shanties of transient seamen. The Irish have contributed much to the local music scene, as the recent boom in Irish pub music attests, but they are only one voice within a wider mixture.[118] Although privileged in heritage and autobiographical accounts, the 'community' mentality of the slummy coexisted with a broader culture, a seafaring cosmopolitanism which made Liverpool particularly receptive to foreign ideas (syndicalism, for example) and to American popular music. Before the Beatles and the advent of the Merseysound, Liverpool had a reputation as the 'Nashville of the North', thanks to the cultural implant of the latest US albums which 'Cunard Yanks', sailors on the Atlantic run, brought back with them – back in the 1930s, indeed, Jimmie Rogers, 'The Yodelling Brakeman', had enjoyed considerable popularity.[119] Strengthened by cross-fertilization with local country bands, Merseybeat arose in similar fashion: 'We used to get the soul records and the rock and roll records long before anyone else got them just because we were here and the sailors would bring them'.[120] The creative receptivity of scouse stands in marked contrast to cockney: rejuvenated by the 'Lambeth Walk', patriotic cockney offered hermetic protection against Americanization or other alien cultural influence.

By no means restricted to music, cosmopolitanism accounts for other Liverpudlian cultural peculiarities, such as the distinctive 'expressionist' nature of working-class fiction in the inter-war years. While writers elsewhere reconstructed the enclosed world of the slum, the Liverpool school – George Garrett, James Hanley and Jim Phelan, all Liverpool-Irish *and* seamen – explored cultural multiplicity in waterfront underworlds, across the globe as they addressed issues of dislocation, rootlessness and alienation.[121] Beyond the 'inland' Irish Sea, Liverpool's private celtic empire, the city looked to the great oceans: as the aptly named Irish-American historian Robert Scally has shrewdly observed, Liverpool at its height drew upon both an inner and outer world.[122]

Unlike dialect culture, scouse thrived through interaction, a process
encapsulated by L.T. Roche's account of the free-flowing wit (and drink)
at the 'Winey' (Yates' Wine Lodge) after work on the docks:

> The Liverpool characteristic became obvious. A soft Irish humour,
> tempered by a Welsh wit. The ability to tell of travellers' tales,
> through personal contact, or from a close relative; brother, nephew,
> uncle, or in-law ... The vast merchant fleet, arriving and departing,
> without a regular time-table, set the base at casual. The immi-
> grants, transients in the main, swelled the complex of Liverpool.
> Songs and stories from lands afar widened and increased the nor-
> mally narrow-based traditions. Mixed religions incensed, or in-
> fused, the inhabitants. Mixed marriages, in religion and colour,
> diffused the conglomeration.[123]

It would be wrong to conclude in uncritical celebration of scouse
cosmopolitanism and otherness. A culture of decline, scouse is unlikely
to rejuvenate the local economy, the post-industrial investment in tour-
ism and heritage notwithstanding.[124] Ironically, the award of Objective
One status, some economists fear, 'may remind some outside Merseyside of the area's relative poverty and record of decline: deterring them
from coming into the area'.[125] As the publicity surrounding the Jamie
Bulger case attested, there is some impatience with Liverpool's 'self-
pitying' insistence on its difference and particular problems. In reporting local reaction to the Heysel and Hillsborough disasters and the
Bulger case, the quality press have constructed an image of Liverpudlian
self-indulgence, self-pity and mawkishness, an unwelcome complement
to the revived tabloid assault, otherwise on the wane in the absence of
industrial and political dispute, against scouse violence, militancy and
arrogance.[126] In the city at the time of the Hillsborough disaster, Alan
Bennett found himself thinking, 'It *would* be Liverpool, that sentimen-
tal, self-dramatizing place'. Bennett, indeed, came to dislike Liverpool:
'Robert Ross said that Dorsetshire rustics, after Hardy, had the inso-
lence of the artist's model, and so it is with Liverpudlians. They have
figured in too many plays and have a cockiness that comes from being
told too often that they and their city are special.'[127] While acknowledg-
ing Liverpool's 'unrivalled tradition in entertainment', its propensity to
exploit the rise of popular art forms over the past thirty-odd years,
cultural critics can still be scathing of its insular style: 'Liverpool resembles an island with arcane customs and rituals, loosely attached to the
north-west coast'.[128]

While this insularity may be called into question by the city's cosmopolitan past, Liverpool lacks a political culture and a historiographical
tradition to incorporate its non-Celtic in-migrants, the long-established
presence of West Indians, Africans and Chinese notwithstanding.[129]

Having captured control of the moribund party machine, Militant chose to operate municipal politics in typical Liverpool 'Tammany' style – Chicago rather than Petrograd on the Mersey. The associational endeavours and representational needs of ethnic, gender, special interest and minority groups, different in composition from the old sectarian and Irish formations, were snubbed and ignored, causing particular offence in the black community.[130] At a time of remarkable ecumenism in the 'hurt city', recent historical studies have attempted a positive reassessment of sectarianism ('Catslicks' and 'Prodidogs'), and of casualism and the continuing propensity to riot,[131] but the 'black struggle for historical recognition in Liverpool'[132] continues:

> the notion of 'scouseness' was, and still is, something Black Liverpudlians are excluded from since to be 'scouse' is to be white and working class. One has only to examine the crowds at Anfield. Such exclusion relates to the broader issue of the way Black people continue to be perceived and treated as if they are immigrants when in reality the majority are Black British. This continues to reflect a deep-rooted racism that is as much a part of Liverpool's character as it is of Britain as a whole.[133]

Although giving a voice to Liverpool and to the casual, non-manufacturing working class, the language of scouse is not without privilege, prejudice and exclusion.

Historical deconstruction of scouse provides a useful corrective to the restricted concerns of conventional labour history. In the reconstruction that lies ahead, however, there is a need to transcend the in-built inequalities of the local vernacular, to establish better communication and understanding between the disadvantaged, exploited and marginalized elements of the post-industrial city.[134] Applied in this way, the 'linguistic turn' might yet reconstitute the working class.

Notes

*   I would like to thank Andrew Hamer, Fritz Spiegl, Jonathan Bate, Tony Lane, Jim Dillon, Eric Taplin, Nick Hardy, Arline Wilson, John Davies, Frank Boyce, Mike Power and Jon Lawrence for their comments on earlier drafts of this chapter.
1.   See my essay 'The peculiarities of Liverpool' in John Belchem (ed.), *Popular Politics, Riot and Labour: Essays in Liverpool History 1790–1940* (Liverpool, 1992), pp. 1–20.
2.   Here the pattern was set by the foundation text of the 'linguistic turn', Gareth Stedman Jones, 'Rethinking Chartism' in his *Languages of Class: Studies in English Working Class History, 1832–1982* (Cambridge, 1983). For a significant broadening of the understanding of 'political' language, see James Epstein, *Radical Expression: Political Language, Ritual and*

Symbol in England, 1790–1850 (New York, 1994). See also Raphael Samuel's two-part essay, 'Reading the signs', *History Workshop Journal*, 32 (1991), pp. 88–109 and 33 (1992), pp. 220–51.

3. There are considerable problems for the historian in recapturing demotic speech, compounded by the tendency for all social groups to move towards a received pronunciation accent in formal contexts, see Andrew Hamer, 'Non-standard accents and the classroom', *Proceedings of the English Association North*, 6 (1992), pp. 56–64.

4. Patrick Joyce, *Visions of the People: Industrial England and the Question of Class, 1840–1914* (Cambridge, 1991); *idem, Democratic Subjects: the Self and the Social in Nineteenth-Century England* (Cambridge, 1994); *idem*, 'The end of social history', *Social History*, 20 (1995), pp. 73–91. James Vernon, *Politics and the People: a Study in English Political Culture, c.1815–1867* (Cambridge, 1993).

5. The definitive linguistic study is Gerald O. Knowles, 'Scouse: the urban dialect of Liverpool', unpublished PhD thesis, University of Leeds (1973). See also, Hilary B. De Lyon, 'A sociolinguistic study of aspects of the Liverpool accent', unpublished M.Phil thesis, University of Liverpool (1981); and Mark Newbrook, *Sociolinguistic Reflexes of Dialect Interference in West Wirral* (Frankfurt, 1986). The study of Merseyside in J.C. Wells, *Accents of English* (3 vols, Cambridge, 1982), vol. 2, pp. 371–3 draws heavily on Knowles.

6. A. Hughes and P. Trudgill, *English Accents and Dialects* (London, 1979), p. 62.

7. Alan Bennett, *Writing Home* (London, 1994) pp. 144, 289.

8. See Gareth Stedman Jones's marvellous study of 'The "cockney" and the nation, 1780–1988' in D. Feldman and G.S. Jones (eds), *Metropolis London: Histories and Representations since 1800* (London, 1989), pp. 272–324.

9. According to Knowles, p. 17, the first reference is to be found in A.J. Ellis, *On Early English Pronunciation. Part V: the Existing Phonology of English Dialects* (1889). By this time, the accent had apparently already crossed the river to Birkenhead and 'Merseyside Wirral', as Ellis disregarded the area north of Bebington in his discussion of West Cheshire usage, see Newbrook, *Sociolinguistic Reflexes*, p. 53.

10. See, for example, *The True and Wonderful History of Dick Liver* (Liverpool, 1824), in which 'Timothy Touchstone', alias the Reverend William Shepherd, condemned the old Corporation and championed Dick Liver, the Liverpool commonalty.

11. *Liverpool Lion*, 14 August, 1847, p. 132.

12. Peter Aughton, *Liverpool: a People's History* (Preston, 1990), p. 214. For the importance of the American connection, see Peter Howell Williams, *Liverpolitana* (Liverpool, 1971), ch. 7.

13. *Notes and Queries*, 7th series, 6 (1888), pp. 124–5, 153, 178, 210.

14. Frank Shaw, *My Liverpool* (Parkgate, 1971; repr. 1988), p. 163.

15. This distinction applies throughout Jack Robinson's autobiography, *Teardrops on my Drum* (London, 1986). Writing of the 1930s and 1940s, by which time Dicky Sam had 'lost its provenance', Ron Garnett claimed that 'Scouse is a generic term applied to Liverpudlian seamen or members of H.M. forces. Whacker is used mainly as a form of greeting between fellow scousers', *Liverpool in the 1930s and the Blitz* (Preston, 1995), p. 124.

16. *Liverpool Echo*, 5 May 1995, p. 30. First coined by George Melly as the title of his autobiography (1984), 'Scouse Mouse' is now a lovable comic character occupying the centrepiece of the world's largest continuous mural, over a quarter of a mile long, painted in a corridor at Alder Hey Children's Hospital, P. Young and J. Bellew, *The Whitbread Book of Scouseology: an Anthology of Merseyside* (Liverpool, n.d.), p. 95.

17. There is no reference to food (or to Liverpool), however, in the entry on scouse in Joseph Wright (ed.), *The English Dialect Dictionary* (London, 1904), vol. 5, p. 264. Here scouse/skouce/skouse is west country dialect for to frolic, frisk about, to run fast; to cause to gallop, to ride hard; and to drive, chase, harry, as in the Gloucestershire usage: 'I skoused the mouse but could not catch it'.

18. See the report of B. Nightingall, 15 September 1837 in a volume of correspondence of the Poor Law Commissioners with the Poor Law Union of Liverpool, in Public Record Office, Kew, M.H. 12/5966. I would like to thank Adrian Allan, University Archivist, University of Liverpool, for drawing my attention to this reference which predates by three years the first recorded use in the *Oxford English Dictionary*.

19. See, for example, *Porcupine*, 6 November 1875, p. 505, a reference kindly provided by Fritz Spiegl.

20. Terry Cooke, *Scotland Road: 'The Old Neighbourhood'* (Birkenhead, 1987), pp. 36, 52.

21. *Clarion* 18 December 1897. For details of the Falkner Street Cinderella Club, see Krista Cowman, 'Engendering citizenship. The political involvement of women on Merseyside 1890–1920', unpublished PhD thesis, University of York (1995), pp. 158–61.

22. Frances Clarke, *At the Heart of It All: an Autobiography* (London, 1993), p. 29.

23. See, for example, Cooke, *Scotland Road*, p. 35, and Robinson *Teardrops on my Drum*, p. 102. Jim Dillon kindly drew my attention to the Park Lane variety.

24. Shaw, *My Liverpool*, p. 15.

25. *Liverpool Repository of Literature, Philosophy and Commerce* (January 1826). See also M.J. Power, 'The growth of Liverpool' in Belchem (ed.), *Popular Politics, Riot and Labour*, pp. 21–37.

26. William Enfield, *An Essay towards the History of Liverpool* (London, 1774), p. 90.

27. A leading merchant in the West India interest (an efficient slaveowner though never a slavetrader), Gladstone possessed an outstanding business brain, but took no interest in the Industrial Revolution, see John Vincent's review of a number of books on the Gladstone family in *Victorian Studies*, 16 (1972), p. 101.

28. See, for example, *The Stranger in Liverpool: or, an Historical and Descriptive View of the Town of Liverpool and its Environs* (Liverpool, 1846), pp. 108–9.

29. William Moss, *The Liverpool Guide* (Liverpool, 1796), p. 1.

30. *Chamber of Commerce. Report of the Select Committee Appointed to Consider What Steps can be Taken for the Purpose of Constituting Liverpool a Self-Dependent Financial Centre* (Liverpool, 1863). As early as 1698, Liverpool had appeared to Celia Fiennes as 'London in miniature', see Power, 'The growth of Liverpool', p. 21.

31. Liverpool's pretensions were acknowledged by outsiders: see, for example, the entry on Liverpool in *Mitchell's Newspaper Press Directory* (1847), p. 161:

> Situated near the mouth of the Mersey, this *second metropolis*, has rapidly advanced in opulence and importance ... The public buildings are in a style of liberal expense and tasteful decoration, superior to those of almost any provincial town in England; and several of its institutions are honourable testimonials of the enlightened spirit by which commercial prosperity has been accompanied.

For the extension of the 'second metropolis' motif into popular fiction, see *The Life, Adventure and Opinions of a Liverpool Policeman, and his Contemporaries* (Liverpool, 1841).

32. See Arline Wilson's forthcoming University of Liverpool PhD thesis on 'The culture of commerce: Liverpool's merchant elite c.1790–1850'.

33. J.A. Picton, *Liverpool Improvements, and How to Accomplish Them* (Liverpool, 1853), p. 24.

34. For a useful survey of societies and institutes, see *Roscoe Magazine*, March 1849.

35. Tony Lane, *Liverpool: Gateway of Empire* (London, 1987) ch. 2.

36. Thomas Baines, *History of the Commerce and Town of Liverpool, and of the Rise of Manufacturing Industry in the Adjoining Counties* (London, 1852), p. 840.

37. *Notes and Queries*, 7th series, 6 (1888), pp. 210–11.

38. Joyce, *Visions*, chs 11–12.

39. Liverpool is 'in a number of ways linguistically as southern as it is northern', Hughes and Trudgill, *English Accent*, p. 20.

40. Ian Sellers, *Nineteenth-Century Liverpool and the Novelists* (Warrington, 1979), p. 3:

> The Liverpudlian, by birth or adoption, confesses to a certain jealousy of Manchester and London and towards the hardened literary convention which sees the Victorian industrial novel as the product of one, and the Urban novel of the other. Now Liverpool is neither 'urban' nor 'industrial', neither Hogarthian/Dickensian nor Mrs Gaskellish, nor certainly was it so tightly-knit and self-contained as to be 'provincial'.

41. Liverpool does not appear in the index of the latest two-volume study of 'gentlemanly capitalism', P.J. Cain and A.G. Hopkins, *British Imperialism: Innovation and Expansion 1688–1914* (London, 1993), and *idem, British Imperialism: Crisis and Deconstruction 1914–1990* (London, 1993).

42. Pat O'Mara, *The Autobiography of a Liverpool Irish Slummy* (London, 1934), p. 17.

43. John Belchem, Vincent Robert and Karl Pohl, 'Grandes villes: Liverpool, Lyon and Munich' in A. Prost, J.L. Robert and F. Boll (eds), *L'invention des syndicalismes* (forthcoming). Wilfred Smith drew attention to the 'illuminating' contrast between Merseyside and Greater Manchester:

> While Merseyside is foreign to and has been superimposed on the rural landscape of South-west Lancashire and Wirral, Greater Manchester is autochthonous and has its roots deep in the roots of South-east Lancashire ... on Merseyside, the life of the place centres on the axial line of the river; in South-east Lancashire, human activity displays similar qualities at many points widely diffused over an extensive industrial terrain. The one represents the outgrowth from a single cell, the other registers the aggregation of a whole mass of similar cells.

Wilfred Smith, 'Merseyside and the Merseyside district', in W. Smith (ed.), *A Scientific Survey of Merseyside* (Liverpool, 1953), pp. 1–2.

44. John Kerrigan, 'Introduction', in P. Robinson (ed.), *Liverpool Accents: Seven Poets and a City* (Liverpool, 1996), p. 2.

45. Knowles, 'Scouse', ch. 2. Areas on the periphery of Merseyside, such as West Wirral, are especially suitable for study since it is possible to identify features as being distinctively 'Merseyside' or 'Cheshire' to a much greater extent than would be possible with the equivalent characteristics for most other urban areas, see Newbrook, *Sociolinguistic Reflexes*, p. 15 and *passim*.

46. J. Langton, 'Liverpool and its hinterland in the late eighteenth-century', in B.L. Anderson and P.M.L. Stoney (eds), *Commerce, Industry and Transport: Studies in Economic Change on Merseyside* (Liverpool, 1983), pp. 1–25.

47. Smith, 'Merseyside and the Merseyside district', p. 2.

48. These cultural and structural factors also facilitated working-class collective action, which perhaps accounts for Liverpool's backwardness in Chartism and other movements, see John Belchem, 'Beyond *Chartist Studies*: class, community and party in early-Victorian populist politics', in D. Fraser (ed.), *Cities, Class and Communication: Essays in Honour of Asa Briggs* (London, 1990), pp. 105–6, 120–21.

49. For an excellent analysis of the construction of Geordie through the interaction of community and culture in the mining villages of the north east, see Rob Colls, *The Collier's Rant: Song and Culture in the Industrial Village* (London, 1977).

50. Walter Dixon Scott, *Liverpool 1907* (1907; repr. Neston, 1979), p. 6, 24.

51. R. Lawton and C.G. Pooley, 'The social geography of Merseyside in the nineteenth century', final report to the Social Science Research Council (Department of Geography, University of Liverpool, 1976).

52. Knowles, 'Scouse', pp. 23–4.

53. W.H. Duncan, 'On the sanitary state of Liverpool' (1842) quoted in G. Kearns, P. Laxton and J. Campbell, 'Duncan and the cholera test: public health in mid nineteenth-century Liverpool', *Transactions of the Historic Society of Lancashire and Cheshire*, 143 (1994), pp. 98–9.

54. Richard Dennis, *English Industrial Cities of the Nineteenth Century: a Social Geography* (Cambridge, 1984), pp. 228–30. C.G. Pooley, 'The residential segregation of migrant communities in mid-Victorian Liverpool', *Transactions of the Institute of British Geographers*, 2 (1977), pp. 364–72. Hall Caine noted of William Edwardes Tirebuck, the most talented of the Liverpool-Welsh novelists, that he 'was only the foster

child of the great city on the Mersey and much as he loved and intimately knew her, at the bottom of his nature he was a Welshman, body and soul', quoted in Sellers, *Nineteenth-Century Liverpool*, p. 52. Another Liverpool-Welsh novelist, Eleazar Roberts assured his readers that the Liverpool setting of his writings would not 'detract in the least from its faithfulness to its Cymric perspective', ibid. p. 59.

55. Quoted in R.J. Scally, *The End of Hidden Ireland* (New York, 1995), p. 189.
56. Charles Dickens, *The Uncommercial Traveller* (final edition, 1869), ch. 5.
57. J.K. Walton and A. Wilcox (eds), *Low Life and Moral Improvement in Mid-Victorian England: Liverpool through the Journalism of Hugh Shimmin* (Leicester, 1991), p. 212.
58. I thank Tony Lane and Jim Dillon for their critical comments and knowledge of oral history.
59. J.R. Walkowitz, *City of Dreadful Delight: Narratives of Sexual Danger in Late-Victorian London* (London, 1992), ch. 1.
60. Dixon Scott, *Liverpool 1907*, pp. 38–9.
61. For the best analysis of waterfront casualism, see Eric Taplin, *Liverpool Dockers and Seamen 1870–1890* (Hull, 1974), and *idem, The Dockers' Union* (Leicester, 1986).
62. Dixon Scott, *Liverpool 1907*, p. 26.
63. L.T. Roche, *Down the Hatch* (Liverpool, 1985), p. 219.
64. Garnett, *Liverpool in the 1930s*, p. 3.
65. John Kerrigan, 'Introduction', p. 3. Noting the relative lack of overland travel eastward from Liverpool Ron Garnett has some interesting observations on the micro-geographical distribution of the Liverpool dialect and the boundaries of 'Liverpool suzerainty':

> Wigan was disparaged by Merseysiders as a joke; Ormskirk, St Helens, Runcorn, Widnes, were on the frontier – beyond which the Lancashire accent held sway. The pattern of incursion of the 'scouse' tongue was largely littoral – Southport, the Wirral, and Chester (despite its well-heeled residents and county town atmosphere) were all in scouse territory. Lancashire was alien and Liverpool did not consider itself to be within the confines of Lancashire. Garnett, *Liverpool in the 1930s*, pp. 13–14.

66. Anthony Griffiths, *Scouse Wars* (Liverpool, 1992), p. 6.
67. Baines, *History of … Liverpool*, p. 769. The rivalry extended to philanthropic and missionary zeal, hence the alacrity with which Liverpool followed London in establishing a Merchant Seaman's Auxiliary Bible Society:

> A corresponding interest to that which the moral want and misery of seamen in London had originated was quickly communicated to Liverpool, and a desire was excited of imitating the judicious bounty of the metropolis, no less than of following hard in the captivating career of its maritime greatness; a holier rivalry was superadded to the energies of commercial speculation.

Eighth Report of the Liverpool Auxiliary Bible Society (Liverpool, 1819), p. 13.

68. Posting-bill in British Library, call-mark 10349f8.
69. One of the lesser Liverpool-Welsh novelists who wrote under the pseu-
    donym Powys Oswin was scathing in his criticism of metropolitan pre-
    tensions of the Liverpool mercantile élite in *Liverpool Ho!* (1857): 'Proud,
    showy imitators of London absurdities ... Liverpool ladies poor players
    upon the second fiddle, weavers of old garbs, pickers up and misers of
    metropolitan cast-offs and farce-robes', quoted in Sellers, *Nineteenth-
    Century Liverpool*, pp. 30–31.
70. Stedman Jones, 'The "cockney"', pp. 280–84.
71. Quoted in Stedman Jones 'The "cockney"', p. 280.
72. C. Colvin (ed.), *Maria Edgworth: Letters from England 1813–44* (Ox-
    ford, 1971), p. 10.
73. Sir Herbert Maxwell (ed.), *Creevey Papers*, vol. 2 (London, 1904), pp.
    256–7.
74. *Notes and Queries*, 7th series, 6 (1888), pp. 124–5, 153, 178, 210. See
    also R.T. Shannon, *Gladstone* (London, 1982), vol. 1, p. 93.
75. Stedman Jones, 'The "cockney"', pp. 284–300.
76. See, for example the innumerable cartoons and articles satirizing the
    club in *Liverpool Lion*, vol. 1 (1847).
77. M. Brogden, *The Police: Autonomy and Consent* (London, 1982), pp.
    43–73.
78. Ibid., p. 276. Tony Lane informs me that shop stewards on the Liver-
    pool docks in the 1960s and 1970s still referred to their London coun-
    terparts (not least Jack Dash) as 'pearlie dockers'.
79. S. Davies, P. Gill, L. Grant, M. Nightingale, R. Noon and A. Shallice,
    *Genuinely Seeking Work: Mass Unemployment on Merseyside in the
    1930s* (Birkenhead, 1992).
80. Quoted in Shaw, *My Liverpool*, p. 25.
81. Ibid., pp. 160–64.
82. Clarke, *At the Heart of It All*, p. 26. For a major reassessment of
    Liverpool and the blitz, see Garnett, *Liverpool in the 1930s*, ch. 6.
83. Frank Boyce has reminded me that the early radio comedians tended to
    come from Protestant backgrounds. More recently, television comedy
    and soap opera have redressed the balance, delighting in Catholic stere-
    otypes and in-jokes (such as the inability of Mrs Boswell, matriarch of
    'Bread', to cross herself correctly). On the absence of sectarianism in
    football allegiance, see Tony Mason, 'The Blues and the Reds: a history
    of the Liverpool and Everton Football Clubs', *Transactions of the His-
    toric Society of Lancashire and Cheshire*, 134 (1985).
84. Jeffrey Richards, *Stars in our Eyes: Lancashire Stars of Stage, Screen and
    Radio* (Preston, 1994).
85. Robinson, *Teardrops on my Drum*, p. 32.
86. Pat Ayers and Jan Lambertz, 'Marriage relations, money and domestic
    violence in working-class Liverpool, 1919–39', in J. Lewis (ed.), *Labour
    and Love: Women's Experience of Home and Family 1850–1940* (Ox-
    ford, 1986). The emergence of Women of the Waterfront during the
    current (1995–96) dock dispute points to an important cultural and
    political change, see Kate Markey, 'Support on the waterfront', *The Big
    Issue in the North*, 2–8 January 1996, and Merseyside Port Shop Stew-
    ards Committee, *Never Cross a Picket Line* (Liverpool, 1996), pp. 23–7.
    Since this chapter was written, a major study of the dispute has been

published; see Michael Lavalette and Jane Kennedy, *Solidarity on the Waterfront: The Liverpool Lock Out of 1995–96* (Liverpool, 1996). On the television, the fist-happy Liverpudlian is to the fore in Harry Enfield's Brookside parody, 'The Scousers'.

87. Bennett, *Writing Home*, pp. 143–4, 289. In their introduction to *The Whitbread Book of Scouseology*, Young and Bellew point out that their 'A–Z of Scouseology isn't just a massive list of facts. It's put together with the humour and the asides Scousers are noted for'.

88. Frank Shaw, *You Know Me Anty Nelly? Liverpool Children's Rhymes* (London, 1970).

89. Fritz Spiegl (ed.), *Lern Yerself Scouse, vol. 1* (Liverpool, 1966; repr. 1988); Linacre Lane, *Lern Yerself Scouse, vol. 2: the ABZ of Scouse* (Liverpool, 1966); Brian Minard, *Lern Yerself Scouse, vol. 3: Wersia Sensa Yuma?* (Liverpool, 1972); and Fritz Spiegl, *Lern Yerself Scouse, vol. 4: Scally Scouse* (Liverpool, 1989). Scouse Press has now been joined by several other heritage and local history publishers, including Countyvise, Liver Press, Bluecoat Press and the Harbour Publishing Company. Mention should also be made of the publications of the Docklands History Project, and of the O'Connor brothers' superb photographic reminders of Liverpool's past: *Liverpool It All Came Tumbling Down* (Liverpool, 1986), 'testimony to our very own "scouse heritage"', Billy Butler writes in his foreword, and *Liverpool: our City, our Heritage*, (Liverpool, 1990). Note the difference in tone and terminology from the earlier heritage publication of the Merseyside Civic Society, *Liverpolitana* (1971).

90. Spiegl, *Scally Scouse*, pp. 5–10.

91. See Fritz Spiegl's 'Preface' to the 1984 reprinted edition of the first volume of *Lern Yerself Scouse*.

92. *Daily Mirror* 11 October 1982 quoted in C.M. Czypull, 'Liverpool's economic decline since World War Two: an approach towards the structural and historical problems of the region', unpublished MA thesis, University of Hannover (1992).

93. In the 1960s, there was a flourishing of pre-tourist 'heritage', focused on the rescue and retrieval not of the local dialect but of the city's commercial and public architecture, best exemplified in Quentin Hughes, *Seaport* (London, 1964), reprinted in 1993 with a 'Postscript' applauding the complementary efforts of the council's Heritage Bureau, the Merseyside Civic Society and the first regional branch of the Victorian Society.

94. 'The quality of Mersey is not strained', *The Guardian*, 6 September 1994.

95. P. Scraton, A. Jemphrey and S. Coleman, *No Last Rights: the Denial of Justice and the Promotion of Myth in the Aftermath of the Hillsborough Disaster* (Liverpool, 1995), p. 226.

96. This is to suggest a later application of the process analysed by Ross McKibbin in 'Class and conventional wisdom: the Conservative Party and the "public" in inter-war Britain', in R. McKibbin, *The Ideologies of Class* (Oxford, 1990), pp. 259–93.

97. Terry Eagleton, *Heathcliff and the Great Hunger* (London, 1995), pp. 1–26.

98. See the essays by David Fitzpatrick, Colin Pooley and Graham Davis in R. Swift and S. Gilley (eds), *The Irish in Britain 1815–1914* (Dublin,

1991). For an alternative perspective on the Liverpool-Irish, see John Belchem, 'The immigrant alternative: ethnic and sectarian mutuality among the Liverpool Irish during the nineteenth century' in O. Ashton, R. Fyson and S. Roberts (eds), *The Duty of Discontent: Essays for Dorothy Thompson* (London, 1995), pp. 231–50.

99. The great north end thoroughfare of nineteenth-century Irish-Liverpool, Scotland Road has established itself as the 'hallowed patch' of Liverpool's heritage and identity, aided by the presence of a local writers' workshop. According to Terry Cooke's *Scotland Road* blurb:

> There was nothing like it anywhere else in the world, and it was known world-wide thanks to the many Scotland Road men who went to sea and talked nostalgically about it. In spite of the many fine buildings that Liverpool possessed it epitomised Liverpool and that special Liverpool spirit that could survive any disaster and then recount the event with typical Scouse humour.

Besides the autobiographies already mentioned, J. Woods, *Growin' Up: One Scouser's Social History* (Preston, 1989) is also set in Scotland Road, 'one of the "rougher" districts of the city'. Written long before the heritage boom, Pat O'Mara's harrowing *Autobiography* (which makes no reference to scouse) is set for the most part in the south end slums. For some unexplained reason, the word 'Irish' has been deleted from the title of the recent (but undated) reprint by the Bluecoat Press.

100. Spiegl, 'Preface' to 1984 reprinted edition of *Lern Yerself Scouse*. See also his 'Foreword' to *The ABZ of Scouse* on how nineteenth-century Merseyside was a Mecca for 'would-be workers who lacked the ability to acquire skills or, being shiftless, lacked the ambition ... Let us face the awful fact: it is from the uneducated and in some respects uneducatable stratum of Merseyside life that Scouse has arisen and developed'.

101. Andrew Hamer, 'Scouse boundaries', paper presented to Liverpool Studies Seminar, 15 November 1995, and his paper, 'Non-standard accents and the classroom', *Proceedings of the English Association North*, vi. See also Knowles, 'Scouse', De Lyon, 'A sociolinguistic study', and Newbrook, *Sociolinguistic Reflexes*.

102. Peter Trudgill, *On Dialect* (Oxford, 1983), pp. 218–19.

103. Knowles, 'Scouse', pp. 14–15, charts its progress north to Southport, north-east to Maghull, Lydiate and Ormskirk, east to St Helens (although Andrew Hamer has noted resistance here – the boundary of woollydom perhaps?), and south-east beyond Halewood to Runcorn and Widnes. See also Newbrook, *Sociolinguistic Reflexes*, for its dominance in West Wirral.

104. Knowles, 'Scouse', ch. 8.

105. 'Liverpudlians are paranoid about what they consider to be "posh"', Matt Simpson, 'Voices, accents, histories', in P. Robinson (ed.), *Liverpool Accents*, p. 167.

106. 'The Fab Fur', *The Observer* 26 November 1995, Life Magazine p. 58.

107. Spiegl, *Scally Scouse* provides a useful introductory manual.

108. Matt Simpson, 'Voices, accents, histories', p. 167.

109. In its preview of 'And the beat goes on', the 'new Scouse extravaganza' on Channel 4, *The Guardian* ('The guide', 16 March 1996) notes how

> from the Liver Birds to Brookside, TV invariably portrays Liverpudlians as plucky underdogs ... a sort of run-down, put-upon natural fighter who's seen it all, done it all, and had it all done to them, but still faces life with a stoic sense of humour and an earthy honesty that's somehow difficult to find elsewhere.

110.   This is not to suggest, of course, that the militant scouser and the scally scouser are mutually exclusive. Jimmy Sexton's narrative of the great dock strike of 1889, the formative moment of Merseyside militancy, is punctuated by accounts of the practical jokes of some of its participants, most notably, one-eyed Blind Riley and the inebriate Christie Kenny. Sexton also appreciated the humour and culture of the old dockers' clubs and societies as they were gradually subsumed into trade unionism, such as the traditional grant of five shillings to coffin bearers at the funeral of a workmate:

> I recall one case where the bearers, anticipating the payment of five shillings, overspent it at the local pub before they had earned it, increased the deficit after they had discharged their melancholy duties, and eventually claimed another shilling piece, under trade union rules, on the ground that their job had been carrying dead meat, for which they were entitled to six shillings a day.

James Sexton, *Sir James Sexton, Agitator: the Life of the Dockers' M.P.* (London, 1935), pp. 93–101, 115.

111.   For a full discussion, see John Belchem and Michael Power, 'Structural change, culture and class in early industrial Liverpool' in R. Schulze (ed.), *Industrial Regions in Transformation* (Essen, 1993), pp. 119–42.

112.   R. Bean and P. Stoney, 'Strikes on Merseyside: a regional analysis', *Industrial Relations Journal*, 17 (1986), pp. 9–23.

113.   Merseyside Socialist Research Group, *Merseyside in Crisis* (Birkenhead 1980). P.J. Waller, *Democracy and Sectarianism: a Political and Social History of Liverpool 1868–1939* (Liverpool, 1981), p. 351. For a critique of the pragmatic new realism of Merseyside workers since the recessionary 1980s, see Ralph Darlington, *The Dynamics of Workplace Unionism: Shop Stewards' Organization in Three Merseyside Plants* (London, 1994).

114.   As Peter Robinson explains in the Preface to *Liverpool Accents*, '*Liverpool Accents* is my attempt to demonstrate that in the field of poetry too, the city's hard years have been a goad to creative vitality and rebirth'.

115.   Robinson, *Liverpool Accents*, pp. 67–8, 90.

116.   Con McConville's introduction to Klaus Schwartze, *The Scouse Phenomenon: the Scrapbook of the New Liverpool Rock Scene* (Birkenau, 1987).

117.   Michael Blackmon, 'Music review', *The Big Issue in the North*, 116, 15–21 July 1996, p. 29.

118.   Kevin McManus, *Céilís, Jigs and Ballads: Irish Music in Liverpool* (Liverpool, 1994).

119.   I owe this reference to Jim Dillon whose uncles worked on Harrison boats and regularly brought back records from Galveston and New Orleans.

120. Kenny Johnson quoted in Kevin McManus, *'Nashville of the North'*: *Country Music in Liverpool* (Liverpool, 1994), p. 2.

121. K. Worpole, *Dockers and Detectives: Popular Reading: Popular Writing* (London, 1983), ch. 4.

122. Scally, *The End of Hidden Ireland*, ch. 5, 'Liverpool and the Celtic Sea' is a masterly reconstruction of mid-nineteenth-century Liverpool.

123. Roche, *Down the Hatch*, p. 111. The tone here is altogether more positive and convivial than in Dickens's famous account of mid-Victorian Liverpool's notorious waterfront drinking-houses (and other clip-joint temptations) in *The Uncommercial Traveller*, ch. 5 where 'Poor Mercantile Jack' is entrapped along with Loafing Jack of the States, Maltese Jack, Jack of Sweden, Jack the Finn and other vulnerable sailors ashore. See also, Matt Simpson, 'Voices, accents, histories', p. 167: 'the lingo and character of Liverpool are the result of cosmopolitan mix. Among the ingredients that go to make up the peculiar Liverpool stew you find Lancashire amiability, Irish blarney, Welsh acerbity, as well as bits of Chinese, German, Scandinavian, to name only the obvious ones'.

124. In '50 Great Merseyside Facts' and other promotional literature to attract investment, the Mersey Partnership places emphasis on 'the renowned warmth and sense of humour of Merseysiders themselves'.

125. P. Minford and P. Stoney, 'Objective One must be growth', *Merseyside Economic and Business Prospect*, 8, ii (1993), p. 4.

126. For an excellent analysis of the media and Hillsborough, see Scraton, Jemphrey and Coleman, *No Last Rights*, ch. 5. For cultural criticism of the 'self-consciously waggish sentimentality of Liverpool', see John Lanchester, *The Debt to Pleasure* (London, 1996), p. 48.

127. Bennett, *Writing Home*, p. 289.

128. Adam Sweeting, 'With a little help from our friends', *Guardian*, 10 May 1995. While the original Liverpool gentlemen aspired to make their city the Florence of the North, contemporary scouse culture resembles the *campanilismo* of Naples: 'Neapolitans, like Liverpudlians, have a way of mythologizing and sentimentalizing the city, their humour, their hospitality, and like the Liverpudlians with some justice; also their songs and their musical and popular culture have put them on the map', Jamie McKendrick, 'One to spare?', in P. Robinson (ed.), *Liverpool Accents*, p. 91.

129. Having enrolled as a Special Constable for the night, Dickens was taken to waterfront entertainment houses where the dancers were black males, 'dancing with a great show of teeth, and with a childish good-humoured enjoyment that was very prepossessing'. Among the audience in other venues, he encountered

> 'Dark Jack, and Dark Jack's delight, his *white* unlovely Nan ... They generally kept together, these poor fellows, said Mr. Superintendent, because they were at a disadvantage singly, and liable to slights in the neighbouring streets. But, if I were Light Jack, I should be very slow to interfere oppressively with Dark Jack, for, whenever I have had to do with him I have found him a simple and gentle fellow. Dickens, *Uncommercial Traveller*, ch. 5.

130.   Gideon Ben-Tovin, 'Race, politics and urban regeneration: lessons from Liverpool' in M. Parkinson, B. Foley and D. Judd (eds), *Regenerating the Cities: the UK Crisis and the US Experience* (Manchester, 1988). John Davies, 'Class practices and political culture in Liverpool' (Lancaster Regionalism Group Working paper 37, 1988). D. Worlock and D. Sheppard, *Better Together: Christian Partnership in a Hurt City* (London, 1989), ch. 8.

131.   As well as Lane, *Liverpool*, Waller, *Democracy and Sectarianism*, and Belchem (ed.), *Popular Politics, Riot and Labour*, see also, Frank Neal, *Sectarian Violence: the Liverpool Experience 1819–1914* (Manchester, 1988); R.S.W. Davies, 'Differentiation in the working class, class consciousness and the development of the Labour Party in Liverpool up to 1939', unpublished PhD thesis, Liverpool John Moores University (1993); and Joan Smith's important comparative analysis: 'Labour tradition in Glasgow and Liverpool', *History Workshop Journal*, 17 (1984), pp. 32–56, and 'Class, skill and sectarianism in Glasgow and Liverpool, 1880–1914', in R.J. Morris (ed.), *British Nineteenth-Century Towns* (Leicester, 1986), pp. 158–215.

132.   Mark Christian, 'Black struggle for historical recognition in Liverpool', *North West Labour History*, 20 (1995–96), pp. 58–66.

133.   Diane Frost, 'West Africans, black scousers and the colour problem in inter-war Liverpool', *North West Labour History*, 20 (1995–96), p. 56.

134.   Paul Gilroy, *'There Ain't No Black in the Union Jack'* (London, 1987), ch. 6.

CHAPTER SIX

Workplace gossip: management myths in further education*

Melanie Tebbutt

Introduction

Gossip has been described as the 'politics of the dispossessed and powerless', and as such seems a good linguistic starting-point from which to examine languages of labour. Talk about other people, be they colleagues or management, is a familiar aspect of workplace experience and the evidence on which much of this chapter is based stems from participant observation and interviews with lecturers within the Further Education (FE) sector. By examining the dynamics of gossip in a contemporary setting, it is hoped to analyse some of the complex ways in which our perceptions of power relationships are moulded and shaped.

This approach draws on the workplace traditions of industrial relations research which produced much useful ethnographic material in the 1970s. By contrast, the investigative trend of recent years has been to adopt a more top-down, survey-based approach largely focused on the experiences of senior managers. Organizational culture has become a dominant theme in management literature where the direction and control of cultural change is frequently seen as vital in ensuring economic survival. The concern to generate commitment and excellence through cultural transformation has been expressed rhetorically in a language of empowerment whose fictional gloss is frequently at odds with workplace experience. These ideas, though often absorbed in a rather piecemeal way, have had a significant influence on organizational change programmes as extensive restructuring has taken place within many UK organizations.[1] Working conditions which would not have been countenanced in the 1970s have been introduced into many areas of industry, often with little overt resistance, leaving many senior managers complacently unaware of the 'demoralised and cynical reality' among their workforce. At the same time, many middle managers are themselves demoralized and cynical. The result has not been to eradicate opposition, merely to 'drive energy sapping dissent underground'.[2] This chapter argues that the nature of such dissent can be analysed through an examination of the role of gossip and rumour. It takes as its subject-matter a specific type of gossip which is largely concerned with lecturers' evaluation of their managers within a context of structural reorganization, budget cuts and redundancies. It is based on the FE sector which has experienced considerable upheaval over the last few years, particularly since all such colleges in England and Wales were 'incorporated' in April 1993 and taken out of local authority control to receive their funding direct from the Further Education Funding Council, (FEFC).[3] This study, which is largely based upon one FE college over a specific period between 1993 and 1996, consequently offers a useful opportunity to examine the role of gossip among such workers at a time of significant cultural change, as the institution moved away from 'traditional' practices, procedures and philosophy.[4]

Organizational context: the 'rumour mill'

Precise numbers of those teaching within the FEFC funded colleges are difficult to determine. The sector covers about 450 colleges which employ some 130,000 full-time and fractional professional staff, although the inclusion of hourly paid, part-time teachers may bring the total to 300,000.[5] The period since incorporation has been marked by rapid change, considerable insecurity and a frequently bitter industrial relations climate which has seen the driving down of lecturers' pay and conditions and the erosion of their negotiating rights. Before incorporation, FE lecturers' conditions were governed by a nationally negotiated settlement whose details were contained in a manual known as the 'Silver Book'. A significant feature of the move to corporate status has been the attempt to alter these working practices via the introduction of new contracts in order to 'respond more flexibly' to a competitive post-16 education market. As Karen Legge has pointed out, such calls for 'flexibility' have become an important part of management's rhetoric, 'a catch-all label to describe on-going efforts to optimise labour utilisation, both qualitatively and quantitatively, in pursuit of competitive advantage'.[6] The initiative in FE was spearheaded by the College Employers' Forum, (CEF), set up in 1992 to deal with pay and employment matters under the leadership of Roger Ward, Chief Executive, who came to the CEF from the Polytechnics and Colleges Employers' Forum.[7] A leader in the *Times Education Supplement* (*TES*) highlighted Ward's approach: 'Hell-bent on changing the culture, smashing the 'Silver Book' conditions of service, which reigned under LEAs, he went further, engineering the deregulation of employment conditions.'[8]

After incorporation, lecturers on 'Silver Book' contracts received only one pay rise, of 1.5 per cent, in September 1993, being excluded from the 1994 increase of 2.9 per cent for those who had accepted new contractual conditions. The average pay increase of college principals over the same period was 11.6 per cent, with the best paid 10 per cent receiving a 19.1 per cent rise. Fifteen principals earned £70,000 or more, with the highest salary £83,500.[9] Colleges were forced to make a push on new contractual conditions by the cash penalty of a 2 per cent budget claw-back imposed by the Treasury on those which failed to introduce new, flexible contracts. After a series of bitter disputes, the sector is now characterized by a variety of employment contracts, some of which have been negotiated locally with union agreement, while others have been imposed. A survey of conditions in roughly one-third of colleges in Autumn 1995 reported that more than 47 per cent of lecturers and senior lecturers were on National Association of Teachers in Further and Higher Education (NATFHE) agreed deals; 25 per cent were still on 'Silver Book' and 28 per cent on CEF contracts.[10] By September 1995, deadlock over national negotiations and the reluctance of members to take national action over pay had led NATFHE, the main lecturers' union, to decide to channel its diminishing resources into fighting local disputes.[11] NATFHE had been badly damaged, with membership falling by 10 per cent since incorporation and income losses in the region of £1 million. An estimated 1,500 redundancies took place in the 1994–95 academic year and membership at the end of 1994 was just under 70,000. By October 1995, 23 per cent of NATFHE paying members were said to be part-timers.[12] The protracted dispute over contracts soured relationships in many colleges, both with management and between staff who had signed new contracts and others who had refused. The principal of one of Britain's largest colleges was reported as saying, 'There's some awful industrial relations in FE and we know it'. Much of FE is testimony to a managerial history which is 'heavily bound up with masculine preoccupations of transforming everything and everyone into an object of control and conquest'.[13] (Roger Ward's own negotiating style has been variously described as 'combative', 'confrontational' and abrasive'.) A climate of suspicion was generated, in which bullying and more 'macho' management styles became noticeably more common and the spreading of malicious rumours a significant weapon in some managers' armoury.[14] Quite apart from the anxiety generated by such methods, general uncertainty was heightened by an awareness that colleges had to operate in a far more competitive manner than in the past. Lecturers were aware of the onus on them to maintain and expand student numbers 'or quite awful things could happen'.[15] Such fears were enhanced by the dire prognoses of some managers that several colleges were likely to 'go under' in the next few years, and by the severe financial difficulties of some colleges which featured prominently in the educational press. As one lecturer who had signed a new contract and was working within what was widely re- garded as a 'safe' curriculum area commented, 'nowhere in the college is secure these days'.[16]

The background to such consciousness was the FEFC funding for- mula which paid little attention to the external influences affecting college success in different areas. Although incorporation guaranteed colleges a 16 per cent growth in funding over three years, it also demanded that student numbers expand by 25 per cent over the same period; when coupled with other efficiency measures, this actually amounted to a 5 per cent cut in income.[17] Not every college had scope for such expansion, yet those failing to grow received only 90 per cent of their core funding the following year.[18] Politically driven to cut costs, even efficient, effective colleges had to make staff redundant.[19]

Several colleges entered the new era in a parlous economic state.[20] Two years after incorporation 48 colleges had aggregate deficits in the region of £20 million, with £16 million of this being owed by 34 colleges on debts accumulated while still with the local authorities.[21] Yet government unwillingness to bail out any college, whatever the circumstances, was illustrated by the refusal to help four colleges in a disadvantaged area of South London which were left with debts on unpaid contracts of between £2 and £3.5 million when South Thames Training and Enterprise Council went bankrupt.[22] One of the colleges, Lewisham, was forced to double its number of redundancies as a result of these losses. Rumours about financial difficulties became common- place in the FE sector, reinforced by the leakage of documents with lobbying to increase funding and alter funding formulae.[23] A climate of insecurity pervaded FE, making individuals at all levels feel vulnerable. Survival language became common, as when exhortations to sign a new contract were accompanied by the dissemination of comments from senior management that 'those who were not on board with us are off the ship' – a metaphor warning those unwary enough to want to rock the boat, yet at the same time undermining other imperatives for every- one to pull together. Staff were aware that FE was likely to be seen as a 'soft target' for future cuts in educational spending, since it had been described as the Cinderella of the education sector, lacking the emo- tional appeal of primary and (to a lesser extent) secondary schooling, and without the friends in high places on whom the universities could call.[24] While Higher Education struggled with an increasing demand for places, FE had to cope with the implications of recent research which suggested that the proportion of 16-year-olds continuing in full-time education had 'fallen for the first time in a decade'.[25] It had to bring in new students and consider non-traditional recruitment areas, yet many

colleges which had a good track record in such areas before incorporation were penalized under the FEFC's funding allocations which took
no account of regional differences or the historical baggage of particular institutions – such as split sites, old buildings and high running
costs.

Competition for students consequently was (and remains) acute. Such
pressure certainly forced colleges to pay more attention to drop-out
rates and mechanisms for tracking students who left before finishing
their courses since they stood to lose so much financially; but as an
editorial in the *Times Higher Education Supplement* (*THES*) put it in
March 1995, 'to go for growth colleges need not just the flexibility of
lecturers but also their goodwill. The great failing of the sector has been
the way the dispute over new contracts has been allowed to fester
unresolved for two years'.[26]

These general pressures and worries within the sector were exacerbated in some colleges by the frequency of reorganizations which were
introduced in a rather piecemeal fashion and meant that established
social and work groups were often broken down or became more
difficult to maintain. Such an atmosphere is not unique, and is to be
found in many sectors moving from a public service ethos into a free
market framework. It is not the aim to argue that gossip is a peculiar
characteristic of such circumstances. What is pertinent is a detailed
examination of how these changes were mediated through the use of
gossip and rumour, as illustrated by the experience of one particular
college during this difficult period.

Subversion or survival?

The FE workplace is not homogeneous and lecturing staff have traditionally tended to define themselves as separate teaching sections rather
than as part of a whole college culture. Aside from administrative and
technical staff who are not the subject here, FE colleges embrace a range
of different subcultures, with an older age profile reflecting the fact that
many lecturers have worked in industry before entering the sector. The
industrial background of some teaching sections has often had a distinct
effect upon their outlook and approach, helping separate them from
other colleagues in college. Many curriculum areas have been largely
constituted according to gender. Masculinist, craft-based traditions –
such as engineering, construction, motor vehicle maintenance – are
probably considered to be most characteristic of FE, although many of
these areas have been contracting for a number of years, reflecting the
decline of the manufacturing sector. Hairdressing, beauty therapy, care

courses and information technology on the other hand have largely comprised women. The styles of different curriculum areas often differs, the relative formality of business studies or catering staff, for example, contrasting with the more relaxed approach of performing arts and art and design lecturers. There may be divisions between teachers of 'academic' subjects and those of more 'vocational' crafts. Incorporation, although the most far-reaching, has not been the only change to affect colleges in recent years, and many staff had already experienced redeployment into new areas of work before the change to corporate status. There have been extensive and sometimes contradictory curriculum developments, often necessitating sudden change at a time of greatly increased student numbers in some areas and declining provision in others. The depth of insecurity which different groups of lecturers experience has consequently varied. In the case study college, some areas had been targeted for redundancy while other apparently growing or static sections felt vulnerable due to changing patterns of enrolment, college priorities and competition from other institutions. Most lecturers probably experienced some degree of insecurity about what the future held.

Gossip tends, under any circumstances, to be an unstable process, often becoming more distorted and exaggerated the further it travels from its point of origin. This tendency is stimulated in an unstable institutional climate when it can serve therapeutic and isolating, inclusive and exclusive functions. Gossip can certainly be acquired and used in active, self-conscious ways, as a means of checking out and exchanging information which is not formally within the public domain, and such strategies became particularly important after incorporation as official channels of communications became distrusted. The in-house news sheet of this particular college, for example, was not untypically named Pravda for the care with which everything appearing in it was vetted. The period after incorporation saw a steady restriction of the open manner in which information had previously been exchanged between senior and main grade lecturing staff, and the consequent development among some lecturers of more self-consciously manipulative approaches to talk and gossip in relationships with management. One lecturer, for example, described how she used gossip to confront managers who would not freely offer information, in order to gauge their reaction. She said:

> It's quite interesting ... to repeat what you've heard and maybe deliberately change it to see how it then affects people you're talking to, to try out, to test ... what they're saying. See how they react to something. So if you've heard something, and you repeat it to someone you don't think has heard it, but who might know

more about it than you, they'll respond to you saying, 'I've heard such and such a thing', and volunteer information from scratch. You see what I mean? If I suspect that somebody knows something after a meeting, I'll say, 'Well, I've heard such and such a thing.' And they'll respond and say, 'Yes, that happened', or, 'Well, it happened, but not quite like that'. Whereas they'd never actually volunteer the information initially. And they may know more about it than the person you heard it from.[27]

The same testing out of stories heard on the grapevine was also recognized and used as a means of reinforcing group solidarity, 'for getting people on your side'.

> Well, I suppose to strengthen like ideas. So if you were encouraging someone to do something in the way that you wanted them to, or, like not signing the contract. Say you want to sort of strengthen the people who don't want to sign it. You'll say, 'Well, I've heard such and such a thing, and if you do', using it like that. To sort of, get people, encourage people to stick together.[28]

However, a suspicious, hostile climate can make this form of solidarity difficult to sustain, for although its intent may be to encourage solidarity, it can also perversely add to the general climate of gloom and uncertainty. Another lecturer, who had reluctantly agreed to sign a new contract, commented how the atmosphere within the college had gradually changed: 'There is more wariness about who you will gossip to and what about', although she was not entirely clear as to why she should feel a need to be more guarded, other than a heightened awareness of how such talk could be misused and a certain fear on other people's behalf. Her college, in line with common practice elsewhere, had inserted a confidentiality clause in her new contract which had also made her far more wary of talking to friends outside college about anything which might even loosely be construed as college affairs. Prior to incorporation she had been involved in several initiatives across the local authority and was used to working closely with colleagues in other organizations. Many of these were now regarded as competitors in the same education market, and this woman experienced some difficulty in defining the boundaries of what might be termed confidential in some of the informal work relationships she had struck up with colleagues outside her institution. 'Are your negative feelings about something that happened, or something that strikes you as ridiculous there supposed to be confidential?' The commercial emphasis of the new contract had little recognition of any conflict of interest between student and corporate needs, with the requirement to act in the best interests of the Corporation at all times, while the comprehensive confidentiality clause was prefaced by the instruction that confidential information should include (but not be limited to) 'any information which you have been told is confidential or which you might reasonably expect to be confidential'. Academic staff retained 'freedom within the law to question and test received wisdom relating to academic matters, and to put forward new ideas and controversial or unpopular opinions about academic matters without placing themselves in jeopardy or losing the jobs and privileges they had at the Corporation', although the phraseology was significant, with its emphasis on privileges rather than rights. The unaccustomed corporate emphasis unsettled many lecturers, and this one worried that having signed the new college contract, she was not supposed to say anything disloyal, yet she had a strong sense that, 'You have to earn loyalty. You don't feel loyal just because someone says to feel loyal'.[29]

Another lecturer also observed how the form which gossip took seemed to have changed as the dispute over contracts hardened. 'People have got more cautious now or less libellous about what they gossip about. And I also think the quality of gossip has actually changed. Because I think it's much more school yard, child like, discussing silly, impossible stories about the Principal.' As another put it, 'It's just like almost maintaining your sanity by, I don't know, making him more human or more vulnerable'.[30] The fear of people tale-telling and of senior managers eavesdropping was particularly strong among those staff who had not signed a new contract. A lecturer who was insisting on staying on the old conditions reflected how, 'There's almost a paranoia developing that people are looking over their shoulder before they say anything. They're really frightened who might overhear them'.[31] A tale circulating among these staff concerned a rumour that the vice-principal had taken to going over to their staff room in the evening, when it was empty, 'to 'ferret about'. The evidence for this was said to be that a whiteboard on which lecturers wrote messages to each other had received replies from her. 'Now whether they were from her in reality or not, I don't know, but I think it's from there that this myth developed. So she's become like this malevolent spirit who walks the staff room at night. (Laughing) But they are genuinely quite paranoid and frightened about what's going to get back to her and how she will use it'. In fact, this story predated the new vice-principal's arrival, and stemmed from how the jokes and scurrilous comments on a so-called 'anarchists' noticeboard' had been cleaned up by another senior manager.[32] The fluid way in which this story was transposed to the new member of senior management to some extent reflected the breakdown of relatively open relationships between senior staff and lecturers. This college, like others, had experienced several restructurings over the previous two or three years, which had helped erode established work patterns and relationships. The number of staff engaged in cross-college activities had been reduced and many had been relocated in new staff rooms and curriculum groupings. The distinction between middle management (most of whom now had responsibility over their own cost centres) and teaching staff had sharpened, while lecturers in staff rooms away from the main site tended to feel remote from and threatened by the rumours passed on by colleagues in other parts of the college. One lecturer somewhat typically described a 'survival strategy' of non-involvement and withdrawal, just doing the job. 'I like my students, and that's what keeps me going. I don't really know what's going on. I just don't listen to the talk.'[33] Another lecturer, one of a minority of staff on old contracts isolated at a minor college site, likened the experience to being exiled in Siberia.[34]

Marchington et al. have pinpointed the role of the grapevine within organizations which come under increasing competitive pressure and whose employees become cynical and distrustful of established or official communication channels when faced with a bleak future of redundancies and increased workloads. It is significant that the 'negative feelings' and 'frustrated expectations' which they chronicle appear to have been most intense in contexts formerly characterized by paternalistic 'caring' and consultative styles. 'In short, the higher the expectations of the employer, the more employees are likely to feel that trust has been betrayed and it would appear that long-standing high trust relations can easily be shattered.'[35]

This insight is usefully applied to colleges such as this, where the erosion and dismantling of traditional approaches and practices was accompanied by a sense that established skills – and by implication, the individual lecturer – were no longer valued. The dissemination of information acquires an enhanced significance under such circumstances, when fears are likely to lead to it being easily misconstrued if not deliberately changed. Insecurity is a fertile ground for the growth of unsubstantiated stories about both individuals and management intentions.[36] Management's own sense of vulnerability often encourages attempts to control more closely the dissemination of information through official channels, rather than in informal discussion. Nevertheless, the more tightly the reins are drawn, the greater the distrust of the 'official line' and the greater the likelihood of gossip being used in rather more subversive ways.[37] Humour, too, often of the 'gallows' type, becomes important, since sharing a malicious (or funny) story about an individual in authority is an important means of deflating status, reinforcing self-respect and letting off steam.[38] Authority figures who represent institutional culture are likely to be a particular focus of such mocking talk, with such stories often conveying an implicit moral message about that culture.[39] The concept of a corporate identity, which many colleges have promoted, was often the subject of mockery. It sat uneasily with many FE lecturers who were more used to focusing themselves upon their students or upon the needs of their particular section. The following story, told with some enjoyment by a lecturer who was still working to old conditions, hinges on the known dedication of two lecturers who were generally acknowledged as hard-working and committed to their students. Both had signed new contracts, although A was a middle manager and B was a main grade lecturer. They are counterpoised against a senior manager, C, who had enthusiastically espoused the entrepreneurial thrust of the new corporation whose FEFC funding depended on enrolling adequate numbers. C was well known for placing recruitment targets before individual student needs, having been heard to remark that it didn't matter finding out if a particular course was right or wrong for them, so long as they were signed up for something; any problems could 'always be sorted out later'.

A and B were working the last of several long days and evenings enrolling students. 'They were completely pissed off by this time.' C 'swanned up, as she does', and asked:

> 'Where is your smile? How can you possibly expect us to enrol students, unless you're here smiling?' And she then went on to demonstrate the corporate smile to them! So apparently, there is now a thing called the corporate smile ... and showed them the corporate smile.
> Q. That's a joke. It must be.
> A. No, that is entirely serious. And B was sort of looking at her as though she was three sheets to the wind. And A just said, 'C, why don't you just piss off?' For A to say that ... because B said she did a double-take, you know. But apparently, he has reached that sort of, desperation.

This short tale, with its focus on the superficial gloss of 'customer care', reflected how far removed members of senior management were perceived as being from the reality of face-to-face dealings with students. Lecturer A was reputed to be a self-effacing and honest manager little known for displays of temper, and his obvious disenchantment was offered up by the story's narrator to highlight the hollowness of the new corporate expectations.

The 'corporate smile' is an important emblem of what has been described as the 'empowerment, skills and growth discourse' in management practice. It is based on ostensibly laudable values such as quality, the needs of the individual, empowerment, efficiency, continual change, flexibility, an emphasis on the necessity of everyone pulling together within an ostensibly more democratic environment known as a 'flattened hierarchy'.[40] However, this public discourse, frequently highlighted in many colleges' publicity, is highly stylized because, despite its democratizing rhetoric, it does not involve any broadening of student/ staff involvement in decision-making. This language also reinforces workers' insecurities, implying that established skills are out of date, and ignoring the problem of how to enhance quality with diminished resources.

Management myths and images: the role of the 'destruction' myth

Organizational culture is not only formed through official policy but also by the informal relationships and gossip which develop within the workplace. Gossip takes place at many different levels, sometimes across hierarchies but also within discrete groups of senior managers as well as among 'ordinary' workers. It disseminates stories about people with whom individuals may have no direct contact whatsoever, and in so doing thereby helps them achieve something of a mythical quality. Peters and Waterman highlighted the importance of 'stories, myths and legends' in perpetuating an institution's values and cultural ethos, and gossip about other people is the medium through which the essence of these myths and stories is transmitted.[41] The role of metaphors within such talk provides useful clues to social consciousness.[42] Tony Watson, for example, has made a distinction between the 'high' stories of corporate mythology which are positive and motivating, and the 'low' stories of an institution's informal culture which are more negative and subversive in intent.[43]

A close analysis of the stories conveyed in gossip helps us evaluate how management reputations are created and diffused among employees.[44] Much has been written in management literature about the role of various super-heroes and so-called 'creation' myths in generating a positive climate in new organizations. However, what might be termed 'destruction' myths can also play a significant part in organizations which are experiencing substantial reorganization and insecurity, as was the situation in the case study institution. The 'disabling' stories of destruction mythology focus, often in a humorous way, upon the more negative aspects of institutional life, externalizing fears and insecurities about change, yet contributing to a collective pessimism which subverts the very positive climate which the 'empowerment, skills and growth' discourse is intended to encourage. Such stories have an ambivalent edge. The college must survive if the lecturer's own future is to be secured. Yet there is a sense that it does not deserve to flourish given the erosion of the 'moral' philosophy underpinning traditional practices and the lack of respect extended to established skills and procedures. The disabling counterpart of the 'inspirational leader' is the intimidat-

ing one, whose aim is to drive the workforce into line with new practices. It is not unusual for organizations to bring in such 'leaders' from
the outside with the intention of developing a new 'strong' culture. At
the case study college, the appointment of a new vice-principal was
soon attended by the rapid development of a strong and ruthless reputation encapsulated in the image of a rottweiler. This reputation began
to circulate even before the new appointee had taken up post. At the
official level, the selection was accompanied by a 'human interest' piece
in the local press and on the main college noticeboard about her background and children.[45] 'That's when she first came and nobody had got
her measure or anything.' As one woman put it, 'A lot of people's initial
suspicions and worries about her were actually placated by that article,
because, it's alright, because she's a mother so she won't be all those
things. Gives her time to get her Doc Martins on before she kicks out
first'.[46] Such retrospective allusions reflected the fact that stories circulating on the college grapevine soon had a rather different emphasis. A
member of the senior management team, who had reputedly seen the
new vice-principal in aggressive action at a conference, used the rottweiler
metaphor in conversation with a member of middle management, who
in turn passed it on to main grade lecturing staff who had not even met
the new manager, and amongst whom the image swiftly became common currency. It was a representation resonant with contemporary
cultural preoccupations – savage, aggressive, uncompromising, unwilling to back down or let go – which projected a reputation based on
attacking the defenceless, particularly children.

Yet the analogy was rather more complex than it might otherwise
seem. It certainly reflected staff fears of their vulnerability in the new FE
climate and the sense of destruction which many felt as old structures
and patterns were broken down, challenged or ignored. However, as
the origins of this metaphor suggest, it is ingenuous to imply that this
exchange of information was wholly unconscious in character. The first
question to attend any new appointment, but particularly one in senior
management is likely to be, 'What are they like?' Workers tend actively
to seek information and impressions from those who may have known
the individual and from those in a position to get to know them, and it
is at this point that new myths start to develop. The dissonant images
conveyed in the soft outline of official publicity and the hard one of
unofficial channels usefully aggravated the sense of unease which defined the post-incorporation climate. The rottweiler story was not received uncritically, being defused by some staff through its humorous
reduction to a cartoon characterization with the nickname 'Bite your
Leg', conveying the idea of a small troublesome pooch rather than
fierce mastiff.[47] Nevertheless, the origins of the story are a reminder

that while barriers may harden as far as the passing on of strategic information is concerned, they often remain permeable to more personal forms of gossip which consciously or unconsciously serve to fortify images which benefit management. The rottweiler reputation did not diminish but was reinforced in stories circulated by and about members of middle management, several of whom, in making presentations to the new vice-principal, were variously reported back as 'receiving a mauling', 'a chewing over' or a 'real grilling'. Such treatment encouraged inconsistency within middle management, with several managers coming down very heavily on their staff in an effort to please. As far as complying with new conditions of service was concerned, a somewhat schizophrenic situation developed in which staff were punished if they signed the new contract and punished if they refused.

> There are people who have signed the contract and then been given horrendous timetables, which really forces others not to sign. And then you don't sign, so you don't get a pay rise and you get a crap timetable but not as many hours as the new contract. So where's the strategy in this?[48]

A certain unpredictability was also encouraged by the new vice-principal's tendency to walk around and appear at unexpected times, without any introductions. An inclination to informal dress meant she did not fit in with status preconceptions of what such a senior manager 'should' look like, so that at least one lecturer tried to enrol her in one of her classes.[49] The approach may have been designed to find out how the college functioned on a day-to-day basis, but in practice it tended to have an unsettling effect, encouraging stories which focused on her 'creeping' round in surveillance mode.

All individuals have complex mental landscapes into which they place the people with whom they work. Those who have been with an organization for a long time have a large number of stories upon which various individual's reputations rest, 'tacit' knowledge shared with other colleagues which may well affect the way in which suggestions etc. are accepted and mediated. Such information can be both a threat and challenge to newcomers, especially to those who aim to break the mould of former practice and introduce new ways of working. The emphasis on flexibility in a rapidly changing market inevitably undermines the relevance of the mental maps which shape existing employee perceptions, and in this particular context, established skills were implicitly devalued in a number of different ways. Working 'smarter' rather than 'harder' found favour as the 'obvious' way of dealing with the heavier demands of the new system. The plodding connotations of the 'hard' worker were at odds with the fast, creative demands of the innovative organization able to keep abreast of and ahead of trends.

Hard-working staff unable to cope with the pressures placed on them were not 'smart' but foolishly responsible for their own stress and anxiety. They were patently not up to their new responsibilities, the fashionable phrasing usefully absolving the institution of responsibility for rising stress-related sickness records. The new vice-principal publicly jettisoned the past at staff meetings, making it clear that the history of what had gone before she arrived was of no interest, the assumption that there were no lessons to be learned there implicitly denying a significant part of her employee's identity. Remarks about the college's 'cosy' atmosphere when she first arrived reflected the 'mission' to 'revitalise' and shake things up.[50] As a college lecturer, implicitly reinforcing the message of the rottweiler story, observed:

> I think the first things I heard about her were that she'd been head-hunted. And that people had concerns about that. Because they thought that she had been head-hunted, which I think is true, as a hatchet-woman, to remove [the principal] from the process ... I mean, that seemed to come from a variety of sources, at the same time. And then, the next thing I hear about her, was that in fact, people who knew staff [at her previous college] who said she was really fair and ... she's tough, but fair. And I certainly don't think that's true of her now.[51]

The story's exposition contained elements almost of self-blame and annoyance at having given the manager the benefit of the doubt and contributing to a powerful reputation. This lecturer, for example, had the 'horrible' feeling that she was responsible for a lingering image of fairness, 'because I know I said it, and I hadn't heard it before that!' This was after a meeting, when she said that she didn't dislike the vice-principal as much as she disliked most of the other managers in the college, because of the honest, upfront approach.

> And so, the thing that I hear most commonly now, what people say about her is, 'Well, she is an absolute and complete bastard, but at least she says that's what she is, doesn't pretend to be anything else. And so most people, I've spoken to loads of people about it this week, and that is the consensus view of her. That she is awful, but at least you know where you are with her. She's only going to do dreadful things to you![52]

It was as if this manager's 'honesty' was perceived as reflecting the inexorability of much broader forces for change which perhaps helped staff justify themselves when they felt they had to cave in to management demands. At the same time it also reflected another common yet contradictory expectation of many new managers brought in from outside the organization, that the changes being implemented had a careerist intent and were just as much the result of a fashionable whim.

'Champions' are often seen as necessary within organizations to introduce cultural change; these are people with the energy and ability to lead new initiatives, to ensure that others are persuaded of their value, and are prepared to commit themselves to embedding strategies on the shop floor or in the office. By their nature, however, champions tend to be mobile and career oriented, often moving to new positions soon after introducing fresh initiatives.[53] Champions make great use of 'impression management', making their activities visible to more senior managers and external audiences, with the result that, soon after making an impression, champions move on to another post, either inside or outside the organization.[54] Those left with responsibility for continuing to progress the new strategies and ideas feel little ownership of them, are less committed to making them work, and in any event want to introduce their own ideas in order to gain promotion themselves. A cycle is set in motion, with the inevitable consequence of fads and fashions, cynicism and short-termism.[55]

Many felt that this senior manager's new position was but a stepping-stone on the way to more prestigious promotion, and there was gossip about bets being placed as to how long she would stay. A lecturer who had left the college summed up a common perception:

> If you really want to hear the most frightening face of FE, go incognito to a vice-principal's two-day residential conference, and listen to the things they say. It is terrifying. They actually legitimately talk about doing something you can put on your CV, and passing off before anybody rumbles to what a mess you've made.[56]

The belief that this senior manager was only passing through contributed to the climate of cynicism, reinforced by the common perception that the Principal was distancing himself in order to maintain a 'moral' reputation while his new deputy did his 'dirty work'. Stories about his removal from everyday college life was common: 'He's withdrawn physically. Nobody has seen him. He gets there in the morning before any staff get in.'[57] Destruction mythology encapsulated the pressure tactics and bullying common to many part of FE. In this college, stories of staff humiliation and surveillance reinforced feelings of being threatened and being backed into a corner. As one lecturer said, 'A lot of us perceived our roles very differently before the new contracts issue came up. What it did was force us backwards rather than forwards. So you got highly committed lecturers arguing about class contact hours when they'd never turned a student down in their lives.[58] With debate stifled and managerial inconsistency, opting out became a form of survival, a means of emotional disengagement. Dozens of staff left this college through retirement or voluntary redundancy, although it is difficult to estimate how many since management refused to give the union any staff lists.

Estimates of those still on 'Silver Book' conditions in 1996 varied for similar reasons. Most union meetings were poorly attended. Those most likely and able to leave were not surprisingly older, more experienced staff on inferior conditions of service. The large round of voluntary redundancies in 1996 saw a vanload of farewell flowers from the management drawing up outside the college. It looked, as several staff wryly observed, 'like a funeral'.

Conclusion

The purpose of this chapter has been to take a slice of experience within one FE college over a particular period of time, to consider the rhetoric of organizational change and how it has been perceived by a specific group of workers, and to raise issues which could also be considered within a more historical context. Early factory discipline, for example, reinforced the idea that talk was idle and that there was a specific time and place for conversation within the workplace.[59] Workplace words have always spun in an imagined landscape which employers are anxious to control, and the sense that such talk was something to be hidden reinforced its subversive aspects as a means of appropriating what was regarded as company time. Modern managers have not surprisingly developed a sophisticated understanding of the power of these words, being urged in management literature to 'understand and harvest the grapevine' in recognition of the richness of the fruit which grows there, although the form it takes is not always the expected one. For the interplay of individual and collective experience is subtle, the process by which 'individual contributions combine and fragment' to make collective myths complex and contradictory.[60] Apprehension and uncertainty pervade the FE workforce at many different levels, including management, and are manifested in the type of gossip which often reinforces fears about the future. This climate does not need to be manipulated consciously in order to serve a useful management purpose by reinforcing the apparent 'inevitability' of otherwise unwelcome change; at the same time, it is also responsible for less compliant impulses which simultaneously erode the moral imperatives and reciprocal aspects of established work culture which are so important for organizational well-being and success. This limited analysis of some of the myths which developed within a particular college during a very specific period suggests the ambivalent forms of resistance which develop under conditions where overt industrial action is difficult to mobilize. In so doing, it illustrates the fragmenting, individualizing tendencies which are encouraged by anxiety and insecurity during periods of rapid institutional change, and which can, in turn, reinforce a subjective, restricting reconstruction of workplace reality.

Notes

*   This research was completed while working as a Research Associate at UMIST. It owes much to discussions with Mick Marchington, Professor of Human Resource Management at UMIST, to whom I am grateful for encouragement and support.

1.   That is not to suggest that earlier ethnographic approaches were flawless. Mostly based on experience within manufacturing industry, they largely ignored the experience of women and tended to focus on the work process rather than upon more diffuse forms of communication within the workplace.

2.   *Observer*, 21 May 1995.

3.   Further and Higher Education Funding Act, 1993. Further education is a large, ill-defined sector which in addition to colleges funded by the FEFC covers a much broader and probably larger constituency including adult education, community work, youth work, prison education and the voluntary sector. It also encompasses over 400 private, non-FEFC institutions which employ something like 40,000 lecturers and tutors. *TES*, 27 October 1995; *NATFHE Journal*, Autumn 1995.

4.   The research on which it is based was conducted between 1993 and 1996.

5.   *NATFHE Journal*, Autumn 1995; *THES*, 17 March 1995. These figures were true at the time of writing in 1996.

6.   Legge (1995), p. 155.

7.   *TES*, 27 October 1995. Ward continually stressed the need to come to terms with the new business culture and press down staffing costs, e.g. *TES*, 13 October 1995. In September 1996 he was appointed Chief Executive of the Association of Colleges, a new 'superbody' formed from the merger of the CEF and the Association for Colleges to represent colleges in England and Wales.

8.   *TES*, 13 September 1996.

9.   *THES*, 17 March 1995. Sir William Stubbs, Chief Executive of the FEFC, reporting to the Public Accounts Committee.

10. *THES*, 29 September 1995; *TES*, 13 September 1996. By September 1996 only 20 per cent of lecturers remained on 'Silver Book' conditions.

11. *THES*, 29 September 1995. A survey revealed only 70 NATFHE branches to be in favour of nationally negotiated co-ordinated action on pay.

12. The take-up of NATFHE membership among part-time staff was actually very low, with only 4–8 per cent of potential part-time members joining. *Lecturer*, October 1995.

13. Knights (1995), p. 3.

14. See, for example, Ian Nash, 'Bullies rise up the ranks', *TES*, 22 September 1995. This article reported how one in seven FE lecturers was believed 'to be the victim of bullying resulting from bad management'. The number of such cases was said to have risen 'alarmingly' under the impact of incorporation, deteriorating work conditions and a tough 'payment by results' formula.

15. Interview with lecturer who had signed the new contract. Respondent 31.1.
16. Respondent 45.1.
17. *TES*, 29 September 1995.
18. Growth in the period 1994–95 was financed at the rate of £14.50 per funding unit, (aka student), which was 'lower than most colleges' actual average levels of funding, (ALFs), which ranged from £14 to £40', *THES*, 17 March 1995.
19. Ruth Gee, Chief Executive of the Association for Colleges, quoted in *THES*, 17 March 1995.
20. *TES*, 17 March 1995.
21. *Lecturer*, October 1995.
22. Lambeth, Lewisham, Southwark and Woolwich. *TES*, 30 June 1995.
23. Fears about many colleges' financial plight received publicity, for example, when figures for 1994 were leaked showing that 58, or more than one in eight colleges, were 'technically insolvent', while a further 303 – more than two-thirds – were 'forecasting operating deficits'. There were anonymous claims that the final figures might 'reveal an even worse position than the one implied in the predictions', although the funding council 'refused to comment on the forecasts' leading to 'questions ... about why such a serious problem remained under wraps', *TES*, 22 September 1995; 29 September 1995.
24. Arguments about quantity being sacrificed for quality were countered by the apparently democratizing (and mass production) analogy of the choice being between a Rolls Royce service for the few or a Mini for the many.
25. Research by London University Institute of Education, quoted in the *TES*, 15 September 1995. A 1 per cent fall in 1994–95 followed an annual growth of 4 per cent between 1987 and 1993. *TES*, 25 August 1995.
26. *THES*, 17 March 1995, p. 13.
27. Respondent 16.1.
28. Respondent 47.1.
29. Respondent 42.1.
30. Respondents 33.1, 21.1.
31. Respondent 13.1.
32. Respondents 11.1, 43.1.
33. Respondent 42.1.
34. Respondent 33.1.
35. Marchington, Wilkinson, Ackers and Goodman (1994), p. 889.
36. Gabriel (1991).
37. For shopfloor rumours at Plessey, see Thompson and Bannon (1985), pp. 39–40.
38. Linstead (1985). Also Boland and Hoffman (1983).
39. Watson (1994), p. 193.
40. Respondent 22.1
41. Peters and Waterman (1982), p. 75.
42. Samuel and Thompson (1990), p. 2.
43. Watson (1994), pp. 22, 192–6.
44. Basso (1990), p. 61.
45. There are undoubtedly gender questions around the fact that this vice-principal was a woman, but they are complex issues which deserve fuller

and separate exploration. The aim of this piece is to highlight aspects of a distinctively 'male' managerial climate common in many FE colleges at this time. Over two-thirds of respondents and all those directly quoted in this chapter about the Vice Principal were women.

46. Respondents 1.1, 12.1.
47. For other examples of nicknames, see Nichols and Armstrong (1976), pp. 49, 82.
48. Respondent 4.2.
49. Respondent 15.1.
50. Anthony (1994), p. 199.
51. Respondent 22.2.
52. Ibid.
53. Ahlstrand, (1990); Rosenfeld, Giacalone and Riordan (1996).
54. Barlow (1989), pp. 499–517.
55. Watson (1994), p. 122.
56. Respondent 4.1.
57. Respondents 7.1, 21.1, 23.1, 26.1, 38.1.
58. Respondent 13.1.
59. Morgan (1986), p. 198; Rules to be Observed by Hands Employed in Water-Foot Mill near Haslingden, September 1851, Rule 9: 'Any person leaving their Work and found Talking with any other workpeople shall be fined 2d for each offence.' Rule 19: 'Any person found away from their usual place of work, except for necessary purposes or Talking with any one out of their own Alley will be fined 2d for each offence.'
60. Basso (1990), p. 61.

Bibliography

Ahlstrand, B.W. (1990), *The Question for Productivity: a Case Study of Fawley after Flanders*, Cambridge: Cambridge University Press.

Anthony, P.D. (1994), *Managing Culture*, Milton Keynes: Open University Press.

Barlow, G. (1989), 'Deficiencies and the perpetuation of power: latent functions in management appraisal', *Journal of Management Studies*, **26**, (5), 499–517.

Basso, R. (1990), 'Myths in contemporary oral transmission: a children's strike', in R. Samuel and P. Thompson (eds), *The Myths We Live By*, London: Routledge.

Boland, R.J. and Hoffman, R. (1983), 'Humour in a machine shop: an interpretation of symbolic action', in L.R. Pondy, P.J. Frost, G. Morgan and T.C. Dandridge, (eds) *Organisational Symbolism*, Greenwich, CN: JAI.

Gabriel, Y. (1991), 'Turning facts into stories and stories into facts', *Human Relations*, **44**, (8), 857–75.

Knights, D. (1995), 'Through the "managerial looking glass": problematising gender in the "new" organisation'. Paper presented at the Management Dissent Conference, Warwick Business School, Coventry, 27 September.

Legge, K. (1995), *Human Resource Management: Rhetoric and Realities*, London: Macmillan Business.

Linstead, S. (1985), 'Jokers wild: the importance of humour in the maintenance of organisational culture', *Sociological Review*, 33, (4), 741–76.

Marchington, M., Wilkinson, A., Ackers, P. and Goodman, J. (1994), 'Understanding the meaning of participation: views from the workplace', *Human Relations*, 47, (8).

Morgan, G. (1986), *Images of Organization*, Beverly Hills and London: Sage.

Nichols, T. and Armstrong, P. (1976), *Workers Divided*, London: Fontana.

Peters, T.J. and Waterman, R.H. (1982), *In Search of Excellence*, New York: Harper and Row.

Rosenfeld, P., Giacalone, R. and Riordan, C. (1996), *Impression Management in Organisations*, London: Routledge.

Samuel R. and Thompson, P. (eds), (1990), *The Myths We Live By*, London: Routledge.

Thompson, P. and Bannon, E. (1985), *Working the System: the Shop Floor and New Technology*, London: Pluto.

Watson, T.J. (1994), *In Search of Management: Culture, Chaos and Control in Managerial Work*, London: Routledge.

PART FOUR
Labour movements

CHAPTER SEVEN

A new language for labour? W. Jett Lauck and the American version of social democracy*

Leon Fink

By the turn of the twentieth century the American labour movement was already moving to adopt rising living standards as its chief objective and justification.[1] Certainly there was something old as well as something new in this development. On the one hand, upholding the minimum 'Standard[s] of Life' had 'from time immemorial', according to Sidney and Beatrice Webb's classic treatment of the subject, served as a central tenet of trade unionism.[2] Similarly, John R. Commons and Associates traced the first strike of American wage-earners to the Philadelphia printers who went out on strike for a minimum wage of $6 a week.[3] Yet such basic material needs had also regularly escalated into wider understandings of the worker's place in the larger world. When the term 'trades union' first appeared in the US in the 1830s, for example, its 'face-mark', wrote Commons, 'is distinctly that of awakened *citizenship* – the first appearance in the history of modern nations of wage-earners as a class exercising the privilege of suffrage'.[4] As evidenced in energetic calls for 'workingmen's democracy', an end to 'wage slavery', and even 'workers' control' of production, the nineteenth-century labour movement sporadically laid claim to radical revisions of the American political economy. On the other hand, the repeated exercise of corporate power and perhaps even more effectively of legal authority against class-based mobilization gradually led the labour leadership to a more modest assessment of its strategic alternatives. Thus it was that the new century witnessed an ever-increasing focus on the goal which American Federation of Labour (AFL) President Samuel Gompers defined in 1912 as 'the best possible conditions obtainable for the workers'.[5] The ensuing decades witnessed a more general public recognition of such objectives as exemplified in the 'living wage' standard of the National War Labour Board (NWLB) (1917) in the First World War, the industrial codes of the National Recovery Act (1933), the preamble to the National Labour Relations Act (1935), the minimum wage of the Fair Labour Standards Act (1938) and, in the post-Second

World War years, the widespread adoption of the automatic cost-of-living adjustment (or COLA) in collective bargaining agreements. The common-sense nature of such progress (for who was not concerned with material improvements?), however, at once belied the strategic genius required to turn a consensual affirmation of values into an effective organizational and political programme and masked the inherent limits of that very same enterprise. With lengthening hindsight, we can begin to identify the key building blocks in the development of both an industrially and politically powerful labour movement as well as the sources of the movement's frailty which is so manifest today.

One critical brace of twentieth-century labour strategy lay in the assimilation of a new economic science (and its accompanying discourse) by labour leaders and a cadre of skilled professional advisers. The creative centres of this enterprise lay in the dynamic paths of the men's clothing workers union on the one hand and the mine workers union on the other. Initially developing separately and then powerfully joining forces in 1936, these twin pillars of what would become the Congress of Industrial Organizations (CIO) had independently discovered the secret trinity to union survival under consumer-capitalist culture: (1) industry-wide organizing; (2) political mobilization and active use of state regulatory powers; and (3) recruitment of representatives of the liberal intelligentsia as part of a larger campaign for public support.

Beginning amid the Progressive reform wave of the pre-First World War era, re-outfitted for the 'new capitalism' of the 1920s, then altered again for the New Deal state of the 1930s, union-centred campaigns for economic growth tied to business regulation and labour standards helped organized labour capture part of the high ground of the nation's political culture. And yet, in the longer run, a 'prosperity'-based unionism hit severe snags. For what happens when 'prosperity' no longer requires a regime of collective bargaining? Upon what other rock will labour stand? The long drop in union numbers and organizational strength, beginning during the heyday of the post-Second World War boom and alarmingly accelerated in recent years of global corporate competition highlights the delicacy of labour's position even in the best of times. Reckoning with the inner logic of the labour movement – and the intellectuals who contributed in important ways to that logic – provides one important index to the state of American democracy.

While John L. Lewis, long-time leader of the United Mine Workers of America (UMWA) and father of the CIO remains one of the best-known, even legendary, architects of the American labour movement, his influential and long-time policy adviser W. Jett Lauck, never much of a public figure, is unknown to all but specialists.[6] Contemporaries were more observant. Looking back on the explosive achievements of the previous few years, labour journalists of the mid-1930s and early 1940s credited Lauck with major influence on labour's political agenda, including at least contributing authorship to the path-breaking Section 7a of the National Recovery Act, which recognized worker rights to 'organize unions of their own choosing' and engage in collective bargaining.[7] Indeed, a 1936 commentary in the *Christian Science Monitor* called him the CIO's 'one-man brain trust' and the 'Sydney [Webb], Beatrice [Webb] and [Harold] Laski' of the American Labour Party'.[8] While this essay does not claim quite so glorious or potent a portfolio for its subject, it does suggest that the deeds and public writings of Lauck, supplemented by a considerable private correspondence and the several-year notations of a daily diary, offer an important window on the world of twentieth-century labour leadership and decision-making.[9] Here I will concentrate on the evolution of Lauck's strategic vision for the labour movement and the ways that the adviser's own very special role and circumstances contributed to the peculiar historical legacy of his chief client

Let me also suggest from the outset that I see Lauck as a fair exemplar of the course of the Progressive vision of democracy carried through the Great Depression and Second World War to the dawn of the contemporary era. Jett Lauck was very much a Progressive reformer, a product of the pre-First World War era of the optimistic application of social science expertise and centralized administrative know-how to the democratic public. Unlike many of the other pre-war Progressives whose ideals and expectations were radically dislocated by the Great War and its aftermath, he readily insinuated himself into centres of power and appeared never to look back with any trace of nostalgia or regret. On the contrary he continued to build on earlier principles, developing his ever more elaborate models of social planning into a full-blown scheme of social democracy – plans which he saw at least partially embodied in institutional form.

It was Lauck's service on the seminal Commission on Industrial Relations (CIR) of 1913–15 which seems to have first sparked the reform instincts of a young professional previously preoccupied with establishing himself as a neutral expert in the sprouting world of applied economics. Born in Keyser, West Virginia, in 1879 into a family headed by a hard-working railway stationmaster William Blackford Lauck – a descendant of German-Protestant refugees from the Thirty Years War who had first come to America in 1750 (and who boasted a soldier under the command of Benedict Arnold at the Battle of Quebec) – Jett, the second of eight children, was the only child of this 'struggling middle-class' family to earn a college degree. A graduate of Washington and Lee University in 1903, Lauck briefly pursued graduate work in political economy at the University of Chicago before returning to Lexington, Virginia to teach at his alma mater and marry his college sweetheart, Eleanor Moore Dunlap, herself the product of an old-stock Scots-Irish farm family.[10] Lauck's graduate school thesis on 'The causes of the panic of 1893' received prize-winning honours when it was published in 1905 as a convincing application of the 'orthodox view that fear of unsettling the gold standard upsets markets'.[11] Despite an academic appointment, Lauck quickly gravitated to the opportunities open to the trained economist in the world of applied research and policy analysis. His early assignments included work as director of industrial investigations for the US Immigration Commission, 1907–10; chief examiner for the Tariff Board in Washington DC, 1910–11; and secretary of the National Citizens League for Promotion of a Sound Banking System, 1911–12. His work in such matters betrayed little sign of social or political unorthodoxy, and within a few years Lauck would already distance himself from his early writings as the conventionally conservative reflections of an economist interested mostly 'in money and banking'.[12] Yet once exposed to the influence of the labour reform community around the CIR (Lauck was first hired as consulting statistician then promoted to managing expert of research after Charles McCarthy was removed by chairman Frank Walsh), Lauck made a permanent career shift. Despite occasional bouts of college teaching, Lauck became a full-time 'labour' expert – as union representative to the railway labour boards (1912–19), secretary to the Walsh-led National War Labour Board (1918–19), and then primarily as consulting economist for John L. Lewis and the United Mine Workers (1919–39).

One of the earliest themes to which Lauck would apply his professional talents was the workers' standard of living. His reports to the Industrial Commission, for example, justified a conventionally restrictionist policy stance on grounds that 'the extensive employment of recent immigrants has brought about living conditions and a standard of living with which the older employees have been unable or have found it extremely difficult to compete'.[13] Indeed, it was a sign of how deeply the concept had already penetrated the larger political culture that Lauck could write off-handedly in his initial application letter to CIR chairman Walsh that 'I am trying to develop work as an independent economist and statistician … . So far, [it has] just about yielded a *living wage* but I am hoping to do better'.[14] While this was not the last time that the economic problems he was investigating at work corresponded to issues in Lauck's own life, his framing of the problem undoubtedly derived from well-established practice in contemporary economic and public policy circles.

By the eve of the First World War, a generation of middle-class social scientists and social reformers, backed by the agitation of the labour unions themselves, had, in fact, placed the problem of the worker's purchasing power squarely on the public agenda. Already by the 1880s labour agitation had begun to turn from a total rejection of the 'wage system' to a concentration on greater earnings, spelled out variously in demands for a 'living wage', a 'minimum wage', or as in AFL President Samuel Gompers' famous expression, 'more'.[15] Carroll Wright, head of the Massachusetts Bureau of Labour Statistics and later US Commissioner of Labour first invoked the notion of a minimum wage in a 1875 report which demonstrated that the traditional male breadwinner could no longer support a family of wife and children on a typical industrial income.[16] The issue had subsequently been pressed through the Roman Catholic Church, as expressed in the call for 'just payment' by Pope Leo XIII's *Rerum Novarum* (1891) and the more explicit appeal by Father John Ryan in his *A Living Wage* (1906).[17] The concept gathered momentum over the next 15 years, as signalled by passage in Massachusetts of the first state minimum wage law in 1912 and the adoption of some version of the measure in party platforms by the Progressives and Socialists in 1912, Democrats in 1916, and even the Republicans by 1920.[18] From a more academic perspective, the economists Simon Nelson Patten and George Gunton had also helped to transform social science discourse from a focus on scarcity to the problem of distribution of a growing economic surplus. As Gunton argued as early as his 1887 work *Wealth and Progress*, escalating consumer desires would prop up a higher standard of living which in turn would be the basis of a higher civilization. The early years of the twentieth century witnessed a whole series of applied studies, determined to demonstrate, as did Robert C. Chapin's *The Standard of Living among Workingmen's Families in New York* (1909), the desperate need for higher and/or minimum industrial wages.[19] The demand for a 'living wage', articulated in the Walsh Report to the CIR as a prerequisite for the national welfare, was thus only the extension of a growing consensus within the labour reform community.

But it was the wartime mobilization and co-ordination of labour by the Government itself that first demonstrated the practical weight of the new discourse of wages and living standards. When the National War Labour Board, jointly led by Frank Walsh and ex-President William Howard Taft, adopted the 'living wage' as an immediate objective, a once vague principle suddenly carried significant implications. As enunciated in a precedent-setting packinghouse decision by Chicago Judge Samuel Alschuler in 1918, wartime arbitration addressed fairness and need as well as market principles in establishing wage standards. Overall, notes one recent historian, NWLB actions, based on 'continuous reappraisals of the cost of living' conducted by an entire division of trained examiners overseen by Board Secretary Lauck, 'significantly raised the standard of living for countless workers,' in effect setting a minimum wage for common labourers.[20] Lauck's direct appropriation of the cost-of-living argument was apparent in his 1920 arbitration testimony on behalf of New York State Street Car Employees, an argument which he pithily summarized in the phrase, 'cheap men make cheap citizens'.[21]

If the wartime pattern of significant governmental intervention in the market-place provided a preview of Lauck's later labour reform strategy, so did one other aspect of NWLB procedures. Lauck's chief conflict during the short tenure of the Board came with women's rights advocate, Marie Obenauer, who sought greater autonomy for her Division of Women Administrative Examiners in pursuing the Board's stated goal of 'equal pay for equal work'. Lauck resisted any challenge to his notion of an 'integrated, cohesive staff directed by the chiefs of existing divisions', who happened all to be men. Indeed, when Obenauer persisted in her complaints of inadequate staff and authority, Lauck abolished her division entirely. Both in his top-down administrative style and in his inclination – demonstrated previously in his attitude towards the new immigrants – to accept traditional social hierarchies (in this case perceiving women as 'mother[s] of the race ... [who] can not be dealt with on the same terms as men workers'), Lauck showed qualities which would define the limits of his democratic commitments in future years.[22]

The war years convinced Lauck that a marriage of economic science with responsible labour leadership offered a guaranteed formula for American social progress. His ideas, moreover, seemed to accord well with such national luminaries as Secretary of Labour William B. Wilson, philanthropist Julius Rosenwald, and Food Administrator Herbert Hoover who endorsed the living wage as the keystone of post-war economic recovery at President Wilson's Second Industrial Conference in 1920. Just how the economist might function as social-political mediator Lauck demonstrated in a characteristic presentation to the Railway Labour Board on behalf of the Maintenance of Way Employees union in 1922:

> When the [workers] insist that they are not now receiving a living wage and therefore can not possibly stand a further reduction, they are not urging their own personal opinions as to what a living wage should be. The approximate amount of a living wage – i.e. the annual income necessary to support a family in mere health and decency – is no longer a matter of conjecture. Scientific studies of the subject have been made by authorities of such undoubted competence that no question can be raised as to the substantial accuracy of the results ... . For a family to attempt to support itself

on a lesser amount does not mean a mere inconvenience, a doing without certain comforts. It means actual deprivation and degradation; either that or a resort to charity. It means insufficient food, unsanitary housing, insufficient clothing for health and simple decency, even the lack of medical care in time of need, and because of the privations imposed sickness is inevitable and more or less chronic ... . For the community, it means child labour and the harmful forms of woman labour. Except when other conditions are extremely favorable, it easily becomes the breeder of disease, unrest, immorality, and crime. In all of these ways, it saps the strength of the nation itself, and undermines the vitality of democratic institutions.[23]

Lauck's simultaneous appeal to moral sentiment and expert authority, exercised as it was before a quasi-political body, captured the optimistic spirit of the Progressive labour reformer in one of his last institutional redoubts. But, as the devastating defeat of the railway shop crafts strike of the same year would demonstrate, time had largely run out on labour agreements based on consensual principles among all the parties. In a memo prepared for the Railroad Labour Board by one of his assistants, Lauck acknowledged that 'now, in the name of "readjustment" America's employers have carried on a propaganda and concerted effort toward wage reduction such as never before was equaled or approached'.[24]

It was during the fading twilight of the Progressive reform era that Jett Lauck first made his connection to the UMWA and their new leader, John L. Lewis. Like Lauck, the young Lewis, who had scratched his way up the union leadership pole from his Illinois base, had initially lent his political allegiance to Woodrow Wilson and a spate of government-sanctioned labour reforms. He continued to back the President, at least until federal troops and a declaration of martial law forced him to accept a compromise settlement ending the 1919 wartime strike and as late as 1921 remained on record supporting government credits to the unemployed, compulsory employer-financed unemployment insurance, and nationalization or at least stringent governmental regulation of the mining industry.[25] But as well as anyone in the labour movement, Lewis read the handwriting on the post-war wall. The Government had evaporated as a potential ally and protector, while soft-coal operators targeted union power and high wages as a source of their chronic instability. A nation-wide showdown in the bituminous fields in 1922 brought home to Lewis just how stacked the odds were against union power; faced with expanding non-union fields and all-out mobilization against the strike by the Harding administration, the UMWA achieved at best a temporary reprieve from the powers determined to roll back union influence in the industry.[26]

It was time, determined Lewis, to cut a deal. The new, 'Republican' Lewis emerged in a full-blown Republican era. Driving his left-wing opposition out of the union, the autocratic UMWA president tried for the rest of the decade to find a common ground of self-interest with both the Republican administration and the big soft-coal operators. For Lewis the connection was both personal and organizatonal. A frustrated entrepreneur himself, Lewis enjoyed the company of men of wealth; his biographers note that his passport through the 1920s read 'executive' not 'labour leader' and his interest in banking (initially cultivated through his friend Jacob Harriman) ultimately spread to the creation of the union-financed United Labour and Bank and Trust Company of Indianapolis with Lewis as president.[27]

Organizationally, the essence of the union's strategy lay in the self-regulation of coal markets – affecting both price and wage structures – as achieved through area-wide collective bargaining agreements. Taking a cue from the 'new capitalism' rhetoric of Secretary of Commerce, Herbert Hoover (himself a former mining engineer), and other corporate leaders, Lewis appealed to business to move beyond the law of the jungle and into an age of managed competition. With the help of Hoover and utilities magnate George G. Moore, the Jacksonville Agreement of 1924, locking the relatively high wage ($7.50 per day) of the Central Field which stretched from Illinois to Central Pennsylvania into place for three years, was the capstone of this era of UMWA voluntarism.[28]

The public and ideological 'cover' for Lewis's move toward business principles was provided by a document drafted by Lauck and other UMWA advisers under Lewis's name in 1925 called *The Miners' Fight For American Standards*. Essentially an adaptation of the law of supply and demand, *The Miners' Fight* took as its premise an American system built on wages high enough to sustain an expanding home market. 'Trade unionism,' it argued, 'is an integral part of the existing system' happily called 'capitalism'. 'Trade unionism is a phenomenon of capitalism quite similar to the corporation. One is essentially a pooling of labour for purposes of common action in production and in sales. The other is a pooling of capital for exactly the same purposes. The economic aims of both are identical – gain.' When things worked right, there was indeed no reason for workers to look beyond their own resources in meeting their material needs: 'The American workingman, no more than the American businessman, wants to be babied by any paternalistic agencies, governmental or private.' But all was not right, for the self-adjusting market equilibrium had come undone. The problem that had regularly disrupted the industry – causing pain to both workers and operators – was over-production: simply put 'too many mines and too many miners'. In the natural scheme of a healthy capitalism, argued the mineworkers' scribes, unsound sectors of the industry would be shut down to allow the healthy, technically advanced sectors to flourish. The cancer of non-union competition – centred in the new pits of Kentucky and West Virginia and the so-called 'captive mines' of the steel companies in Pennsylvania – however, interrupted this logic, for 'lowering wages and breaking unions would serve only to prolong the maladies of the industry, while sacrificing the rights of the miners'. Only the maintenance of an 'American wage standard', said the authors, could save the industry by forcing a 'reorganization ... upon scientific and efficient lines'.[29]

While the guiding hand of Jett Lauck as UMWA economist is written all over *The Miners' Fight*, it is nevertheless interesting that he chose not to complement the union-as-capitalist-partner theme of the collaborative work with ideas evoked in a book of his own the following year. In *Political and Industrial Democracy, 1775–1926*, Lauck gave voice to an older idealism of the Progressive past which played little role in the UMWA's history or immediate future. Harnessing the findings of the 1920 Industrial Conference to a roster of similar expressions from religious leaders, *Political and Industrial Democracy* focused on the 'aspirations towards participation by workers to exert a larger and more organic influence upon the processes of industrial life'. Lauding individual examples of cooperation and industrial self-management initiated in the pre-war period, Lauck seemed at once to recognize that time was running out on such idealistic models and yet to regret their passing. In Lauck's extensive corpus of public and private writing, the book stands as an uncommon projection of his hopes for the active enfranchisement of ordinary working people.[30]

As it happened, the 1920s' mining industry was not kind to either the industrial democracy or capitalist collaboration fantasies of their labour union creators. Even while professing common interests with the mine owners, *The Miners' Fight* was, in fact, an attempt to stem an already rapid seepage of operators away from the Jacksonville Agreement. But neither the appeal to business logic nor to the good offices of Secretary of Commerce Hoover to stem the tide paid any tangible dividend.[31] Expanding southern production combined with competing fuels, including natural gas, petroleum and electricity, weakened demand and depressed both prices and profits. Even the Mellon-owned Pittsburgh Coal Co., union-operated for 35 years, shut down and reopened non-union in 1925.[32] Throughout the decade the number of miners employed dropped as did hours of work. As for the union, Melvyn Dubofsky and Warren Van Tine describe the UMWA by 1928 as 'in a headlong race for oblivion'. From a peak of 500,000-plus bituminous members in 1921, a bare 80,000 (two-thirds from Lewis's Illinois home district) survived on the rolls, and employers were regularly paying 30–50 per cent below union scale. Altogether bloodied and broke, the organization faced its most desperate hours.[33]

For reasons only partly connected to the union's slide, economist Jett Lauck's fortunes also worsened appreciably during the nation's 'prosperous twenties'. It certainly was not foreordained that a union professional, let alone a union leader, should suffer according to the vicissitudes of the union's organizational health. President Lewis, for example, survived the decade navigating between three houses in his private Cadillac and supporting a large extended family with a combination of union and bank salary as well as successful stock market investments.[34] But Lauck was not quite so lucky. Supporting a wife and three children on a large Chevy Chase estate with three servants, Lauck clearly aspired to a level of professional middle-class respectability that was not so easily accommodated by union consulting work.[35] While regularly retained by a few union patrons, Lauck depended, sometimes to the point of desperation, on the UMWA for his bread and butter.[36] As early as July 1923, for example, he beseeched Lewis for a spot in the upcoming anthracite negotiations, 'because I have done nothing practically since the close of the [1922] coal strike but to accumulate liabilities'.[37] Then, a few months later, Lauck took a fateful gamble, borrowing nearly $10,000 from the Harriman Bank against the signatures of Lewis and UMWA Vice-President Philip Murray to help purchase an office building in Washington DC. He had jumped into a pit from which he never fully escaped. Through the end of the decade and beyond, his relations with his boss (and others with whom he was professionally involved) would become complicated by personal debts. The building proved an albatross: in 1926 he was again seeking 'temporary financial help' (this time while awaiting completion of a cotton deal he had arranged for a southern cooperative marketing association), hoping to sell the building which had never proven creditworthy and determined as he told Lewis 'to be a free man once more'. 'You know my interests and inclinations are not towards the accumulation of property or an oppressive amount of wealth,' Lauck explained. But escape from this 'recent financial jam' – and refusal to declare personal bankruptcy – had become 'a matter of honor'.[38] With the Harriman Bank pressing in on him in a 'quite hard-boiled' manner, Lauck, self-confessedly at his 'lowest ebb' by the end of the decade, was forced to sell his beloved Chevy Chase home and relocate to Fredericksburg to an older house overlooking the Rappahannock River.[39]

Against the background of such private discomforts, one passage from Lauck et al.'s *Miners' Fight* may have rung with special meaning for its ghost writer: '[The American workingman] may submit when he has to, to a feudal overlord in industry. He may even for a time, accept philanthropic largesse dispensed in that manner, but he will never like it. He will never become spiritually reconciled to such conditions.'[40]

Whatever toll they may have taken emotionally, Lauck's private troubles seemed only to stimulate his intellectual contributions to labour's organizational rebirth in the 1930s. Overall, it is noteworthy that the two liveliest centres of New Deal-era labour strategy derived from 'sick' industries of the pre-Depression era – namely Lewis's mineworkers and Sidney Hillman's clothing trades. In both cases adversity led to broadly inventive strategies for industrial planning and regulation, efforts designed to restore economic stability on the back of an American living standard for an organized labour force.[41]

The first step, as Lauck had recognized and pressed on a reluctant boss since the official expiration of the Jacksonville Agreement in 1927, was to get the federal government involved in the control of runaway free markets. John L. Lewis's official break with his prior commitments to 'voluntarism' came in 1928 when he threw the union's remaining leverage behind the proposal of Indiana Republican Senator, James Watson, to use the interstate regulatory authority of Congress to establish a coal commission which would in turn regulate wages, prices, and profits and guarantee collective bargaining.[42] Updated as the Davis-Kelly bill of 1932, such initiatives, while doomed to failure under President Hoover (whom Lewis had mistakenly expected to come to the union's aid in 1928 and still backed in the election of 1932) formed the intellectual and political crucible for the path-breaking National Industrial Recovery Act (NIRA) of 1933.[43]

Once Lauck had gotten Lewis to reject what he called Hoover's 'old rugged individualism', an array of possibilities opened for the imaginative union strategist. As the stock market crash of 1929 began dragging the entire domestic economy into the ditch already long occupied by the soft-coal industry, Lauck produced a steady drumbeat of advice in President Lewis's ear. Hoover's 'big-man theory' of economic progress – the idea that the way to 'help the underdog is to first help the man on top with the assumption that the big man ... will drag the lower levels up with him' had come to naught.[44] The times demanded a leader and a plan, insisted Lauck, and no one was better positioned than Lewis to provide both. 'In this period of depression,' Lauck wrote Lewis in July 1930,

> it is necessary for you above all other considerations to take advantage of the psychology of the business world and the great mass of people outside of the organized labour movement ... The fundamental consideration ... is for you to be the first to give voice to a plan of real constructive industrial statesmanship to lead the country out of the Wilderness.[45]

To clinch the issue, Lauck appealed to his patron's artistic soul as well as his vanity: 'You are a Shakespearean scholar and you know that "there is a tide in the affairs of men which taken at its ebb leads to victory" or words to that effect.' Seated as he was as but one constituent within the leadership council of the larger American Federation of Labour, Lewis initially demurred, responding that he could not 'with propriety' act as a spokesman for industries beyond coal, yet allowing that 'one or two' of Lauck's ideas demanded further thought.[46]

Over the course of the new decade Lauck would, in fact, lay out before Lewis an almost mind-boggling set of reform ideas, an agenda which, accepted as it was even in part, helped to transform the political discourse of the New Deal era. That Lewis had seized the political moment was first apparent with the NIRA. Negotiated through a variety of advisory committees to President Roosevelt (in one of which Lauck toiled tirelessly under the supervision of Sen. Robert Wagner), the basic licensure authority of the resulting industry boards, together with the commitment to collective bargaining, drew heavily on the Watson and Davis-Kelly coal stabilization bills as well as Lewis's testimony to the Senate Finance Committee in February 1933.[47] Lewis, in short, knew what he was doing when he immediately trumpeted the Blue Eagle as the equivalent to the Emancipation Proclamation in the coalfields. Temporarily freed from the downward pressure on wages and the iron heel of employer resistance, the men in the pits responded *en masse*. Virtually every miner in the state of West Virginia had joined the union by the end of the first week of the new regime, and an industry-wide campaign begun on 1 June was all but complete (except for the captive mines) two months later.[48] Not surprisingly, it was precisely the two outposts of organized labour who had intellectually prepared for the Government's new role in the economy – namely the mine and garment workers – who alone were able to take advantage of the NIRA regime.

Yet even as the first stage of the New Deal programme took hold, Jett Lauck was already dreaming bigger thoughts involving drastic changes in the American economy. 'Socialization,' he wrote in 1934 notes intended for John L. Lewis, 'had ceased to be an academic question.' 'We know that a continuance of the capitalistic system as we have had it, is impossible. Profit motive and profit system must be eliminated. Otherwise there is no hope for humanity or democracy.'[49] The stabilization of industry needed for recovery and reform required, in Lauck's view, either nationalization ('state socialism') or strict regulation on a 'public utility basis'. For political reasons, Lauck proposed the second alternative, a kind of super NIRA for the nation's 15 or 20 basic industries, including explicit profit limitations, shorter hours, higher wages, and control of credit facilities by the Government.[50]As if to underscore the direction of his own proposals, Lauck carefully copied into his notes the following words from a 1936 *New Republic* editorial:

> The real question is not whether we go back to laissez-faire...also not whether we shall go forward to economic planning. This is inevitable under either private or public auspices...But what about planning to increase production, to raise the material and cultural standards of life? What about planning under a government expressing the interest of the masses, rather than those of a profit-seeking business? Would that not be democracy of a high order?[51]

Soon, Lauck had even the old voluntarist Lewis singing out of his liberal-statist hymnbook. Perhaps the most convincing public unveiling of the 'new Lewis' came in a forum on 'What I expect of Roosevelt' in *The Nation* just after the 1936 election. Starting with the premise that the goal of public policy was 'a life of plenty' for all groups of people, Lewis argued [in a script obviously written by Lauck] that the nation's experience since 1933 'conclusively demonstrated that our financial and industrial leaders are unable of themselves to govern our economic life in the public interest'. The necessary role of the federal government for the future was thus to guarantee 'economic feedom and democracy to wage and salary workers, accompanied by a high degree of economic planning and regulation for both industry and agriculture'.[52] By 1937 the adviser was openly taking pride and partial credit for the 'evolution' of Lewis 'from a reactionary labour leader to a liberal constructive statesman'.[53]

Although his interactions with President Lewis only occasionally strayed from issues of public policy to matters of direct union administration, it is clear that Lauck himself projected his long-held 'living wage' commitments into a full-scale battle plan for the emergent CIO. Only two months after Lewis had socked Carpenters' leader William Hutcheson in the jaw at the October 1935 AFL convention, Lauck, responding to a direct request for advice, pressed his boss to turn the fledgling Committee for Industrial Organization into a practical reality. What was needed, Lauck suggested, were 'mass meetings' like the crusade which had swept the coalfields in 1933, this time beginning in the steel towns. The argumentative touchstone for such organizing should be the 'living wage idea' which he believed would offer 'a terrific impetus for success somewhat akin to the Townsend old age movement'.[54] Lauck followed up such thoughts with a more elaborate statement of 'objectives of labour', a list which indicated the neat intersection of workplace, political, and broader economic themes in its author's mind:

1. Organize the unorganized, develop economic-political strength
2. Organizing campaign itself requires political action, right to organize and bargain collectively.
3. Formulate constructive policy for ...
a. industrial freedom and liberty, free America from judicial oligarchy, from financial oligarchy.
b. industrial policy – stability, abundance, leisure, security.[55]

Through the CIO and the New Deal, it seemed, Lauck had found the perfect vehicle to pursue the question of living standards which had inspired his work since the pre-war days.

In many respects, Lauck's connection of economic recovery with the strengthening of the labour movement resonated with the most far-reaching of actual New Deal measures. In the case of the newly enacted National Labour Relations Act (on which Lauck consulted with Senator Wagner), robust economic growth served in the legislation's preamble as the justification for the whole enumerated set of labour rights. To wit:

> The inequality of bargaining power between employees who do not possess full freedom of association or actual liberty of contract, and employers who are organized in the corporate or other forms of ownership association substantially burdens and affects the flow of commerce, and tends to aggravate recurrent business depressions, by depressing wage rates and the purchasing power of wage earners in industry and by preventing the stabilization of competitive wage rates and working conditions within and between industries.[56]

Likewise, Lauck's expressed fear of 'judicial oligarchy' linked long-standing labour concerns over injunctions and annulment of hours legislation with the administration's alarm at the Supreme Court's evisceration of its farm relief and industrial recovery acts. While President Roosevelt (FDR) proposed only to dilute the Court's conservative bloc with the power of additional appointments, Lauck and the CIO leadership pushed strongly for a constitutional amendment to eliminate the power of judicial review.[57] Although neither idea bore legislative fruit, the Court's own switch (beginning with acceptance of the Wagner Act in 1937) towards a more pliant respect for federal economic initiative was well understood at the time as a response to a shifting political climate.[58]

But in other respects – as hinted at in his rhetorical determination to free the nation from 'financial oligarchy' – Lauck clearly wanted to go much further than most of his contemporaries in either government or the labour movement towards a social democratic state.[59] His focus on the banks was not a new theme. Together, ever since the breakdown of the Jacksonville Agreement in the coalfields, Lauck and Lewis had regularly identified the 'Morgan interests' (or a broader Morgan–Mellon–Dupont–Rockefeller nexus) as the ultimate source of reactionary politics in the country.[60] The captive mines controversy regularly added fuel to the fire until it was tentatively resolved in 1933. Then, with the newly created CIO gearing up to take on the mass-production industries, Lewis and Co. again addressed the evil power behind the employers' throne. As early as his preparations for a July 1936 radio broadcast scheduled to open the steelworkers' organizing drive, Lauck urged Lewis 'not [to] leave Morgan & Co. out of speech but should attack this banking house as the seat of economic dictatorship of the country'.[61] He further sent Lewis a memo 'reiterating' and 'emphasizing this point', always connecting the steel drive to talk of 'finance-capitalism, the living wage, and economic planning'.[62] Uncharacteristically, Lauck literally threw himself into the centre of a radical attack on the financial sector.

> [I] suggest you have CIO meeting pass a motion instructing W. Jett Lauck to report to next meeting ... a plan for bringing under public control and direction our so-called investment banking or banking having to do with the underwriting and distribution of corporate and other securities, such a plan to have for its purpose the substitution of a permanent public agency modeled possibly after the emergency Reconstruction Finance Coroporation to do the banking normally performed by J.P. Morgan, Dillon, Read, and Co., and similar private banking groups. Let the resolution recite further that Morgan & Co ... dictate the reactionary labour policies of steel, motors, rubber, and other basic industries ... and that under a public fiscal institution such industries will have enlightened labour policies and function in the public interest.[63]

And this was just the beginning. When FDR momentarily shifted his own rhetoric leftward in 1938, promising to investigate monopoly enterprises, Lauck positively exulted. Such an investigation, Lauck counselled Lewis, 'could be utilized to show that there was no hope for the Labour Movement until the Morgan or Investment Banking Control were eliminated from industrial and other corporations'.[64] Indeed, in the same period, Lauck advised a New York *Times* reporter that the financial problems of the nation's railroads also derived from the same investment bankers 'who rooked the railroads in times of prosperity and threw them back upon the government ... for increased freight rates or upon wage reduction of employees in times of adversity'.[65]

Why such a sustained rhetorical assault upon the banks when there was little immediate expectation of major political reform in this area? One answer may be that it served immediate tactical as well as long-term strategic ends. Thus, after outlining his proposed CIO initiative for a new finance system, Lauck added the justification to Lewis that 'if you take the above action in the Committee [CIO] and you give it out to the press, the big banking interests will be so alarmed over the threat to the continuance of their power that they will agree to the unionization of steel, motors, rubber, etc'.[66] Indeed, when US Steel's Myron Taylor stunned the country with his willingness to recognize the Steel Workers Organizing Committee, Lauck rationalized the decision as the culmination of exactly the pressure he had helped bring to bear, a matter of the corporation finally seeing 'the handwriting on the wall' and taking the only 'realistic course' available.[67] From one angle, therefore, Lauck's 'bank-war' strategy towards the steel companies appears to have anticipated the later-day 'corporate-campaign' approach to union-organizing, whereby pressure is brought to bear on stockholders or banks to bring an offending employer to heal.[68]

Still, tactical advantage in the steel campaign alone cannot explain Lauck's continuing preoccupation with restructuring of the banking system. His hopes were most clearly revealed in the programme of the American Association of Economic Freedom (AAEF), a tripartite organization of church leaders, academics, and independent 'public' representatives, which Lauck formed and presided over (with substantive help from the UMWA treasury) as 'acting chairman' from 1938 to 1940.[69] Acting as a political battering ram on economic policy, the AAEF officially spoke through a National Policy Board including such liberal luminaries as Monsignor John Ryan, Rabbi Stephen S. Wise, journalist William Allen White, and university president, Frank Porter Graham. But its message reflected vintage Lauckian craftsmanship. 'Late at night,' his diary entry of 26 January 1938 read, 'I began the preparation of an outline of a Bill for democratizing our investment banking system ... to be used in connection with [a] Bill for expansion of recovery on basis of planned economy of abundance.'[70] As Lauck stressed in a letter to President Roosevelt urging him to include the AAEF in a 1940 recovery conference, the organization

> has devoted a great deal of time to the preparation of a concrete plan to bring about reemployment and general well-being under governmental controls ... Our attitude is that there must be positive ... governmental action requiring the expansion of industry upon the basis of shorter hours and higher rates of compensation.[71]

At the core of the AAEF reconstruction plan stood a prescription for 'an economy of plenty' based on public control of investment capital. Private investment banks would give way to a 'capital-issues' banking system charged with maintaining 'purchasing power ... in approximate balance with increasing production'. Bureaucratically, an 'Industrial Reconstruction Commission' appointed by the President would preside over a vast network of planning boards, industry councils, an assurance and marketing corporation, and banks which would alone underwrite all securities affecting interstate commerce. To guarantee a rising floor under wages and workplace practices, the plan stipulated that 'no articles, commodities or goods produced in the major industries shall be shipped, transported or delivered in interstate commerce, if produced, manufactured, processed or distributed by any business which has not been licensed by the Industrial Reconstruction Commission'.[72] Lest there be any mistake about the animus of the financial reform plan, Lauck chastised so-called bank reformers within the administration and Congress for climbing 'on all fours towards Big Business'.[73] The AAEF's preferred bill, which he hoped to make a 'fundamental issue of the New Deal', sought no less than to 'tax private bankers out of business'.[74]

It does no disservice to Lauck's political commitments (which of course could not have been advanced without at least tacit support from John L. Lewis) to note that his own public financial radicalism likely derived at least in part from his unhappy private economy. The same day in 1938, for example, that he vowed to tax investment bankers 'out of existence', a survey of his own finances revealed that while his expenses averaged $3,000 per month, his income barely reached $1,300 per month.[75] Indeed, the formation of the visionary AAEF corresponded to a second act of downward mobility in the Lauck family estate. Following a devastating 1938 flood, Lauck was forced to put his Fredericksburg 'Island' home on the auction block and move again, this time to a modest farmhouse in Port Royal.[76] Although ostensibly aimed at working people who lived on far more meagre incomes than did he, Lauck's recurrent emphasis on 'plenty', 'abundance', and 'security' surely possessed a personal meaning as well.

There is no doubt that Lauck pictured himself as a radical democrat, helping to 'meet the challenge of Fascist and Communist dictatorships' with 'the idea of industrial democracy and economic planning'.[77] In the context of his times (or our times for that matter) the institutional enfranchisement of working people which the CIO–New Deal effected in both industry and government, did indeed constitute a massive shift toward social power-sharing. But it is also worth taking stock of the limits of the message of democratic abundance promulgated by Lauck, Lewis, and the CIO. Both in theory and practice, the message betrayed a characteristically circumscribed sense of 'democratic process' and popular self-government.

To begin with, of course, no one ever accused John L. Lewis, to whom Lauck was indelibly linked, of an overzealous concern for democratic procedure. From the bruising leadership wars of the UMWA during 1910–19 to his ousting of the left opposition in the 1920s, Lewis had made clear his insistence on undivided power within his organization. Even as he reached out to respond to the aspirations of mass production workers in the 1930s, the same top-down organizational instincts prevailed. The Steel Workers' Organizing Committee (SWOC) for example, the most direct extension of the Lewis-centred organizing mission, was notoriously autocratic in internal structure, a virtual political machine controlled by Lewis' hand-picked adjutant general, Philip Murray.[78] The evidence suggests, however, that Jett Lauck was no mere conduit of his master's will when it came to matters of union decision-making. Rather, as adviser and strategist he actively aided and abetted Lewis's tendencies to achieve desirable ends by the most efficient means possible. It was to Lauck, for example, that John L. Lewis's younger brother, Dennie, repaired for advice on how 'to obtain closer contact and control over districts' in the often unruly UMWA.[79] Similarly, at the dawn of the CIO, it was Lauck who helped design a plan 'on [the] precipitation [of] organization of Industrial Unionism by having mine workers convention direct him [Lewis] to take up steel', a mandate which quickly allowed a hefty $500,000 in UMWA funds to be pumped into the SWOC drive.[80] Moreover, as his own AAEF first took shape, recruiting some 150 leading church and academicians in a campaign for economic democracy, Lauck advised Lewis, 'It is very important for me to control the program and the organization in its initial stages'.[81]

Perhaps the clearest signals of Lauck's taste for hierarchy emerged in his 1937–38 consultancy to United Auto Workers President Homer Martin, who in the aftermath of the astounding sitdown victory over General Motors (GM) at Flint, Michigan was contending at once with recalcitrant GM bargainers and a growing rank and file opposition movement led, among others, by the Reuther brothers.[82] Lauck, undoubtedly with Lewis's blessing, judged the erratic but charismatic Martin the 'best man' available for UAW leadership, agreed to help him 'write a strong centralized constitution for the Union – like the United Mine Workers', and favoured quick accommodation with GM.[83] In the face of recurrent wildcat sitdown threats, Lauck even sketched a plan to move Martin and other UAW officers from Detroit to Washington DC 'to remove them from constant direct contact and interference with by local person and committee[s]'.[84] Despite such basic sympathies, Lauck also readily perceived the weaknesses of the erratic Martin and his ideologically overzealous strategist, Jay Lovestone. The factional threat from UAW 'reds', Lauck advised Lewis, had been greatly exaggerated by the Martin–Lovestone forces, and fearing disruptive internal blood-letting, counselled against impending purges of middle-level union staff.[85] By January 1939, Martin had left the UAW in a shambles, having greeted union opponents with a pistol, accepted an utterly concessionary contract with GM, arranged a secret, sweetheart deal with the Ford Motor Company, and then fired most of the union's executive board members. Lauck for his part, had officially severed his ties with the Martin faction a year before, alienated at once by Martin's political incompetence and his managerial irresponsibility in delaying Lauck's salary checks.[86]

A clue to the underlying ideological assumptions upheld by Lauck and other left-progressives in the late 1930s is revealed in the work of business writer and reformer, Ordway Tead. An Amherst College graduate (1912) who spent three years at Boston's South End settlement house before entering a career as social worker, industrial relations consultant, writer-editor and educational administrator, Tead collected his reform-minded wisdom in a 1939 volume entitled *New Adventures in Democracy Applications of the Democratic Idea*. Attracted to the book by a newspaper review, Jett Lauck was so taken with its message that he corresponded with the author and invited him to testify for the AAEF in public hearings.[87] Combining a general sympathy for the union shop with an economic focus on rising levels of consumption for all, Tead provided a fitting theoretical complement to Lauck's policy priorities. The emphases within Tead's schema are especially suggestive. The first principle of democracy in Tead's accounting was 'representation of interests' such that 'every group which has a clearly identifiable set of interests is safeguarded in its dealings with other groups'; further tests of the 'maturity' of the industrial system, Tead argued, were demonstrated by such practices as uniform wage rates for newcomers, seniority rights, safeguards against arbitrary discharge, quality of output, medical care, vacation pay, a safe workplace and limitations on overtime. Tead made clear, in ways that both Lauck and John L. Lewis would surely have approved, that *democratic results* combined with a *procedure of group representation* defined the significant measures of democratic practice. 'What is a democratic approach to economic problems?' Tead asked rhetorically. The answer was simple. 'A democratic approach ... is that approach which puts the welfare of the great majority of people above the welfare of any small group in the community.'[88] By such logic, rising living standards and the closed shop were the surest and safest tests of democratic progress. Government of the people and for the people, by all means, Tead and Lauck might have said, whereas government *by* the people was a luxury which might have to wait.

Unfortunately for Jett Lauck, just as his vehicle of economic democracy took on a refined and ever more concrete shape, his designated driver deserted him. Throughout the 1930s, from Lauck's point of view, no one was more crucially situated to effect historic social change than

John L. Lewis. As both the New Deal and CIO gained in staying power, offering the opportunity for ever more intense co-operation between labour and the state, Lauck had taken it upon himself to turn Lewis into the perfect prod to stir the diffuse forces behind the New Deal coalition towards institutionalized social democracy. With Lauck's help, ever since the NRA, Lewis had operated as both crucial supporter and critical goad to President Roosevelt, ensuring that issues of union rights and worker welfare were constantly present on the nation's political table. Yet, all too soon, the approach of a Second World War raised the stakes on labour's delicate political balancing act. As FDR turned away from domestic reform plans in deference to both foreign policy and a rapprochement with business leaders, so Lewis the Welshman determined not to allow 'British imperialists' and the 'Morgan interests' to sidetrack the nation into a new military conflict. By 1940 Lewis's attacks on administration policy (including labour's governmental liaison, Sidney Hillman) grew ever more harsh even as the President called for reconciliation of domestic conflicts (including a vain attempt at reunification of the AFL and CIO).[89] Lauck was caught in the middle. In rapidly changing political circumstances, his strategic antennae proved at once keen and useless.

Anticipating the inevitable expansion of governmental regulatory powers in wartime, Lauck attempted both to grab Roosevelt's ear on behalf of labour-friendly measures and to corral the irrepressible Lewis into a more patient posture that would serve his (as well as his members') long-term interests. In early October, 1940, for example, Lauck confided to his diary that he had

> had a confidential talk with Lewis today relative to my proposal for a National Defense Labour Board and about Labour policies for the future. He approved the proposal, thought highly of it as a constructive measure, but did not believe the President would approve it, because of its fundamental provisions for reemployment and well-being ... Said that Big Business had been practically allowed to write there [sic] own ticket for the Defense Program. Said that he had told Pres[ident Roosevelt] after 1936, if he would issue Executive Order to enforce compliance for government contractors with NLRB, etc, he [Lewis] would organize 5 million men back of him, but refused because he feared an imperium in imperio. Said F[air] L[abor] Standard Act was not being enforced properly now because of Pres. order ... to pass on only 2000 cases a month or 1/ 16th of those seeking actions. Then talked briefly with him as what should be the role of leaders of organized labour during the next 4 years and left memorandum with him on this subject, stating that English labour was going to take a dominant position after [the] War, and should a leader like himself advocate a program of fundamental reform in principle here in America he would attain great

> prestige and possibly high political preferment, because [of the] present lack of such leadership.[90]

Once again playing Machiavelli to his would-be Prince, Lauck tried to turn Lewis's justifiable frustration with FDR labour policies into an extended war for political position.

Just how little patience Lewis had for 'progressive' strategy of any kind was revealed just two weeks before the presidential election when, to Lauck's chagrin, the CIO chieftain publicly endorsed Republican Wendell Willkie for president and promised to resign as CIO president if Roosevelt was reelected. 'I did not approve of the speech,' Lauck noted privately, 'principally on account of [the] bad effect it would have on Lewis' future career and usefulness because of his deal with [the] Wilkie [sic] Democrats – representing the most reactionary banking groups ... [I] decided to continue to support and vote for Roosevelt.'

In an instant, the whole social-democratic project to which Lauck had dedicated himself came crashing down. Inseparably attached to Lewis professionally, he could not and did not openly break with his patron.[91] Yet Lauck knew that in his willing detachment from the Democratic Party masses of the CIO, Lewis had rendered himself – and thereby Lauck as well – a political nullity. He wrote:

> [I] had hoped to prevent this but could not get to Lewis ... My thought was to attack the New Deal but say that the CIO would support [it] and make it a success during the next 4 years. This attitude would have retained progressive groups in support of CIO and laid the way open to Lewis becoming a progressive leader – and possibly obtaining high public office in the future. [I] considered his action tragic from this perspective.[92]

Several days later, after again playing back to himself his unsuccessful efforts to reach and dissuade Lewis from a suicidal course, Lauck confided simply, 'Result broke my heart'.[93]

Just as Lauck feared, the war years were not happy times for policy-makers who stuck with John L. Lewis. Consumed at first with internal union fights leading first to resignation from the presidency, then total withdrawal from the CIO which he had created, a resentful Lewis retreated to the bulwark of the UMWA. But it was in direct defiance of presidential orders as well as AFL and CIO no-strike policy that Lewis went from mere maverick to outcast in much of the public mind. His running confrontation with the War Labour Board over the Government's right to set wage ceilings – climaxed by extended walkouts in 1943 – effectively cut Lewis off from the larger left–liberal coalition he had cultivated since the beginning of the Depression. While he had permanently consolidated the loyalty of his own UMWA base (a constituency that would rapidly shrink in the post-war decades with the declining use of coal), Lewis, for all practical purposes, had surrendered his claim to national economic policy or political influence. Len De Caux, one of several left-wingers Lewis had recruited onto his CIO organizing train, recalled the pathos of these years: 'I saw and felt how alone Lewis was, most of all in 1940, when others fled from him – in ways he recognized, if not formally. In his period of wartime defiances, Lewis must have felt all the more alone.'[94]

While dutifully maintaining his UMWA consultancy, Lauck's own portfolio of operations grew increasingly constricted throughout the 1940s. Intellectually he remained as ambitious as ever. As early as 1943, for example, Lauck seized with a passion on plans for a post-war world government, reading everything he could get his hands on about possible replacements for the discredited League of Nations. His own 'preamble for a Constitution for a World Federation' tellingly extended the pronouncements of the Atlantic Charter and Allied summits to 'prevent imperialism and the causes of war by permitting international cartels under governmental control' – a kind of worldwide NRA![95] Even regarding domestic affairs, he had not entirely abandoned hope for a progressive resurgence. FDR's 'Economic Bill of Rights', enunciated in the President's Annual Message to Congress in January 1944, Lauck hailed as a modern-day equivalent to 'Jefferson's Bill of Rights' and immediately began lobbying to incorporate the new charter as amendments to the Wagner Act.[96] Such moments of bubbling enthusiasm, however, were inevitably quieted with doses of political reality. At a luncheon in December 1943, for example, Lauck ventured the thought that 'Pres. Roosevelt's reelection and post-war success in establishing a new World Order was dependent on a unified labour support under Pres. Lewis. [Consulting economist, Hugh] Hanna agreed with me, but with me also, could not think of any successful way of bringing this about at the present time'.[97] Most of Lauck's business time was now devoted to comparatively mundane advice on union contracts and energy industry developments; the reform ideals that had once sparked endless rounds of active engagement had become matters of idle speculation.

Moreover, at a personal as well as programmatic level, Lauck was experiencing hard times. His son Peter recalls an emotional 'rift' in the household over his father's loyalty to Lewis while his mother remained a 'big fan' of FDR. The tensions were likely exacerbated by Lauck's long absences from home. Since the 1930s, in fact, the pressures and passions of his public role often made Lauck a near-stranger to his own children. As son Peter remembers, 'All he did was work'.[98] Lauck's diary entries confirm the stress of days which might begin with a bus ride from Port Royal to Fredericksburg, Virginia where he caught a crowded train to Washington DC, then spent the 'rest of day catching up on accumulated articles and miscellaneous matters at offices … taking data home at night to go over', then 'reading to midnight in evening'.[99] Nor had Lauck ever escaped the burdens of debt under which he had laboured for many years. Of the three Lauck children, only the oldest son, William (who became an architect) could afford the advantage of a professional education. The youngest child, Eleanor, who never attended college, suffered particularly during the family's Depression-era privation and (according to her brother Peter) bore emotional scars which led to her later institutional confinement.[100]

In the face of mounting obstacles Lauck soldiered on. A day after Roosevelt's electoral victory in November 1944, Lauck was still strategizing, anticipating 'the final constructive policies' of the President's agenda, including 'an assured program of industrial expansion, full employment and plenty'.[101] But constantly borrowing new money and covering old loans, Lauck himself was pressed financially to the wall. In 1944 he spent a frantic week vainly preparing his entry for a Budweiser Beer Company contest on the 'best plan of post-war revival'.[102] By 1945 he realized that he did 'not have resources sufficient to pay apartment and office rents'.[103] In desperate straits, he joined in 1947 with John L. Lewis in a speculative scheme for oil exploration in Wyoming.[104] But Lauck had no time to wait for the ripening of investments. Unbeknownst to his family and friends, he had been diagnosed several years before with arteriosclerosis of the brain. Only when they noticed a sudden fall-off in his work routine did his loved ones learn of his condition. Nursed at home by his family in his final months, he died at age 69 on 18 June 1949.

In one sense Lauck departed at an appropriate moment. For, not only the people he relied on but basic assumptions he had subscribed to since the Progressive era had been dramatically displaced from the centre of American public life. As historian Alan Brinkley makes clear in a most penetrating treatment of the denouement of New Deal liberalism, the structural tinkering with capitalism envisioned by earlier twentieth-century reformers – linked variously with anti-monopoly initiatives, the associative or regulatory state, as well as direct state planning – had all but disappeared from pragmatic political discourse by the end of the Second World War. What had taken its place (beginning in the aftermath of the 1937–38 'Roosevelt recession' and then consolidated through *de facto* wartime pump-priming and after) was Keynesian fiscal policy. Economists and political reformers alike changed their focus from controlling Big Business to guaranteeing a continuingly expanding economy.[105] Social welfare, by post-war liberal standards, became less a matter of balancing power at the point of production than ensuring

higher living standards on the principle later enunciated by President
Kennedy as 'a rising tide lifts all boats'.[106]

Even the labour movement – the century-long champion of capitalist
restructing – was in no position, and for the most part in little mood, to
buck the tide. UAW President Walter Reuther's 1945 proposal for a
guaranteed annual wage for auto workers like AFL President William
Green's call 'for the maintenance of a high national income – [and]
equilibrium between producing and consuming power', accepted the
new orthodoxy of high consumption divorced from structural economic
reforms.[107] Even James Matles of the left-wing United Electrical Workers of America defined his union's aim by 1944 in 'one proposition –
more money'. 'Bring home the gravy to your people,' declared Matles,
'that's all you have to worry about.'[108] All in all, the world of liberal
fiscal policy and even post-war collective bargaining was far removed
from the crusades for 'economic democracy' or 'public utility capitalism' conducted by W. Jett Lauck and an entire generation of Progressive
intellectual reformers.

And yet, as Lauck's career also neatly illustrates, there was at least
one important point of continuity, a theme that postwar liberals owed
their interwar and even Progressive era forebears. 'Consumerism' itself
– or the preoccupation with mass consumption and rising living standards as the chief test of social progress – was hardly the brainchild of
those fiscal reductionists Brinkley calls the New Liberals.[109] Rather,
decades before the Roosevelt recession and its aftermath, strategists of
Lauck's generation had already fashioned the brilliant synthesis between a democratic social movement like organized labour and the rise
of a corporate-centred consumer capitalism in America. The chief difference in reform projects, pre- and post-Keynesian synthesis, was that
Lauck and Company were convinced that an Economy of Plenty required 'democratic planning' or tight restrictions on capitalist institutions, while the extended post-Second World War boom lent dramatic
credence to an opposite conclusion – the less internal meddling the
better. No doubt, Lauck's much belaboured AAEF plans for recovery
would have appeared irrelevant five years after their creation and utterly unrecognizable antiques of social thought ten years later. By Lauck's
calculus, the sustained recovery, rising living standards, and heightened
consumer power of the post-war years must have seemed like the right
answer to the wrong question. The Angel of Plenty, whose arrival he
had so ardently anticipated and championed, proved a most ungrateful
guest.

Now, nearly a half-century after Lauck's death, the tables have turned
again. Stretching far into the once affluent middle-classes, American
living standards regularly stumble and fall. A fiercely competitive inter-

national economy, accompanied by neo-liberal principles, has largely consigned Keynesian liberalism itself – and with it much of organized labour's accumulated strength – to the historical scrapheap. And just as the Great Depression opened but an impermanent window for a labour–State alliance, so the Boom's socially conciliatory politics has met its temporal end. The moment, indeed, may have arrived for a re-examination of the social democratic project built in a time of economic pain and scarcity. In an era when capital investment regularly crosses borders in search of cheaper labour markets, when downsizing and concession bargaining define a downward spiral of income and benefits for employees, might not Lauck's call for minimum living standards, controls on investment capital, and even an 'economic United Nations' carry renewed relevance? Might social economic stagnation combined with the 'death of Communism' reinvigorate international left–liberal alternatives? If so, an alliance of popular forces and reform-minded intellectuals may again play a vital role in public affairs. Yet, if such far-flung changes carry any realistic potential, they will have to rely on another change to which Lauck gave relatively little thought. Democratic ends, in short, must be supported by democratic institution-building. After all, when abundance finally arrived for the great mass of the American people, it proved a frail reed upon which to perch a democratic culture. Will it be different next time?

Notes

* My connection to the 'language' theme of this collection of essays is less motivated by the ongoing historiographical debates over language-and-class (or non-class) than by a more general interest in the roles that intellectuals have played inside and outside labour movements in help-ing to define the 'terms' upon which workers would lay claim to the body politic. The following piece is drawn from a larger work entitled *Progressive Intellectuals and the Dilemmas of Democratic Commitment*, forthcoming from Harvard University Press.

1. In preparing this chapter, I am especially indebted to Peter B. Lauck for adding his memory of his father's world to the written record otherwise available to the historian. I also am grateful for the able research assist-ance of David Anderson and to Tom Dublin, Robert Gallman, and Nelson Lichtenstein for specific suggestions and helpful leads. Finally, librarian Christina Deane of the Special Collections Department at the Alderman Library, University of Virginia greatly facilitated my work in the Lauck Papers.

2. Beatrice Webb and Sidney Webb, *The History of Trade Unionism* (New York, Longmans, Green and Co., 1920 [1894], p. 369.

3. John R. Commons and David J. Saposs, *History of Labour in the United States*, vol. 1. (New York, Macmillan, 1926 [1918], p. 25.

4.   Commons, Saposs, et al., *History of Labour*, p. 12.

5.   On labour's late-nineteenth century political culture, see Leon Fink, *Workingmen's Democracy: the Knights of Labour and American Politics* (Urbana, University of Illinois Press, 1983). For the influence of the courts on labour actions, see William E. Forbath, *Law and the Shaping of the American Labour Movement* (Cambridge, MA, Harvard University Press, 1991); Victoria C. Hattam, *Labour Visions and State Power: the Origins of Business Unionism in the United States* (Princeton, NJ, Princeton University Press, 1993); and Karen Orren, *Belated Feudalism: Labour the Law and Liberal Development in the United States* (Cambridge, Cambridge University Press, 1991). The earlier ideological claims, to be sure, regularly reappeared in the form of workplace-centred 'control' struggles and continuing calls for 'industrial democracy', staunched by the influence of a strong socialist minority within the organized labour movement. See, e.g. David Montgomery, *Workers Control in America: Studies in the History of Work, Technology, and Labour Struggles* (New York, Cambridge University Press, 1979), and Nelson Lichtenstein and Howell John Harris (eds), *Industrial Democracy in America: the Ambiguous Promise* (New York, Cambridge University Press, 1993); Gompers as quoted in Louis S. Reed, *The Labour Philosophy of Samuel Gompers* (Port Washington, NY, Kennikat Press, 1966), p. 12.

6.   I found no previous studies of Lauck's writing or larger work, and while several historians have made excellent use of fragments of the huge Lauck Papers, housed at the University of Virginia, none have focused squarely on Lauck himself. To date, the magisterial biography, *John L. Lewis: a Biography* by Melvyn Dubofsky and Warren Van Tine (New York, Quadrangle/New York Times, 1977), (abridged edition, Urbana, University of Illinois Press 1986) offers the best available, albeit quite brief, assessment of Lauck's overall contributions, including his authorship of 'most ... of Lewis' speeches and publications in the 1930s' (p. 556, fn. 11, 1977 edition). Outside of brief mentions in other biographical treatments of Lewis, the only scholarly references I have encountered for Lauck are incidental citations in descriptions of the policy machinations behind the National Industrial Recovery Act, to be referred to below. Even the biographical sketch at the front of the W. Jett Lauck Papers describes its subject as a 'somewhat mysterious figure'. His son Peter B. Lauck, reached at age 78 for an interview by telephone by the author in 1995, had never previously been questioned about his father's role for scholarly purposes.

7.   Cecil Carnes, *John L. Lewis: Leader of Labour* (New York, Robert Speller, 1936), p. 240; James A. Wechsler, *Labour Baron: a Portrait of John L. Lewis* (New York, William Morrow and Co., 1944), p. 46.

8.   *Monitor* quotation cited in personal diaries, 17 November 1936, W. Jett Lauck Papers, University of Virginia Library, Charlottesville, Virginia.

9.   In addition to some four hundred boxes of records, the W. Jett Lauck Papers (hereafter LP), housed at Special Collections, Alderman Library, University of Virginia include Lauck's personal diaries, 1935–47, preserved on three reels of microfilm.

10. Peter Lauck interview by telephone by the author, 30 October 1995.

11. 'Scrapbook', box 29, LP.

12. 'Testimony of W.J. Lauck, 1920', New York State Board of Arbitration on the Differences Between the New York State Railways and the Employers' Associations, box 12, LP.

13. Jeremiah W. Jenks and W. Jett Lauck, *The Immigration Problem: a Study of American Immigration Conditions and Needs* (New York, Funk and Wagnalls Co., 1922 [1911], p. 202; As an Immigration Commission researcher, Lauck was singularly responsible for a careful comparison of standards of living between northern immigrant and southern US textile workers. 'Labour conditions in cotton mills in north and south: preliminary report', US Immigration Commission, 1910, box 242, LP; Lauck's Immigration Commission also suggested that his West Virginia roots had already made him respectful of the basic aims of trade unionism. As demonstrated in his work with co-researcher Jeremiah Jenks, Lauck defended the restriction of Southern and Eastern Europeans and outright exclusion of 'Orientals' in part on grounds that the influx of new immigrants (many of whom would later indirectly employ Lauck as UMWA members) – has 'had the effect of weakening the labour organizations of the original employees, and in some of the industries has caused their entire demoralization and disruption' ('Labour conditions', 202–3).

14. W. Jett Lauck to Frank Walsh, 21 July 1915, Frank Walsh Papers, New York Public Library (emphasis added).

15. Louis S. Reed, *The Labour Philosophy of Samuel Gomperrs* (Port Washington, NY, Kennikat Press, 1966), pp. 11–53, quotation p. 12; the last great attack on the wages system itself had been raised by the Knights of Labour in the 1880s. For the logic of this earlier movement, see Leon Fink, *Workingmen's Democracy: the Knights of Labour and American Politics* (Urbana, University of Illinois Press, 1983), esp. pp. 3–37.

16. Daniel Horowitz, *The Morality of Spending: Attitudes Toward the Consumer Society in America, 1875–1940* (Baltimore, Johns Hopkins University Press, 1985), pp. 16–18.

17. Lawrence Bennett Glickman, 'A living wage: political economy, gender and consumerism in American culture, 1880–1925', PhD dissertation, University of California-Berkeley (1992) provides the most sustained treatment of these issues.

18. Glickman, 'A living wage', pp. 323–35.

19. Horowitz, *The Morality of Spending*, pp. 30–66.

20. Valerie Jean Conner, *The National War Labour Board: Stability, Social Justice, and the Voluntary State in World War I* (Chapel Hill, UNC Press, 1983), pp. 50–67, quotation pp. 66–7.

21. 'Testimony of W.J. Lauck, 1920', Board of Arbitration on the Difference Between the New York State Railways and the Employers' Associations, box 12, LP.

22. Conner, *The National War Labour Board*, pp. 143–7, quotations pp. 143, 146.

23. 'Harmful effects of low wages upon the family, the individual, and the community', testimony on behalf of the Maintenance of Way Employees, Railroad Labour Board, 1922, box 185, LP.

24. 'The national income and the practicability of the living wage', memo prepared for hearings of the Maintenance of Way Employees case before the Railroad Labour Board, 1922, box 180, LP.

25. Dubofsky and Van Tine, *John L. Lewis* (1986 edition), p. 56.
26. Ibid., pp. 56–71; James P. Johnson, *The Politics of Soft Coal: the Bituminous Industry from World War I through the New Deal* (Urbana, University of Illinois Press, 1979), pp. 92–108.
27. Dubofsky and Van Tine, *John L. Lewis* (1986), pp. 72–5.
28. Johnson, *The Politics of Soft Coal*, pp. 118–23; For the most cogent assessment of the UMWA's long-term strategy of market regulation, see David Brody, 'Market unionism in America: the case of coal', in *In Labour's Cause: Main Themes on the History of the American Worker* (New York, Oxford University Press, 1993), pp. 131–74.
29. John L. Lewis, *The Miners' Fight for American Standards* (Indianapolis, Bell Publishing 1925), pp. 24, 39–41, 130–31.
30. W. Jett Lauck, *Political and Industrial Democracy, 1775–1926* (New York, Funk and Wagnalls, 1926), pp. 25, 28–38, 42–3, 53–7, quotation p. 25.
31. Dubofsky and Van Tine, *John L. Lewis* (1986), pp. 101–3.
32. Johnson, *The Politics of Soft Coal*, pp. 95–8.
33. Dubofsky and Van Tine, *John L. Lewis* (1986), p. 110.
34. Ibid., p. 112.
35. Jett Lauck's son, Peter B. Lauck, remembers the Chevy Chase home as a 'grand' white-framed mansion surrounded by 2 acres of gardens and a pond just at the end of the DC streetcar line. Interview 30 October 1995.
36. Although he held a UMWA membership card, Lauck resisted entreaties to practise within the union headquarters, preferring to maintain his own independent Washington DC office under the name William Jett Lauck and Associates, Consulting and Practicing Economists. (Peter Lauck interview; personal diaries, 22 February 1937, reel 1, LP; personal diaries, 25 August 1938, reel 1, LP); in addition to UMWA and later special CIO-related projects, Lauck continued to advise other labour groups, particularly the New York Public Building Service Employees and the Brotherhood of Locomotive Firemen and Engineers.
37. Lauck to John L. Lewis, 3 July 1995, box 39, LP.
38. Lauck to John L. Lewis, 26 November 1926, 10 December 1926, box 39, LP. For his part, Lewis was patient but not without limits in his responsiveness to Lauck's requests. While he regularly signed the requisite bank forms to extend the time frame for Lauck's debt repayments, he declined to cover further loans on the grounds that his own personal financial standing did not warrant 'added risk'. Lewis to Lauck, 2 December 1926, 29 November 1928, 5 May 1929, box 39, LP.
39. Although Lauck first talked of selling his estate (with an estimated worth of $115,000) in 1927, the evidence suggests that he most likely made the transaction in 1931. Lauck to Morris L. Ernst, 13 August 1927, box 35, LP; Lauck to Lewis, 2 May 1929, 2 May 1931, box 39, LP. By 1927, Lauck had exhausted his bank credit and was forced to turn to the 'outrageous' rates of independent moneylenders. In his desperation he appealed for loans to his active associates in the labour reform world, including the attorney Morris L. Ernst and Pennsylvania Governor Gifford Pinchot. Gifford Pinchot to Lauck, 21 July 1931; Lauck to Pinchot, 27 August 1931, box 43, LP; Lauck to Morris L. Ernst, 13 August 1927, box 35, LP. In the end, according to his son,

Lauck actually 'traded down' his Chevy Chase home (to an officer of the virulently anti-union National Association of Manufacturers, no less!) for the lesser riverfront home plus $15,000 cash. Peter Lauck interview; By the end of the decade, when Lauck's Lenox Building-related debt approached $75,000 dollars, even the usually gruff Lewis grew openly worried and counselled his friend not to 'become melancholy or depressed by what I am sure is only momentary embarrassment'. Lauck to Paul Brissenden, 13 October 1938, box 33, LP; John L. Lewis to Lauck, 16 July 1930, box 39, LP.

For the Lauck family, to be sure, the material deprivation involved in the move was only relative. Lauck estimated his average annual income during the 1920s (perhaps slightly inflated to reassure his creditors) at $32,000, a figure in 1925 dollars that my economic historian colleague Robert Gallman translates to a handsome $276,000 in 1995 prices, or effectively within the top 1 cent of family incomes of the day. Even when forced to economize, as Peter Lauck recalls, the family dropped to one servant in the Fredericksburg riverfront home called 'The Island'. Meanwhile, Lauck maintained membership in both the Chevy Chase Country Club and the Cosmos Club in Washington DC, although, according to Peter Lauck, 'my father hardly went there'. Both his parents, Peter recalls, were rather 'like children', unrealistic and always overextended when it came to money matters.

40. Lewis, *The Miners' Fight*, pp. 130–31.
41. Ellis W. Hawley, *The New Deal and the Problem of Monopoly: a Study in Economic Ambivalence* (New York, Fordham University Press, 1995 [1966]), p. 28 makes this point most succinctly. For an excellent, and largely parallel, treatment of the Hillman side of the equation, see Steve Fraser, *Labour Will Rule: Sidney Hillman and the Rise of American Labour* (New York, Free Press, 1991).
42. Robert H. Zieger, *Republicans and Labour, 1919–1929* (Lexington, University of Kentucky Press, 1969), p. 257; Johnson, *The Politics of Soft Coal*, p. 123.
43. Johnson, *The Politics of Soft Coal*, pp. 132–3. Lauck himself rejoiced in the election of Franklin Roosevelt over Hoover. Lauck to Lewis, 10 November 1932, box 39, LP.
44. Lauck to Lewis, 13 May 1930, box 39, LP.
45. Lauck to Lewis, 8 July 1930, box 39, LP.
46. Lewis to Lauck, 31 August 1931; 26 May 1930, Box 39, LP.
47. Dubofsky and Van Tine, *John L. Lewis* (1986), pp. 131–3; Johnson, *The Politics of Soft Coal*, pp. 142–4; Lauck's central role in the NIRA drafting process is evident from his correspondence with Lewis, copious notes, draft proposals, and subsequent outline of the 'Origin and history of the Recovery Act' which he prepared on 11 Novemebr 1936, box 29, box 46, LP. In April 1933 Lauck was assigned by Senator Wagner to work with Dr Harold Moulton of the Brookings Institution in drafting a recovery plan. 'My effort,' Lauck wrote President Lewis ... would be similar boards for each major industry ... in accordance with provisions of the [Davis-Kelly] Coal Bill.' Lauck to Lewis, 27 April 1933, box 39, LP. For Lewis's own recognition of Lauck's role in the creation of Section 7A/NRA, see Saul Alinsky, *John L. Lewis: an Unauthorized Biography* (New York, G.P. Putnam's Sons, 1949), pp. 65–6.

48. Dubofsky and Van Tine, *John L. Lewis* (1986), pp. 133–5, 149.
49. Lauck notes on 'Socialization', 1934, box 29, LP.
50. 'Formula for the NRA', 18 October 1934, box 29, LP.
51. Lauck notes and memoranda, *New Republic* editorial, 'Landon on Planning', 23 September 1936, box 29, LP.
52. John L. Lewis, "What I expect of Roosevelt," *The Nation*, **143** (14 November 1936), pp. 571–2.
53. Personal diaries, 5 December 1937, Reel 1, LP. Lauck here summarizes a conversation with New York *Times* reporter, C.L. Sulzberger, who was researching his forthcoming *Sit Down with John L. Lewis* (New York, Random House, 1938).
54. Lauck memorandum to Lewis, 17 December 1935, box 164, LP; Lauck Diaries, 12 December 1935, reel 1, LP; Dr Francis E. Townsend's Old Age Revolving Pension scheme (which helped to spur Roosevelt's Social Security Act of 1935) advocated payments of $200 per month to persons 60 years of age and older, the pensions to be drawn from a national 2 per cent tax on commercial transactions.
55. Lauck memorandum to Lewis, 'Objectives of labour' [1936], box 29, LP.
56. J. Joseph Huthmacher, *Senator Robert F. Wagner and the Rise of Urban Liberalism* (New York, Atheneum, 1968), p. 167. Text of NLRA as quoted in Charles J. Morris (ed.), *The Developing Labour Law: the Board, the Courts, and the National Labour Relations Act* (Washington, DC, American Bar Association, 1971), appendix A, p. 895.
57. Personal diaries, 5 February 1937, 6 March 1937, reel 1, LP.
58. On the politics of the court's shift, see, e.g. James MacGregor Burns, *Roosevelt: the Lion and Fox* (New York, Harcourt, Brace and World, 1956), pp. 303–8; and William E. Lauchtenburg, *The Supreme Court Reborn: the Constitutional Revolution in the Age of Roosevelt* (New York, Oxford University Press, 1995), pp. 213–36.
59. Perhaps Lauck's most explicit plan in this regard lay in his proposals for the Commonwealth of Pennsylvania based on his work as chairman of the state's Anthracite Industry Commission in 1937–8. The recommendations (which proved a legislative non-starter) included creation of a Public Service Commission to regulate prices of anthracite at the mine, public corporations to redirect coal bootleggers to legitimate operations under regulated prices and wages, co-operative marketing organizations among operators to reduce freight costs, and ultimately, authority to reabsorb unemployed miners via TVA-like public development projects. *Report of the Anthracity Coal Industry Commission* (Harrisburg, 30 July 1938), reference courtesy of Thomas Dublin.
60. For reference to what they call the 'Lauck–Lewis demonology' of the bankers, see Dubofsky and Van Tine, *John L. Lewis* (1977), pp. 192, 197, 250, 252.
61. Personal diaries, 3 July 1936, reel 1, LP. Lauck had begun in December 1935 to keep a daily 'diary' of his work activities.
62. Personal diaries, 11 August 1936.
63. 'Memo to Mr. Lewis on investment banking', 7 November 1936, box 29, LP.
64. Personal diaries, 20 June 1938, reel 1, LP. For a shrewd overview of the 'anti-monopoly moment' as led by Thurman Arnold within the New

Deal, see Alan Brinkley, *The End of Reform: New Deal Liberalism in Recession and War* (New York, Alfred A. Knopf, 1995), pp. 106–36.

65. Personal diaries, 23 June 1938, reel 1, LP.
66. Memo to Mr Lewis on investment banking, 7 November 1936, box 29, LP; in his diary Lauck noted that Lewis' left-wing lieutenant John Brophy 'did not seem to grasp' the significance of Lauck's anti-bank manoeuver. Personal diaries, 11 November 1936, reel 1, LP.
67. Personal diaries, 3 March 1937, reel 1, LP.
68. Most closely associated with union consultant, Ray Rodgers, the corporate campaign became famous in the Farah and J.P. Stevens campaigns by the Amalgamated Clothing Workers in the 1970s and the Austin meatpackers' strike against Hormel in the mid-1980s. The idea involved 'a combination of tactics such as consumer boycotts, legal appeals, attempts to broaden the issues from simple labour relations to moral or social matters, and pressure on interlocking sectors of the business and financial community in hopes of isolating the offending employers'. Kim Moody, *An Injury to All: the Decline of American Unionism* (New York, Verso, 1988), pp. 306–7, 317–19. See also Peter Rachleff, *Hard-Pressed in the Heartland: the Hormel Strike and the Future of the Labour Movement* (Boston, South End Press, 1993), pp. 53, 109–10; Historical accounts of US Steel's decision to recognize the union make no mention of the CIO's 'bank war' as a possible influence on its action. But neither does the issue seem ever to have been researched. For the best existing account of these events see Walter Galenson, *The CIO Challenge to the AFL: a History of the American Labour Movement, 1935–1941* (Cambridge, MA, Harvard University Press, 1960), pp. 75–96. That Lewis, in particular, may have viewed the bank reform talk more as a negotiating tactic than a serious political programme is suggested by his willingness to meet, at President Roosevelt's request, with Thomas W. Lamont of the House of Morgan in 1938 in an effort to arrive at a 'cooperative' recession-fighting programme. Brinkley, *The End of Reform*, pp. 88–90.
69. Originally funded at a rate of $800 per month from the union, the AAEF struggled to maintain an 'independent' public posture. Personal diaries, 30 September 1938; 5 July 1939, reel 1, LP.
70. Personal diaries, 26 January 1938, reel 1, LP.
71. Lauck to President Roosevelt, 30 January 1940, box 383, LP. There is no sign that the AAEF received a positive reply to its request.
72. W. Jett Lauck, 'After the New Deal: a program for America', *The New Republic*, 99 (5 July 1939), pp. 243–6.
73. Personal diaries, 29 August 1938, reel 1, LP.
74. Personal diaries, 13 May 1938, reel 1, LP.
75. Personal diaries, 30 April 1938, reel 1, LP.
76. The $35,000 realized from the sale went to the mortgage holders. Peter B. Lauck interview. Personal diaries, 17 May 1939; 6 June 1939, reel 1, LP.
77. Lauck, 'After the New Deal' p. 243; Lauck to John L. Lewis, 5 November 1937, box 39, LP.
78. On SWOC, see e.g. Len De Caux, *Labour Radical: from the Wobblies to CIO, a Personal History* (Boston, Beacon Press, 1970), pp. 280–81.
79. Personal diaries, 29 February 1936, reel 1, LP.

80. Personal diaries, 17 December 1935, reel 1 LP; Zieger, *Republicans and Labour*, p. 36.

81. Lauck to John L. Lewis, 5 July 1937, box 39, LP.

82. For an extended discussion of these issues, see the definitive political biography on the subject by Nelson Lichtenstein, *The Most Dangerous Man in Detroit: Walter Reuther and the Fate of American Labour* (New York, Basic Books, 1995), esp. pp. 116–18.

83. Personal diaries, 14 August 1937, reel 1, LP.

84. Personal diaries, 14 August 1937, reel 1, LP.

84. Personal diaries, 15 November 1937, 18 November, reel 1, LP.

85. Lauck to John L. Lewis, 20 November 1937, box 39, LP; Personal diaries, 16 January 1938, reel 1, LP; Lichtenstein, *The Most Dangerous Man*, pp. 117–18.

86. Personal diaries, 26 February 1938, reel 1, LP.

87. 'Ordway Tead', *Current Biography Yearbook* (New York, H.W. Wilson Co., 1942), pp. 817–18; Personal diaries, 25 October 1939, reel 1, LP.

88. Ordway Tead, *New Adventures in Democracy: Practical Applications of the Democratic Idea* (New York, Whittlesey House, 1939), pp. 5, 92–3, 95, 142, 149. Tead, no more than Lauck, seemed to know what to do with workers' actual powers on the shop floor (let alone within their union). Along with the representation of different interests in industry, he suggested vaguely that 'we should go further and create situations in which the working staff become virtual partners in the enterprise'. But not only did Tead admit that there was 'no easy formula to apply here', he tied such worker participation to considerations of 'high output' as much as 'democratic intention' (p. 152).

89. On Lewis's growing conflicts with the Administration, see Robert H. Zieger, *The CIO, 1935–1955*, (Chapel Hill: University of North Carolina Press, pp. 106–7, and Dubofsky and Van Tine, *John L. Lewis*, (1986), pp. 147–53.

90. Personal diaries, 12 October 1940, reel 2, LP.

91. Rather sheepishly, Lauck confided to his diary that following Lewis's speech, he 'decided not to do anything about it because I was economic and not political advisor to Lewis'. Personal diaries, 26 October 1940, LP.

92. Ibid. Lewis's daughter Kathryn normally regulated official access to her father, but in this case even she (according to Lauck) expressed frustration at her father's self-isolation on the eve of a momentous decison. See also Zieger, *The CIO*, pp. 96–7.

93. Personal diaries, 6 November 1940, LP.

94. Len De Caux, *Labour Radical*, p. 386. Like many who worked with Lewis, De Caux viewed him with a mixture of awe and mystery:

> Lewis usually knew which way the wind blew. He took account of the tides. He knew which was the safe and easy course. Yet sometimes he chose to chart a course against the wind, to follow it stubbornly, come shipwreck or glory. Only a fool, or a red, or a man like Lewis, does things like that (p. 390).

95. Personal diaries, 5 October 1943, 19 November 1943, reel 2, LP; quotation Personal diaries, 19 February 1944, reel 3, LP.

96. Personal diaries, 14 January 1944; 22 January 1944, 24 January 1944, reel 3, LP.
97. Personal diaries, 31 December 1943, reel 2, LP.
98. Peter B. Lauck interview.
99. Personal diaries, 6 July 1943, 30 December 1943, LP.
100. Peter B. Lauck interview. Peter Lauck himself served as a Navy airplane mechanic during the Second World War and settled later on a career as small-town newspaper writer and editor.
101. Personal diaries, 8 November 1944, reel 3, LP.
102. Personal diairies, 28 January 1944, 29 January 1944, 1 February 1944, reel 3, LP.
103. Personal diaries, 4 November 1944, reel 3, LP.
104. Personal diaries, 15 March 1947, reel 3, LP.
105. Alan Brinkley, *The End of Reform: New Deal Liberalism in Recession and War* (New York: Alfred A. Knopf, 1995), esp. pp. 128–36; pp. 170–74, 198–200, 265–71.
106. Kennedy made the first of his oft-repeated references to the 'rising tide' in an Address in the Assembly Hall at Paulskirche, Frankfurt, West Germany, 25 June 1963. Suzy Platt (ed.), *Respectfully Quoted: a Dictionary of Quotations Requested from the Congressional Research Services* (Washington, DC, Library of Congress, 1989), p. 313.
107. Reuther and Green as quoted in Brinkley, *The End of Reform*, p. 224.
108. Ronald W. Schatz *The Electrical Workers: a History of Labour at General Electric and Westinghouse, 1923–60* (Urbana, University of Illinois Press, 1983), p. 155.
109. By crediting 1930s new liberals with the shift to 'a world in which both the idea and the reality of mass consumption were becoming central … gradually supplanting production as the principal focus of popular hopes,' Brinkley, I think, gives too much credit (and blame) to his subjects. It is important to acknowledge the continuum in consumerist thought as well as the key transitions. Brinkley *The End of Reform*, p. 4.

CHAPTER EIGHT

Political identities in the West Virginia and South Wales coalfields, 1900–1922

Roger Fagge

In recent years labour historians have produced a far more complex picture of working-class experience and behaviour, with many rejecting the use of abstract theory, or models, in favour of multicausal analyses of specific historical situations. The teleological reading of the relationship between class and politics has been a major casualty of this process, notably with regard to the theory of US working-class exceptionalism. The latter has been undermined both by a growing body of research questioning assumptions about universal class-consciousness in Europe, and a more sophisticated appreciation of working-class radicalism in the US. This has led to a position where some historians of British labour, for example, have argued in favour of non-socialist continuities in working-class politics, while some of their counterparts looking at the US have proferred a view of workers articulating a language of Americanism which could incorporate the aspirations of labour.[1]

In the light of these revisions, this chapter will offer a comparative perspective on political identities in the coalfields of West Virginia and South Wales. Both regions were major producers, and both also experienced high levels of industrial conflict in this period. However, the patterns of conflict were different, with West Virginia witnessing explosions of unrest amounting to virtual 'civil wars', while South Wales saw constant, less spectacular strike activity. Crucially, in the context of this paper, industrial conflict was backed by contrasting political identities. The West Virginia miners voiced their protests through a language of Americanism, while the South Wales miners moved towards labourist and class politics. This contrast allows an analysis of the meaning and coherence of different political identities, and their ability to express working-class demands.

This chapter will suggest that, although it has been claimed that the political language of the West Virginia miners conformed to the image of a radical, class-conscious, Americanism,[2] the evidence would suggest otherwise. The appeal to American rights was generally vague and loosely defined, and ignored the fact that the ideological implications of these rights were hotly contested. Moreover these appeals were not backed by political organization, in either its electoral, or non-electoral forms. In contrast, the mining communities of South Wales were able to establish a more clearly defined, located and radical identity, drawing on their occupational position in an industrial capitalist society; an identity supported by an emerging pattern of independent political organization, and the expression of collectivity through the ballot box.

The key to understanding these different identities lies in the contrasting social structures, cultural formations and power relationships within the two coalfields. The West Virginia miners were able to overcome a number of formidable barriers in order to organize strikes and huge armed marches, however, these barriers proved much more significant when it came to the more difficult realm of politics. The majority of the West Virginia miners lived in functional company towns, dedicated to the production of coal, which were both geographically and culturally isolated. In the early years, in particular, they were rarely integrated into an established political framework, nor, as new communities, could they draw on an existing political culture. These characteristics were reinforced by the rootless, transitory nature of life in the communities, with inhabitants frequently moving between towns, to other states and industries, and, in some cases, back to their rural origins.[3]

The instability, and isolation at community level obviously worked against the emergence of a collective identity. This tendency was reinforced by the distinctive cultural mix of the mining population, which was made up of black and white Americans and European immigrants. Whilst these groups were sometimes able to unify around a set of specific demands relating to the coal operators' abuses, the cultural differences were more significant on a political level. For example, the foreign-born miners, most of whom were from southern and eastern Europe, were made up of various nationalities and hence, cultures and languages.[4] At a practical level this inhibited the spread of political ideas within the mining communities, beyond demands which clustered around the United Mine Workers of America (UMWA). Moreover, the fact that many of the foreign-born miners intended only a temporary stay in the coalfields, and were not naturalized citizens, limited the electoral strength of the miners as a whole.[5]

For the black miners, West Virginia offered a less oppressive, although by no means equal, social environment than further south. In particular they were able to exercise the vote, which they did, along race lines, for the Republican party. For historical reasons, the Democratic Party did not attract black votes, and the Socialist Party of America (SPA) with its at best equivocal line towards racism, also secured little black support.[6]

Indeed, the link between the black vote and the Republican party was so strong that there were allegations throughout this period that the operators in southern West Virginia recruited blacks to shift the state's political balance.[7] This had the effect, as Trotter has shown, of allying the black miners with the small black middle class, and the coal interests.[8]

The native West Virginians within the mining communities discovered that, as with every other aspect of their lives, the coming of the new industrial order destroyed the traditional pattern of politics. Previously their independent, rural way of life had been marked by local political identities, usually based on kinship. Elections were treated as social occasions, often taking place on Sundays or public holidays.[9] The new political framework, created and dominated by the coal interests, ran counter to this in almost every sense. The former mountaineers, therefore, isolated within the coal towns, often clung to their identity as 'descendants of the pioneers' who had first settled the region and who still had a right to own the land.[10] Although this did not necessarily rule out the formation of a common politics with other groups, it did, when combined with the other barriers, make such a process more difficult.

Great though the above were as barriers against the formation of a common political identity, or political organization, it was the overarching power of the operators which proved most significant. From mining town to state government, a formidable network of repression was in place to deal with recalcitrant UMWA organizers, and any other what coal-operator Justus Collins termed as 'undesirable people' from organizing meetings or distributing propaganda.[11] This obviously applied equally to advocates of political change, particularly if they were outsiders.[12]

At state level, the distinction between industrial and political activity became confused behind a blanket paranoia about 'reds' and 'radicals'. This was particularly true of the war and immediate post-war period when, giving an extra twist to the anti-socialist campaign in the wider nation, the state Governor, John J. Cornwell, considered the most limited of demands as cause for the deportation of foreign-born miners, while the response to small quantities of radical literature led to state/federal activity, and the passing of legislation such as the iniquitous 'Red Flag Act'.[13] Nor were these pressures restricted to the era of the 'red scare'. Although the intensity of repression was greater then, other Governors were equally dismissive of the right to free speech. Thus Governor H.E. Hatfield responded to criticism of his imposed 'settlement' of the 1912–13 Paint Creek strike, by smashing the presses and arresting the editor of the Huntington *Socialist and Labor Star*. West Virginia was not welcome territory for the political organizer or activist.[14]

The operators also interfered with the conduct of elections, particularly those for county posts which provided the basis for the control of the local mining communities. In 1922, for example, a US attorney wrote to the Attorney-General to complain that politics in Logan county was under the control of the operators' infamous appointee, Sheriff Don Chafin, with 'election results figured up and given out in advance as to what the county will do'.[15] While Logan was probably the worst example of such excesses, electoral abuses were rife, particularly in other southern counties. Thus in 1920, a store owner in McDowell county appealed to W.B. Wilson for federal aid to ensure fair elections. He reported that mine guards had assaulted local citizens, leaving him concerned that some 'voters in this county will be afraid to go to the poles (sic)'.[16]

The operators' control of the political apparatus of the state, which the electoral frauds helped perpetuate, was also a cause of political alienation, and hence a barrier against political action. Both the Democratic and Republican parties were subservient to the coal interests, as were many of the county and state political offices.[17] This led to the defeat of legislation of which the operators didn't approve or, when such legislation was passed, as in the case of laws covering scrip and mine guards, non-enforcement.[18] Consequently there was a tendency for the miners to withdraw from the political process and instead focus on the UMWA.[19] This helps explain why the pattern of industrial conflict, most notably in the armed marches, was so intense and in many ways amounted to politics by another means. Indeed the intensity itself helped further focus attention on the specifics of battles in the industrial arena at the expense of a broader, more politicized outlook.

Considering the remarkably inhospitable circumstances which have been described, it is perhaps surprising that the West Virginia miners engaged in the level of political organization they did, rather than vice versa. Although never consistently successful, this activity took place both within the existing party framework and through third party politics.

Prior to this period, in the late 1880s and 1890s, certain areas of the West Virginia coalfield had shown some interest in independent radical politics. Parts of the Kanawha region, in particular, supported the Greenback party, and later the Populists.[20] Later on there were also attempts at working through the mainstream parties. Labour sympathizer, Samuel B. Montgomery, was elected as a state senator in 1904, while in 1906, District 17 President, John Nugent, and UMWA attorney, Adam B. Littlepage, were elected to the state Senate on the Republican and Democratic tickets respectively. The latter elections led the editor of the Charleston *Labor Argus* to announce 'we have elected two of labor's greatest champions to offices where they can compel our enemies to show their hands.'[21] However, this soon turned sour, when

Nugent resigned the District 17 leadership in 1907, to become state Immigration Commissioner – a post financed and controlled by the operators.[22] The following year also saw the defeat of Montgomery in a Preston county Republican primary, and Littlepage fail to gain the Democratic nomination for the Governorship. Montgomery's bill to remedy the abuses of the mine guards was also defeated.[23]

These events underlined the operators' stranglehold on the political system and the two established parties, and the difficulties of working within such a framework. Other politicians did run with labour support, such as Democrat Matthew M. Neely, former mayor of Fairmont and future state Governor, who established himself in northern West Virginia due to splits in the Republican vote during the 'progressive era'. He went on to become a federal Senator in 1922, with UMWA support, although he reneged on this as the decade progressed.[24] Similarly, local UMWA officer Fred Mooney was defeated in 1920 and 1922 as a Republican candidate for the House of Delegates.[25] The black coalminer, John V. Coleman, was slightly more successful, securing election to the House of Delegates in 1918, where he helped influence the passage of a limited anti-lynching law. However, Coleman was unusual, with most black mining votes going to buttress the emerging black middle class.[26]

The most vigorous challenge by labour, however, was Samuel B. Montgomery's campaign for the 1920 Republican nomination for Governor, which was defeated amidst allegations of electoral irregularities.[27] Indeed so strong was the disgust at the manipulations of the ballot that a 'non-partisan' electoral ticket was drawn up for the subsequent elections, with Montgomery at the head, and six Republican and six Democratic candidates for the main state offices. Although defeated by E.F. Morgan, who secured 150,000 votes, Montgomery came second with a remarkable 81,000 votes, beating the Democrat into third place on 42,500.[28] A similar independent campaign was run four years later when the veteran radical Robert M. LaFollette, backed by various labour/left/progressive groups, ran against the major parties for the Presidency, and secured nearly 5 million votes (16.5 per cent).[29] In West Virginia, however, despite efforts by local union leaders, including Mooney who once again ran for the House of Delegates, this time on an independent ticket, the total vote was only 37,724.[30]

Notwithstanding the Montgomery and LaFollette campaigns, the most consistent attempt at creating a genuinely independent labour politics, outside the established parties, was made by the SPA which was at its strongest in the state around the middle of this period. Although partially a response to disillusionment with the political situation within West Virginia, the advance of the SPA was also linked to the national political context, where the party was, by 1912, offering an increasingly significant political alternative. Under the inspirational, if sometimes inconsistent, leadership of Eugene V. Debs, the SPA had not only made electoral advances, but increased its influence within the trade unions, including the powerful UMWA.[31] This influence proved short-lived, however, as divisions within the SPA, the war, state repression, and social and political changes led to a precipitous collapse in support[32] This affected West Virginia as much as the rest of the US.

The rise, and indeed fall, of the socialist vote in West Virginia may have mirrored the national pattern, but it did so at a lower level. In 1904 Debs secured only 1,573 (0.7 per cent) votes in West Virginia compared with a national vote of 402,283 (2.98 per cent). This increased to 1.4 per cent (compared with 2.82 per cent nationally) four years later, reaching a high point of 15,248 (5.7 per cent) votes in the election of 1912. This coincided with the national SPA vote of 900,672 (5.99 per cent).[33] Even at the height of the SPA's electoral power, therefore, West Virginia was recording less than the national average, and well below states which had a more vigorous socialist electoral presence. In the same election, for example, Debs received 16.5 per cent of the vote in Nevada, 16.4 per cent in Oklahoma, 13.5 per cent in Montana, 13.4 per cent in Arizona, 12.4 per cent in Washington, 11.7 per cent in California and 11.3 per cent in Idaho.[34] In the 1916 election the SPA candidate, Allan L. Benson, polled less than half the 1912 vote with 6,144 (2.1 per cent), while nationally the vote dropped to 518,113 (3.18 per cent). In 1920, with the incarcerated Debs again the candidate, a further drop to a dismal 5,609 (1.1 per cent) was recorded in West Virginia, compared with a small real increase nationally to 919,799 (3.42 per cent).[35]

The weakness of the SPA vote revealed in these figures in many ways speaks for itself, underlining the lack of correlation between industrial conflict and socialist voting patterns. After all the 1920 vote was secured at the height of the Mine Wars, with Logan county, at the centre of the struggle, recording a miniscule 27 votes for Debs.[36] Of course it would be wrong, especially if we take into account the difficulties involved in mounting an electoral challenge in West Virginia in these years, to completely write off the socialist influence solely on these electoral figures, revealing though they are. An active socialist press helped publicize abuses within the state, and encouraged the miners to resist them – hence the unsolicited attention of Hatfield during the Paint Creek strike. Furthermore, some of the newer generation of local leaders who came to the fore during the Paint Creek strike, most notably Frank Keeney and Mooney were, for a time at least, associated with the SPA,[37] and several visits by Debs and other socialist leaders, including in 1912 the MP for the Merthyr Boroughs, Keir Hardie, all raised the profile of the socialists.[38] However, despite these examples, the overwhelming impression remains that socialist support was marginal, submerged within a broader non-class based Americanism.

This is further underlined by the lack of support for the Industrial Workers of the World (IWW) which, as the main left-wing revolutionary alternative, might have been expected to pick up support from socialists disillusioned with, or intimidated from using, the ballot box. However, although Cornwell, Debs and some historians have seen the IWW hand lurking behind the coal tipples,[39] there is little evidence to support this. As IWW activist Ralph Chaplin, in West Virginia at the time of the Paint Creek strike wrote, 'there was little use in proclaiming the virtues of the IWW', as the miners 'had a union already and an industrial union of sorts', and 'were more interested in remaining alive' than hearing about dual unionism.[40] This was something which even an FBI agent in Charleston, at the end of this period, agreed with. He reported that he 'never believed that there has been much, if any, outside political agitation at work' in the state.[41]

Not only did the FBI agent refute the suggestion of widespread outside agitation among the West Virginia miners, but he also described what he believed lay behind the miners' actions. The local union leadership, he argued, were of 'an extremely radical type'. However, crucially, he continued that,

> All of the radicalism seems to find vent in state issues and the radical elements have been almost completely absorbed in this struggle ... little or no interest has been manifested in radical issues having a national or international application. Their minds and lives are fully occupied with the struggle immediately at hand ... teachings and propaganda are directed almost solely against the coal operators of the State, rather than against capitalistic interests everywhere.[42]

The fact that an IWW activist and an FBI agent both stressed the way the miners focused on the specific state issues is as unusual as it is significant, underlining the previous evidence which suggested that due to the significant barriers within the state, the extension of the formidable displays of solidarity and direct action into a wider political movement did not take place, and there was no sustained political activity by the miners either within the existing political framework, or through independent alternatives.

Instead, the focus on the 'struggle immediately at hand', rather than broader class concerns, led to an emphasis on the denial of rights; particularly the right to join the UMWA. The union thus became doubly significant, both as an example of operator interference in the miners' freedom of action, but also, as the only 'alternative source of institutional power', as the potential vehicle, symbolically and practically, for bringing about change.[43] To those engaged in the struggle to establish the union in West Virginia, the compromises and contradictions of union policy were often lost beneath a more general faith in the power of the idea of unionism, and its role in remedying the wrongs they experienced. As journalist, Winthrop D. Lane put it, 'Keeney has no carefully thought out philosophy of a class struggle … His experience is his philosophy. He believes in unionism'.[44]

This struggle for the union and the restoration of rights was placed within the context of what were seen as American values. The system of relations within the state was seen as a throwback to the past, or to the 'old world', what Samuel Gompers's stridently called 'Russianized West Virginia'.[45] UMWA Vice-President Frank J. Hayes spoke in 1913, of how 'conditions in West Virginia are different from those in other states … that find no comparison except in the feudalism of the middle ages'.[46] Similarly, Mother Jones cited the abuses of monarchy when she was incarcerated during the Paint Creek dispute, claiming that it was 'just what the old monarchy did (to) my grandparents 90 years ago in Ireland'.[47]

To those both native-born and foreign-born this was seen as un-American, and a betrayal of the meaning of republican America. Polish-born UMWA organizer, Albert Manka, complained that 'I always thought this was a free country, but I have found there isn't much liberty in the state of West Virginia for a poor working man'.[48] Similarly underneath the headline 'Slave Drivers', the *Labor Argus* reported that a mass meeting on Cabin Creek had described the guard system as 'unnecessary and un-American'.[49] Most graphically, UMWA Vice-President Phillip Murray was told by a group of miners who took part in the 'Battle of Blair Mountain', in 1921, that 'we, in West Virginia, are not really and truly in America … Let us win West Virginia back to America'.[50]

On the surface at least, the evocation of America and its symbols seemed straightforward. Independence day was usually marked by marches,[51] and the flag was also prominent during strikes.[52] More specifically the miners appealed for their rights as citizens via the application of the Constitution and the Bill of Rights. Miners at Bower appealed to the state Governor for 'a greater sense of justice and a full measure of the workers' constitutional guarantees to the protection of their rights to organize and combine'.[53] In the same year a local union at Mammoth told the Secretary of Labor that the 'miners ask little', just fair weighing, the abolition of the mine guards and 'to be treated as Citizens of this Great Republic and knot (*sic*) Slaves … all we wont (*sic*) is justice and fair play'.[54] Heroic figures from the past were also cited in support of the miners' demands. Margaret Fowles, a miner's wife from Scottdale, concluded an eloquent appeal to President Harding, with the words 'no man is fit to preside over the destiny of this republic who does not recognize with Lincoln that the voice of the people is the voice of God'.[55] Others, like Keeney and Mother Jones, used the example of such historical figures to justify the miners' call to arms.[56]

The lessons taken from the past and, indeed, the whole appeal to American rights and values were, however, far more ambiguous than they at first seem. Were the miners fighting to receive the same treatment as the rest of America, or were they appealing to a more radical, historical, ideal of America? Moreover, what did this ideal mean – Gompers and Keeney, for example, had very different definitions. In fact these issues were never really worked out and instead the overwhelming impression is of the assertion of these rights and symbols as being somehow absolute and self-evident – as if the myth and reality of America somehow coincided, or were interchangeable.

Yet those responsible for the miners' exploitation in West Virginia themselves espoused Americanism, and laid claim to the same rights and traditions as justification for their actions. This similarity in language is apparent, for example, in the operators' involvement in the American Constitutional Association at the end of this period. They published *The American Citizen* twice monthly, and claimed to support 'American Ideals' and 'real patriotism and love of country', as opposed to the (mythical) 'tide of bolshevism'.[57]

The claim that they were upholding law and order was central to the operator and state governments' arguments. Thus Morgan replied to the miners at Bower, 'I assure you that every effort possible is being made to secure the people, and when I say "people" I mean *all the people* of Mingo county, the rights guaranteed to them by our state and federal constitutions'.[58] It is clear that this definition of America, its constitution, and the meaning of citizenship, involved opposing unions, socialists and any others who attempted to protest against the unfettered excesses of business. In their view, it was the UMWA which was un-American.

And it was this definition of the meaning of America, rather than that of the miners, which was closest to that held by those in power in the US generally. In reality, the US labour movement had consistently appealed to the republican tradition and the constitutional order, yet had been restrained by hostile court and government decisions. It was not only in West Virginia in this period, therefore, that workers discovered that they 'did not live in a world shaped according to their preferred version of Americanism'.[59]

However, the contested terrain of Americanism was never addressed. The West Virginia miners did not espouse a clear, class-conscious version of Americanism, but rather a vague political language constructed against the odds amidst a severely fragmented social and political culture. With no political movement to help construct a genuinely radical language, or connect it to a wider political discourse, the heterogeneous workforce were only able to unite around a broad belief in law and order, and their rights as citizens of a 'Great Republic' which submerged the ambiguity of such beliefs, and failed to clarify, or place in context, the underlying economic basis for their exploitation.

If political identities in the West Virginia coalfield were shaped by the different cultural formations and power relationships found in the region, the contrasting patterns of community in South Wales enabled a different, and more effective political identity to emerge. The generally larger, older, less isolated, more permanent mining communities in South Wales provided a firmer base for the nurture and spread of political activity. Similarly the overwhelmingly collective culture which developed within these communities was underpinned by the greater cultural homogeneity and the location of this culture within existing traditions of radical political activity which, due to the greater age of the communities were, by the start of this period, part of the miners' common heritage.[60]

Different power relations in South Wales also meant these communities were fully integrated into a political framework and therefore much freer to express the political dimension of this collectivity through party organization and at the ballot box. Indeed, although the franchise did not admit all miners to the vote throughout this period (and no women were able to vote until 1918), their sheer weight of numbers within certain constituencies gave the mining communities a great deal of electoral influence. Moreover, in contrast to West Virginia, the fact that the union was established proved vital, particularly as the South Wales Miners' Federation (SWMF) and Miners' Federation of Great Britain (MFGB) were both actively involved in politics, first through the Liberal Party and then, after 1909, via the Labour Party. This presented a political structure which, although operating within a far from sympathetic political system, could reflect and help create a political identity to a far greater extent than in West Virginia. In addition other, nonelectoral, alternatives were available when the shortcomings of the system became apparent.

The South Wales miners created a strong tradition of radical political activity during the nineteenth century, playing a part in the underground 'scotch cattle' movement, 1831 Merthyr Rising, and Chartist movement.[61] They were also keen supporters of Henry Richard, who stood as 'a Welshman, an advanced Liberal and a Nonconformist', and the candidate for 'Wales and the Working Man' for a Merthyr Boroughs seat in 1868. He secured election with the support of miners in Dowlais and Mountain Ash, and represented the constituency until his death in 1888.[62]

Richard was more radical than the vast majority of the Liberals who began to sweep Wales from the 1850s, backed by the rising tide of radical nonconformity, and franchise changes.[63] However, it was through the Liberals that the South Wales miners first made their electoral presence felt. The franchise reforms and the redistribution of constituencies in 1884–85 radically altered the nature of electoral politics, giving a larger section of the working class a vote, and establishing a number of seats where they were in the majority.[64] Almost immediately, in the election of 1885, miners' leader, William Abraham ('Mabon') was returned as the member for the Rhondda, amid near riotous scenes, defeating Liberal F.L. Davis with over 56 per cent of the vote.[65] Soon after the election, however, it became clear that Mabon and the miners were keen to remain within the Liberal tradition and a joint Liberal and Labour (Lib–Lab) Association was formed.[66]

Mabon's hold on the constituency was such that he was unopposed at the next three elections and won comfortably when challenged by Conservative Robert Hughes in 1900.[67] Described in a miners' manifesto as the 'Labour member for Wales' and 'the key of the South Wales miners to the British House of Commons',[68] the SWMF President received enthusiastic support from various quarters during the 1900 election, including Sir Henry Campbell-Bannerman and D.A. Thomas.[69] He was again unopposed until 1910.[70]

A more genuine attempt at establishing an independent labour politics in South Wales came at the 1900 election. The impetus for the challenge came from the Independent Labour Party (ILP) who had established themselves, if somewhat shakily, within the constituency during, and in the immediate aftermath of, the momentous 1898 coal strike.[71] With socialists active within newly formed Trades Councils in Aberdare and Merthyr, and the election of ILP member C.B. Stanton as Aberdare miners' agent, the support for running an independent candidate increased.[72] The ILP National Administrative Council (NAC) heard in July 1900 that ILP men within the Trades Council were 'endeavouring to get that body to bring out a Labour candidate'. Moreover they were also told that Keir Hardie, 'had been suggested as a candidate', something which he personally favoured.[73]

Although, under pressure from Bruce Glasier, Hardie decided to accept the nomination to run for Preston, supporters in Merthyr, building on the personal popularity Hardie had gained during the 1898 strike, secured his selection.[74] Pessimistic about his chances, Hardie concentrated on the Preston seat, leaving ILP activists like S.D. Shallard and

S.G. Hobson to conduct his campaign. The former recalled that Hardie was 'in the division for exactly one afternoon and two evenings before the polling day',[75] but he nevertheless won a remarkable victory and became the first ILP MP in Wales.

In 1915, looking back on Hardie's first victory at Merthyr, the *Merthyr Pioneer* (newspaper of the local ILP) suggested that seat had been won because of 'the impression that he (Hardie) had created on people; on the zeal of his workers; and on the fact that Mr. Pritchard Morgan [his Liberal opponent] was largely out of court with the people'.[76] As a summary of the reasons for Hardie's success this was undoubtedly accurate. However, the strongest factor was Hardie's ability to represent, and develop, the radical traditions of Merthyr. As he told one audience in 1898, 'my programme is the programme of Labour; my cause is the cause of Labour – the cause of humanity – the cause of God ... I first learnt my socialism in the New Testament where I still find my chief inspiration', thus combining evangelical fervour and independent working-class politics.[77]

This appeal was not primarily over policy, as Hardie and Liberals like the other Merthyr MP, D.A. Thomas had, in 1900 at least, much in common. Thomas was, after all, one of the more radical Liberals in the coalfield.[78] What Hardie represented, however, was the embodiment of independent working-class politics, Labour with a capital 'L', rather than labour within the paternalistic embrace of the Liberal Party. 'Vote for Labour' he told the Merthyr electorate, then give the second vote to 'the least dangerous man of the other two'.[79] While this suggestion was not universally accepted, as Hardie's second place in the polls behind Thomas (31.3 per cent to 46.9 per cent) revealed,[80] if we take into account that a large number of miners were disenfranchised due to the 1898 strike,[81] it is clear that his appeal struck some chords within the mining communities.

The ILP success at Merthyr was very much the exception to the general pattern of South Wales politics at the 1900 election. The only other independent labour candidate was John Hodge of the Steel Smelters union who stood in the Gower constituency. He ran only after being rejected as a Liberal candidate, and then proceeded to present a programme which K.O. Morgan suggests was 'nebulous in the extreme'.[82] Despite, or perhaps because of this, Hodge polled a more than respectable 3,853 (47.4 per cent), only 423 behind Liberal J.A. Thomas.[83] Even Mabon's hold on the Rhondda was an exception in 1900, as he was the only sitting Lib–Lab within South Wales. Moves were made to change this in 1903, however, when, under pressure from Liberal chief whip Herbert Gladstone, the South Glamorgan Liberals selected SWMF Vice-President William Brace to run at the next election. A year later, with similar pressures applied, SWMF General Secretary Tom Richards was selected to fight a by-election in the West Monmouth seat. He won easily with over 70 per cent of the vote.[84]

In the 1906 general election the Liberal party further tightened its grip on Wales, winning 32 out 34 seats.[85] Within this Mabon, Richards, and Brace – newly elected with over 63 per cent of the vote – ran as Lib–Labs. Another SWMF activist, John Williams, did run in a three way contest in the Gower constituency, building on the precedent of Hodge. Standing as an independent Lib–Lab, Williams defeated the second placed Liberal by only 319 votes. On entering Parliament, however, he took the Liberal whip. Thus the only genuine independent labour candidate, and one of only two non-Liberals in Wales, was once again Keir Hardie in Merthyr.[86]

The fact that both the 1900 and 1906 elections saw only two direct confrontations between Liberal and independent labour candidates was testimony to the links between the SWMF and the Liberal Party. As early as 1902, the MFGB had devised a scheme to secure greater Parliamentary representation for miners which the SWMF adopted the following year. However, although 11 South Wales seats were targeted, and under a later MFGB scheme, which urged one candidate for every 10,000 members, 12 were 'scheduled' in 1906, in practice the SWMF Executive Committee (EC) would only allow challenges when seats became vacant.[87] The caution over standing miners' candidates as either Liberals, or as independent labour representatives, is all the more remarkable if we consider that there were, by 1910, 11 constituencies (12 seats) in South Wales where miners made up over 10 per cent of the electorate. These ranged from the Rhondda seat, which had the largest national proportion of miners with 76 per cent (13,590 out of 17,760), to the Brecon seat with 10 per cent (1,400 out of 13,342).[88]

On the surface at least it might have been expected that the 1910 elections would have seen a change in the electoral pattern of the previous decade. After all, following a second national ballot in May 1908, the MFGB officially affiliated to the Labour Representation Committee and the union's MPs took the Labour whip. Within South Wales the enthusiasm for the move was shown by the huge vote of 74,675 to 44,615 in favour of affiliation, an even larger majority than the 1906 margin of 41,843 to 31,527 (when nationally the move was defeated).[89] However in the January election, the SWMF EC withdrew candidates for East and Mid Glamorgan, and East Carmarthen, claiming that they did not want to split the progressive vote while the 'People's budget' was at stake (it also meant that the four Lib–Labs would not be opposed by Liberals).[90]

As a consequence little changed at the election. Thus Mabon claimed his 9,000 majority was 'a tribute to Mr. Lloyd George and the cause of progress'.[91] Likewise Brace seemed more interested in maintaining old alliances than pursuing the independence of the party he now represented. He told an audience at Tonypandy that 'Mr. Lloyd George was simply the advance guard of a mighty Welsh nation … It required a man to have been born in Wales to have produced such a budget – a budget which breathed a passion for the people'.[92] Only Hardie continued to pursue a genuinely independent course. He told a meeting at Aberdare on New Years' Eve 1909 that, 'so long as the workers were in a minority, the Liberals did not think of protecting the rights of the workers. When the workers were being victimised, they did not hear much talk about protecting the rights of the individual'.[93]

By the time the issue of the Parliament Bill led to a second election in 1910, the South Wales coalfield had been disrupted by the Cambrian Combine dispute. Although the strike saw miners facing up to the Combine owner, the former MP for Merthyr, D.A. Thomas, and the Tonypandy riots of November, there was no large-scale shift away from the Liberals. The SWMF did back Labour candidates in Mid and East Glamorgan, but these were unsuccessful.[94] Of the sitting MPs, only Williams and Hardie faced Liberal opposition and, once again, only the latter stuck to campaigning on a distinctly Labour platform. On what turned out to be Hardie's last candidacy, he polled his highest percentage with 11,507 (39.6 per cent) votes, compared with Liberal, Edgar Jones' 12,258 (42.2 per cent) – only 751 votes between them.[95] In the Gower seat Williams, according to the *Labour Leader*, passed through 'a series of changes of opinion which would do no discredit to a chameleon',[96] but managed to hold his seat with a much reduced majority. The other three former Lib–Labs were easily re-elected (Richards was in fact returned unopposed).[97]

By 1910, therefore, despite the rising tide of industrial conflict and a vote for affiliation to the Labour Party, the South Wales miners were, in the electoral sense at least, still committed to Lib–Labism rather than Labour. Other than in Merthyr, only Williams could secure election against Liberal opposition, and this was done with a 'chameleon' appeal to the Lib as well as the Lab.

The limited success of the independent Labour vote at Parliamentary elections was underlined by mixed success in terms of party organisation and local elections. As we saw earlier, a number of ILP branches were formed during the 1898 strike, many of which collapsed soon afterwards.[98] In the years that followed, the ILP never successfully established a mass presence in the valleys.[99] Labour candidates were, however, making advances in certain parts of the region at a local level. In Merthyr in 1905, for example, 12 Labour candidates were elected in the November elections.[100] In the Rhondda, Labour gradually increased its representation to the point that, but for the death of three Rhondda SWMF EC members (and Labour councillors) in 1911, they would have assumed control of the Rhondda Urban District Council (RUDC) before the outbreak of war.[101]

More widespread Labour advances in local and national elections were hampered by the ineffective organization of the broader Labour forces, and in particular the slow pace of development of Labour Representation Committees.[102] The lack of cohesion between ILP branches, SWMF lodges and Trades Councils was partly due to the inevitable problems surrounding the creation of a new political organization. However, it was also exacerbated by the miners' unwillingness to yield influence over the selection of candidates.[103] In fact, where there were successes prior to the war, as in the Rhondda, this was not due to a broad Labour alliance, but to the fact that the SWMF completely dominated the local Labour organization, paying MPs salaries, and selecting and financing local candidates.[104]

This began to change when the SWMF EC allowed a broader base for the selection of a Labour candidate, which was symptomatic of a more vigorous approach to independent Labour politics immediately prior to the war. Although the Labour Party constitution of 1918 established proper constituency-based structures, Stead suggests that 'the meaningful existence of a local Labour Party' in most of Wales 'dates from 1913', when the SWMF EC took advantage of the Trades Union Act of 1913, to declare its commitment to fighting on genuine Labour lines with the backing of Labour organization in the localities.[105] The SWMF decided to fight eight seats, but the outbreak of war delayed the next election, postponing a genuine battle between Labour and Liberal.[106]

As a consequence the results of the December 1910 election, which was itself fought amid special circumstances, stand somewhat unrealistically as the pinnacle of Labour pre-war electoral strength. If we recall, this consisted of five Labour MPs, of whom only two were elected against Liberal opposition, and only one of these on a genuinely independent line. In reality this probably underestimated Labour support before 1914 (particularly as the SWMF was taking a more militant line after 1910), and helps explain why there was such a dramatic shift in electoral politics after the war. Certainly the war itself was to be a major influence on change, however, we would do well to remember that changes prior to the outbreak of hostilities could only be expressed at the electoral level from 1918.

This point is of great significance in the comparison with West Virginia, where the SPA made its strongest showing in this period. This advance, however, as we saw, was a temporary, exceptional trend to the general pattern of electoral politics. In contrast the South Wales miners, even at this artificially low point, had established a greater political presence, rooted within the framework of community, providing the building block for further advances. South Wales was headed in an entirely different political direction to West Virginia.

With the outbreak of war, politics in the coalfield was seemingly thrown into turmoil. As with the national Labour movement, the Labour Party, somewhat reluctantly at first, lined up behind the war effort, leading to divisions with elements of the ILP.[107] These splits were more than apparent in the South Wales coalfield where there was, initially at least, general support for the war.[108] This came to the fore in a by-election at Merthyr in November 1915, caused by the death of Hardie. Labour candidate, ILPer James Winstone, was defeated by militant, turned nationalist miners' agent, Stanton, following an acrimonious campaign.[109]

However, the loss of Hardie's seat was more symbolic than significant, and as the war progressed opinion began to turn against the conflict. The first chance to voice such feelings came shortly after the war ended, when Lloyd George called the first general election for eight years. The so-called 'coupon' election of December 1918, however, was hardly a typical election and, to quote Pelling, 'was inevitably a virtual plebiscite for or against Lloyd George, as the architect of victory'.[110] Nevertheless, Labour made significant gains within the newly redistributed seats in industrial South Wales. Candidates at Rhondda East, Rhondda West, Abertillery, Ebbw Vale and Ogmore were all elected unopposed; while at Caerphilly, Gower, Ogmore, Bedwellty and Pontypool, victory was secured against Liberal opposition.[111] All of those elected, however, had been prominent in supporting the war effort.[112] In contrast those Labour candidates who had opposed the war, like Winstone, who had been a prominent critic after the 1915 by-election, went down to defeat.[113]

By 1922, the war issue had faded, and the new spectre of economic decline taken centre stage. In an election in which the divided Liberals were generally routed, Labour captured six more mining seats.[114] Cemented by the elections of 1923 and 1924, Labour had become overwhelmingly the party of the South Wales miners, and South Wales generally. Backed by a domination of local government,[115] these constituencies became some of Labour's safest in Britain. Indeed, in Rhondda East in the 1930s, for example, the only serious challenge to the Labour Party came not from the Liberals, but the Communist Party of Great Britain (CPGB).[116]

The contrast with West Virginia could not be more stark. Throughout the period 1900–22, the West Virginia miners were unable to sustain independent political activity, even under the umbrella of the two existing parties. The only major independent activity centred on the SPA which momentarily mounted a minor challenge, but could never overcome the barriers in its path. In South Wales, in contrast, from Merthyr in 1900 to November 1922, the Labour Party was gradually building a political hegemony based on the votes of the mining valleys. This difference also extends to other more radical political activities. Whereas the IWW and other syndicalist organizations were virtually non-existent in the West Virginia valleys, in South Wales, proponents of revolutionary politics were influential at certain times throughout this period.

The most prominent example of these were the activists in the Rhondda, who worked through the Plebs League, Industrial Democracy League (which was active 1912–13), Central Labour College, Rhondda Socialist Society (which became the South Wales Socialist Society in 1919), and most prominent of all, the Unofficial Reform Committee (URC). The Social Democratic Federation were also a minor influence in the valleys,[117] although it was the CPGB which pulled most of these strands together at the end of this period, and proved the most influential revolutionary party organization.[118] Indeed the contrast with West Virginia is made even more pertinent if we consider the fact that some of the inspiration for these organizations came from across the Atlantic. For example, Noah Ablett was one of those influenced by Daniel De Leon of the US Socialist Labor Party,[119] while IWW leader, Big Bill Haywood, was also well received on visits to the valleys.[120]

The level of support for the revolutionary element was never consistently high, even in the Rhondda, where it was at its strongest.[121] But although a minority, these groups were at times extremely influential. As G.A. Williams suggested, writing of the election of the imprisoned Arthur Horner as the Mardy checkweigher in 1919, a 1917 rule committing the union to the abolition of capitalism, and the decision to affiliate to Red International of Labour Unions, 'This was a spasmodic and minority trend, but at moments of high temper it could carry a majority',[122] What this 'trend' built upon was the mixture of anger and frustration at the aggressiveness of the South Wales owners, as well as the potential power of the solid, homogeneous mining communities of, in particular, the Rhondda. As Egan has pointed out, the Rhondda district had a membership of 41,000 prior to the war which, 'taking their families into account (was) virtually the whole population of the Rhondda Valleys'. This represented a far more direct democracy than the machinations of 'distant Parliaments', as well as a logical fighting unit against the coal owners.[123] Moreover the strength of numbers in the Rhondda, which made up a third of the SWMF, which was in turn the largest region in the MFGB, gave the miners a national influence.[124]

With a sense of such power it is easy to understand why the industrial unionism of the URC could, at times, strike a chord within the steam coal region. As Ablett told one audience, 'the industrial union did not need the backing of the political organisation, therefore it was foolish to swim the river to fill the bucket on the other side'.[125] The emphasis was placed upon strengthening the union and turning it into a revolutionary instrument; a view which received its most famous elucidation in *The Miners' Next Step*.[126] Yet the industrial unionist position was more flexible than Ablett's comments suggest. For a start, even at its most syndicalist, as in the URC in the middle of this period, it was, as Foote has suggested, 'not necessarily incompatible with labourism, or even the electoral success of the labour movement'.[127] This is graphically underlined by the fact that *The Miners' Next Step* itself noted that 'Political action must go on side by side with industrial action'.[128]

Distinctions were also blurred by the fact that many of the organizations which had syndicalist elements, for a time at least, also contained ILP activists. For example, in 1911 the *Rhondda Socialist* newspaper was started by both ILP and syndicalist sympathizers.[129] Inevitably friction over political tactics were voiced in the paper, as in May 1912, when the secretary of the Rhondda Socialist Newspaper Committee described syndicalism as 'Neo-Anarchism'.[130] However, this should not dispel the impression that, except for the most militant exponents, the Labour left and the syndicalists had a good deal in common. This is further illustrated by the way many individuals moved between the two groups. Thus, for example, Ablett was a member of the Labour Party until 1907, as was A.J. Cook until 1913.[131] Similarly Will Mainwaring, George Barker and Frank Hodges moved in the opposite direction to become Labour loyalists.

Moreover such changes did not, necessarily, require an ideological about turn, just a juggling of the equation balancing industrial and political power. After all, Aneurin Bevan, who was influenced early on by the syndicalist movement, was later able to articulate within the Labour Party a brand of socialism in which the 'belief in the class struggle stayed unshakeable'.[132] Key to this was his understanding that 'politics was about power'.[133] As he put it on the first page of *In Place of Fear*;

> A young miner in a South Wales colliery, my concern was with the one practical question, where does power lie in this particular state of Great Britain, and how can it be attained by the workers? No doubt this is the same question as the one to which the savants of political theory are fond of addressing themselves, but there is a world of difference in the way it shaped itself for young workers like us. The circumstances of our lives made it a burning luminous

mark of interrogation. Where was power and which the road to it?[134]

Nor was this preoccupation with power restricted only to the Labour left and the self-confessed revolutionaries. Virtually all the political activity in this period was concerned with the same question; the differences concerned which roads to take and what power actually meant. This was as true for the Lib–Lab leaders as for those further left; they may have preferred conciliationism, but they were no strangers to strikes or political activity.[135] As William Brace put it in his 1914 Presidential address, the 'Government and the owners, having failed to accept conciliatory methods, must accept demands enforced by industrial and political power'.[136] Nor were the militant elements blind to this. For example, on the death of Tom Richards in 1931, Ablett remarked 'We have lost the greatest man in the Federation: the greatest man in Wales'.[137]

What underpinned this common strand was the sense of power within the mining communities, and the hostility of the coal owners. This was why Arthur Horner was described as a miner and trade unionist first, and a Communist second.[138] It also explains why the miners' politics concealed a barely disguised arrogance towards other elements of the labour movement for much of this period.

Although the syndicalists and later the CPGB were at times able to seize the initiative in this common strand, the eventual road which the mass of miners across the South Wales coalfield chose was that of the Labour party. What Labour actually came to mean, however, was more complicated. The socialism of the ILP, and later of the Labour left was one important, but by no means dominant influence. Another input came from the Lib–Labs who had been reluctantly dragged into the party in 1909. As several historians have shown, the continuities in style and content of leadership left an indelible mark on the Labour Party that emerged after the war.[139]

Indeed in the 'translation' of the Liberal past into the Labour future[140] the most common beneficiary were the likes of Vernon Hartshorn and D. Watts Morgan, where the '"middle position" continually redefined itself and maintains its dominance'.[141] In this sense the shift to Labour was about the independence implied by the capital 'L', which Keir Hardie successfully proffered in Merthyr. It was also the general political expression of the growing self-confidence of these valleys, hardened by the conflict which had torn through the coalfield in the previous decades. In an increasingly national political framework, the web of identities – Welsh, English, British, radical, socialist, working class, miner – which were the substance of these communities became redefined, and reshuffled around the appeal of the, in many ways, pragmatic Labour Party. Where the militant minority, particularly the

CPGB, were successful, as in the structures of the SWMF, this success owed more to a reputation for strong and able leadership than their revolutionary credentials.[142] In Labour South Wales they were elected as miners first, Communists second.

In contrast to their counterparts in West Virginia, therefore, the South Wales miners were able to organize politically, as they had industrially, and establish a political presence firmly rooted within party organization and electoral representation. This reflected a broader divergence in the political identities of the two regions; for in South Wales, the miners drew on their stronger sense of community and greater civil freedom to form a coherent political identity resting on their occupational and class position. In contrast, the culturally fragmented and politically restricted world of the West Virginia miner, while allowing momentous displays of industrial militancy, could only sustain a fragile and ambiguous alliance around notions of citizenship and exceptionalism, which while relevant to the expression of political protest, were largely unrelated to the position of miners and workers in an aggressive industrial capitalist society.

In a broader sense, this would suggest that while different political languages might reflect similar experiences, this is not always the case. In this instance, the appeal to the American tradition seemed more a sign of weakness than strength, when compared with the labourism of South Wales. This should not be interpreted as meaning that US workers were never able to use such a language in a coherent manner, but it would suggest this such a programme would be difficult. For, by the end of the nineteenth century, whether radicals liked it or not, business and their supporters had seized control of the meaning of America, almost as effectively as they ruled economic life.

The irony, of course, is that the differences described above neatly conform to the old arguments about US exceptionalism. However, while this chapter is willing to wave a warning flag about simply equating Americanism with labourism, it is not intended to resurrect the truly dead. While a little more structure might be appealing in history, and in political life, we are forced back to our melting reality, and the glaring question, exceptional to what? After all, it could be South Wales that was exceptional, rather than West Virginia. Now there's an idea.

Notes

1. On Britain see, for example, R. McKibbin, *The Ideologies of Class* (Oxford, Oxford University Press, 1990); E.F. Biagini and A.J. Reid (eds), *Currents of Radicalism: Popular Radicalism, Organised Labour*

and Party Politics in Britain, 1850–1914 (Cambridge, Cambridge University Press, 1991); and G. Stedman Jones, *Languages of Class: Studies in English Working Class History, 1832–1982* (Cambridge, Cambridge University Press, 1983). Important US studies include, S. Wilentz, *Chants Democratic: New York City and the Rise of The American Working Class, 1788–1850* (New York, Oxford University Press, 1984); L. Fink, *Workingmen's Democracy: the Knights of Labor and American Politics* (Urbana, University of Illinois Press, 1983); and D. Montgomery, *Citizen Worker: the Experience of Workers in the United State with Democracy and the Free Market during the Nineteenth Century* (Cambridge, Cambridge University Press, 1993). For a summary of the debate on Exceptionalism, see E. Foner, 'Why is there no socialism in the United States?', *History Workshop Journal*, 17 (1984), pp. 57–80; and S. Wilentz, 'Against exceptionalism: class consciousness and the American Labour Movement'; N. Salvatore, 'Response to Sean Wilentz'; M. Hanagan, 'Response to Sean Wilentz'; all in *International Labour and Working Class History*, 26 (1984), pp. 1–24, 25–30, 31–6 respectively; and Wilentz 'A reply to criticism', *International Labour and Working Class History*, 28, (1985), pp. 46–55. The debate on Americanism is considered at length in Wilentz, 'Against exceptionalism'. He argues against the 'counter-progressive' approach of Hofstadter and Hartz, and its stress on the consensual nature of the practice and discourse of US radicalism. Instead he proffers a view of a genuinely class-based politics, rooted in the American language. See also his *Chants Democratic*. This debate is also touched upon in L. Fink, 'The new labour history and the powers of historical pessimism: concensus, hegemony, and the case of the Knights of Labor', *Journal of American History*, 75 (1988), pp. 115–36.

2.   This has been argued by Corbin, who has suggested that the West Virginia miners espoused a language of 'Americanism' based on 'an ideology, containing values, beliefs, principles, and goals, as coherent, radical, and understanding of an exploitative and oppressive system, as any ideology announced by Socialists, Communists and Wobblies'. D. Corbin, *Life, Work and Rebellion in the Coal Fields*, (Urbana, University of Illinois Press, 1981), p. 244–6.

3.   R. Fagge, *Power, Culture and Conflict in the Coalfields: West Virginia and South Wales, 1900–1922* (Manchester, Manchester University Press, 1996), pp. 27–108.

4.   In 1910, the West Virginia Department of Mines reported 30 different nationalities among immigrant miners. They made up approximately 30 per cent of the state's miners, compared with 46 per cent white American, and nearly 20 per cent black American, West Virginia Department of Mines, *Annual Report, 1910* (Charleston, 1910), p. 104.

5.   By the end of the period under discussion only 10 per cent of this group had become naturalised citizens. E.E. Hunt, F.G. Tyron and J.H. Willits (eds), *What the Coal Commission Found* (Baltimore, Williams and Williams Co., 1925), p. 137.

6.   F. Barkey, 'The Socialist Party in West Virginia from 1898–1920: a study in working class radicalism', unpublished PhD dissertation, University of Pittsburgh (1971), p. 168; I. Howe, *Socialism and America* (San Diego, Harcourt Brace Javanovich, 1985), pp. 19–22; S. Miller, 'Socialism and race'; T. Kornweiber, 'A reply'; both in J.H.M. Laslett and S.M.

Lipset (eds), *Failure of a Dream? Essays in the History of American Socialism* (Berkeley, University of California Press, 1984 edn), pp. 223–8, 231–40.

7. W.A. MacCorkle, *The Recollections of Fifty Years of West Virginia* (New York, G.P. Putnam's Sons, 1928), p. 479; R.L. Lewis, *Black Coal Miners in America, 1780–1980*, (Lexington, University of Kentucky Press, 1987), pp. 126–7.

8. J.W. Trotter Jr, *Coal, Class and Color: Blacks in Southern West Virginia, 1915–32* (Urbana, University of Illinois Press, 1991), pp. 216–58.

9. J.C. Campbell, *The Southern Highlander and his Homeland* (Lexington, University of Kentucky Press, 1969 edn), pp. 100–103; R.D. Eller, *Miners, Millhands and Mountaineers: Industrialization of the Appalachian South, 1880–1930* (Knoxville, University of Tennessee Press, 1981), p. 235.

10. F. Mooney, *Struggle in the Coal Fields* (Morgantown, West Virginia University Library Press, 1967), p. 16; US Senate, *Conditions in the Paint Creek District, West Virginia*, 63 Congress, 1 Session (Washington, DC, 1913), pt. 1, p. 790; R. Chaplin, 'Violence in West Virginia', *International Socialist Review*, 13 (April 3 1913), pp. 730–31; J.L. Spivak, *A Man and his Time* (New York, Horizon Press, 1967), p. 57.

11. Collins to Wolfe, 27 December 1915, Morgantown, West Virginia University (WVU), West Virginia and Regional History Collection, Justus Collins Papers (A+M 1824), series 1, box 13, file 93.

12. For example, when an IWW activist arrived in Logan Town in 1921, he was arrested and later 'shot down in cold blood'. L.K. Savage, *Thunder in the Mountains: The West Virginia Mine War, 1920–21* (Charleston, Jalamp Publications, 1984), pp. 123–4.

13. Fagge, *Power, Culture and Conflict in the Coalfields*, pp. 130–35.

14. Ibid., p. 123.

15. US Attorney Northcott to Attorney-General, 18 December 1922, National Archive (NA), Department of Justice (RG 60), file 16–130–83, folder 4.

16. W.H. Cline to Wilson, Secretary of Labor, 12 October 1920, Washington National Records Centre (WNRC), Records of Federal Mediation and Conciliation Service (FMCS) (RG 280), file 170/1185, part one.

17. J.A. Williams, *West Virginia and the Captains of Industry* (Morgantown, West Virginia University Library Press, 1976), pp. 3–16; Eller, *Miners, Millhands and Mountaineers*, pp. 211–17; Corbin, *Life, Work and Rebellion in the Coal Fields*, pp. 12–13.

18. H.B. Lee, *Bloodletting in Appalachia: the Story of West Virginia's Four Major Mine Wars and Other Thrilling Incidents of its Coal Fields* (Morgantown, West Virginia University Library Press, 1969), pp. 10–11; Eller, *Miners, Millhands and Mountaineers*, pp. 217–18; J.B. Thomas, 'Coal country: the rise of the southern smokeless coal industry and its effect on area development', unpublished PhD dissertation, University of North Carolina (1971), pp. 224–5.

19. Eller, *Miners, Millhands and Mountaineers*, pp. 234–5; J.A. Williams, *West Virginia: A History* (New York, W.W. Norton and Co., 1976), pp. 142–3.

20. Williams, *West Virginia and the Captains of Industry*, pp. 122–4; J.H.M. Laslett, *Labor and the Left: a Study of Socialist and Radical Influences*

in the American Labor Movement, 1881–1924 (New York, Basic Books, 1970), p. 201.

21. *Labor Argus*, 8 November 1906, pp. 1–2.
22. Ibid., 30 May 1907, p. 1.
23. E.L.K. Harris and F.J. Krebs, *From Humble Beginnings: West Virginia State Federation of Labor, 1903–57* (Charleston, West Virginia Labor History Publishing Fund, 1960), p. 47.
24. Ibid., p. 82; Williams, *West Virginia*, p. 146.
25. Mooney, *Struggle in the Coal Fields*, pp. 129–30.
26. Trotter, *Coal, Class and Color*, pp. 47–9; 226–7; 251–2.
27. Spivak, *A Man and his Time*, pp. 86–7.
28. Harris and Krebs, *From Humble Beginnings*, p. 177; R.D. Lunt, *Law and Order vs. The Miners: West Virginia* (Hamden, Archon Books, 1979), p. 117.
29. D.P. Thelen, *Robert M. La Follette and the Insurgent Spirit* (Boston, Little Brown Co., 1976), pp. 181–92; N. Salvatore, *Eugene V. Debs: Citizen and Socialist* (Urbana, University of Illinois Press, 1983), pp. 335–7.
30. Harris and Krebs, *From Humble Beginnings*, pp. 179–80; Mooney, *Struggle in the Coal Fields*, pp. 129–30.
31. Salvatore, *Eugene V. Debs*, pp. 220–302; Howe, *Socialism and America*, pp. 3–35. UMWA, *Proceedings of 23rd Annual Convention, 1910*, pp. 191, 215–46, 433–41; Laslett, *Labor and the Left*, pp. 216–19.
32. Laslett, *Labor and the Left*, pp. 218–31, and 'End of an alliance: selected correspondence between Socialist Party Secretary Adolph Germer, and UMW of A leaders in World War One', *Labor History*, 12, 4 (1977), pp. 570–95; Howe, *Socialism and America*, pp. 36–48; Salvatore, *Eugene V. Debs*, pp. 262–345; J. Weinstein, *The Decline of Socialism in America, 1912–1925* (New York, Monthly Review Press, 1967).
33. US Congress, *Presidential Elections since 1789* (Congressional Quarterly, Washington, DC, 1983), pp. 99–107; M.A. Jones, *The Limits of Liberty: American History 1607–1980* (Oxford, Oxford University Press, 1983), p. 650.
34. *Presidential Elections since 1789*, p. 102.
35. Ibid., p. 99–107; Jones, *The Limits of Liberty*, p. 102.
36. M. Nash, *Conflict and Accommodation: Coal Miners, Steel Workers and Socialism, 1890–1920* (Westport, Greenwood Press, 1982), p. 146.
37. Corbin, *Life, Work and Rebellion in the Coal Fields*, p. 240; interview with Bert Castle, WVU, Oral History Collection.
38. *Wheeling Register*, 6 October, 1912, p. 20.
39. E.V. Debs, 'Debs denounces critics', *International Socialist Review*, 14 (August 1913), pp. 105–6; Salvatore, *Eugene V. Debs*, p. 257; Nash, *Conflict and Accommodation*, p. 143; S. Bird, D. Georgakas and D. Shaffer (eds), *Solidarity Forever, the IWW: an Oral History of the Wobblies* (London, Lawrence and Wishart, 1987), p. 126.
40. R. Chaplin, *Wobbly: the Rough-and-Tumble Story of an American Radical* (Chicago, University of Chicago Press, 1948), p. 121.
41. Report of Agent H. Nathan, NA, Records of War Department General Staff (RG165), Military Intelligence Division Correspondence, 1917–41 (entry 65), box 3649, file 10634–793, folder 5.
42. Ibid.

43. Lewis, *Black Coal Miners in America*, pp. 156–7.
44. W.D. Lane, *Civil War in West Virginia: a Story of Industrial Conflict in the Coal Mines* (New York, B.W. Heubsch, 1921), p. 85.
45. S. Gompers, 'Russianized West Virginia', *American Federationist*, 20, 10 (October 1913), pp. 825–35.
46. *Socialist and Labor Star*, 30 August 1913, p. 3.
47. M. Jones to Borah, n.d., NA, General Records of the Department of Labor, file 16–13 E. box 24.
48. *United Mine Workers' Journal*, 11 October 1990, p. 4.
49. *Labor Argus*, 8 July 1909, p. 1.
50. *Wheeling Register*, 3 September 1921, p. 6.
51. For example, at the start of this period miners paraded at Loup Creek on Independence day 'wearing the miners badge', *UMWJ*, 19 July 1900, p. 4.
52. E.M. Steel, 'Mother Jones in the Fairmont Field, 1902', *Journal of American History*, 57 (1970), p. 294; see *UMWJ*, 12 September 1912, p. 2, on the flag during Paint Creek.
53. Bower Committee to Morgan, 14 July 1921, WVU, E.F. Morgan Papers (A+M 203), box 8, file 2.
54. L.U. 404 to Secretary of Labor, 12 September 1921, FMCS, file 170/1185 A.
55. Fowles to Harding, 6 January 1922, FMCS, file 170/1185 A.
56. *West Virginia Federationist*, 26 February 1920, p. 1. *Conditions in the Paint Creek District*, pt. 3, p. 2264.
57. See leaflet 'The work of the American Constitutional Association', WVU, John J. Cornwell Papers (A+M 952), series 35, box 135.
58. Morgan to A.M. Wimer, Bower Local, 16 July 1921, Morgan Papers, box 8, file 2.
59. L. Fink, 'Labor, liberty and the law: trade unionism and the problem of American constitutional order', *Journal of American History*, 74, 1 (1987), pp. 904–25, 906.
60. Fagge, *Power, Culture and Conflict in the Coalfields*, pp. 27–108.
61. G.A. Williams, *When was Wales? A History of the Welsh* (London, Penguin, 1985), pp. 191–7; G.A. Williams, *The Welsh in Their History* (London, Croom Helm, 1982), pp. 135–50.
62. K.O. Morgan, *Wales in British Politics, 1868–1922* (Cardiff, University of Wales Press, 1980 edn) pp. 23–4; Williams, *When Was Wales?*, pp. 213–17; G.A. Williams, *Peace and Power: Henry Richard, a Radical for our Time* (Cardiff, CND Cymru, 1988), pp. 1–7.
63. Williams, *When Was Wales?*, pp. 213–17; K.O. Morgan, *Wales in British Politics*, pp. 1–27.
64. K.O. Morgan, *Rebirth of a Nation: Wales 1880–1980* (Oxford, Oxford University Press, 1980), pp. 27–8.
65. *Rhondda Leader*, 13 October 1900, p. 4, compared the peaceful election in 1900 with that of 1885, when crowds fought with police and the Riot Act was read.
66. Morgan, *Wales in British Politics*, p. 66.
67. F.W.S. Craig, *British Parliamentary Election Results, 1885–1918* (London, Macmillan, 1974), p. 480.
68. Miners' manifesto in support of Mabon, *South Wales Daily News*, 26 September 1900, p. 6.

69. Campbell Bannerman sent his 'heartiest wishes', *Rhondda Leader*, 6 October 1900, p. 5; D.A. Thomas was actually one of Mabon's constituents and 'supported Mabon's colours in his way to the booth', *Rhondda Leader*, 13 October 1900, p. 3.

70. Craig, *British Parliamentary Election Results, 1885–1918*, p. 480.

71. For a summary of ILP activity in Wales generally from the 1890s to 1906, see D. Hopkin, 'The Rise of Labour in Wales, 1890–1914', *Llafur*, 6, 3 (1994), pp. 125–9.

72. D. Howell, *British Workers and the Independent Labour Party, 1888–1906* (Manchester, Manchester University Press, 1983), pp. 245–6; K.O. Morgan, *Keir Hardie: Radical and Socialist* (London, Weidenfeld and Nicholson, 1984 edn), pp. 97, 112; K.O. Fox, 'Labour and Merthyr's khaki election of 1900', *Welsh History Review*, 2, 4, pp. 354–7.

73. ILP NAC, 28 July 1900, ILP Minute Books, 1893–1909, (m/film edition), Cambridge, University Library.

74. Morgan, *Keir Hardie*, pp. 112–14; ILP NAC, 21–24 September 1900, ILP Minute Books, 1893–1900; *Labour Leader*, 29 September 1900, p. 309; Fox, 'Labour and Merthyr's khaki election of 1900', pp. 354–7.

75. *Labour Leader*, 20 October 1900, p. 334.

76. *Labour Leader*, 30 September 1915, p. 28.

77. K.O. Morgan, 'The Merthyr of Keir Hardie', in G. Williams (ed.), *Merthyr Politics: The Making of a Working-Class Tradition* (Cardiff, University of Wales Press, 1966), p. 67.

78. D. Tanner, *Political Change and the Labour Party, 1900–1918* (Cambridge, Cambridge University Press, 1990), pp. 208–9.

79. *South Wales Daily News*, 29 September 1900, p. 6.

80. The result in terms of votes was: Thomas 8,598; Hardie 5,745; Morgan 4,004. Craig, *British Parliamentary Election Results, 1885–1918*, p. 458.

81. Howell, *British Workers and the Independent Labour Party*, pp. 249–50; *Western Mail*, 27 September 1900, p. 3.

82. Morgan, *Wales in British Politics*, pp. 202, 207.

83. Craig, *British Parliamentary Election Results, 1885–1918*, p. 478.

84. R. Gregory, *The Miners and British Politics, 1906–1914* (Oxford, Oxford University Press, 1968), p. 122; Morgan, *Wales in British Politics*, pp. 209–10; Craig, *British Parliamentary Election Results, 1885–1918*, p. 485.

85. F.W.S. Craig, *British Electoral Facts* (Chichester, Parliamentary Research Services, 1981 edn), p. 18.

86. Craig, *British Parliamentary Election Results, 1885–1918*, pp. 480, 485, 481, 478; D. Cleaver, 'Labour and Liberals in the Gower constituency, 1885–1910', *Welsh History Review*, 12, 3 (1985), pp. 388–410; K.O. Morgan, 'The New Liberalism and the challenge of Labour', *Welsh History Review*, 6, 3 (1973), p. 285.

87. Gregory, *The Miners and British Politics*, pp. 123–7; Morgan, *Wales in British Politics*, pp. 246–7.

88. Gregory, *The Miners and British Politics*, see table, p. 138. The double seat constituency was, of course, Merthyr.

89. R.P. Arnot, *South Wales Miners; a History of the South Wales Miners' Federation, 1898–1914* (London, Allen and Unwin, 1967), p. 149.

90. Gregory, *The Miners and British Politics*, pp. 127–30.

91. *South Wales Daily News*, 22 January 1910, p. 8.
92. Ibid., 11 January 1910, p. 6.
93. *Aberdare Leader*, 1 January 1910, p. 8.
94. Fagge, *Power, Culture and Conflict in the Coalfields*, p. 242.
95. Craig, *British Parliamentary Election Results, 1885–1918*, p. 458.
96. *Labour Leader*, 9 December 1910, p. 774.
97. Craig, *British Parliamentary Elections Results, 1885–1918*, pp. 478, 480, 481, 485.
98. Howell suggests a drop from 31 to 9 branches: *British Workers and the Independent Labour Party*, p. 245.
99. Fagge, *Power, Culture and Conflict in the Coalfields*, p. 243; P. Stead, 'Establishing a heartland – the Labour Party in Wales', in K.D. Brown (ed.), *The First Labour Party, 1906–1914* (London, Croom Helm, 1985), pp. 73–6.
100. Howell, *British Workers and the Independent Labour Party*, p. 252.
101. Williams, '"An able administrator of Capitalism"?: the Labour Party in the Rhondda, 1917–21', *Llafur*, 4, 4, p. 22.
102. Stead, 'Establishing a heartland', pp. 78–9.
103. SWMF EC Meeting, 23 February 1914, SWMF Minutes, 1914, Swansea, South Wales Coalfield Archive (SWCA), C.1.
104. Williams, '"An able administrator of capitalism"?', p. 20.
105. Stead, 'Establishing a heartland', pp. 83–4.
106. Gregory, *The Miners and British Politics*, pp. 136–7.
107. For a concise account of Labour and the war see H.M. Pelling, *A Short History of the Labour Party* (London, Macmillan, 1985 edn), pp. 35–51.
108. Morgan, *Wales in British Politics*, p. 276.
109. Fagge, *Power, Culture and Conflict in the Coalfields*, pp. 246–8.
110. Pelling, *A Short History of the Labour Party*, p. 46.
111. F.W.S. Craig, *British Parliamentary Election Results 1918–1945* (Chichester, Parliamentary Research Services, 1983 edn), pp. 538–68.
112. Morgan, *Wales in British Politics*, p. 283.
113. Winstone died in July 1921, having never gained a seat in Parliament. 25,000 attended his funeral: J.M. Bellamy and J. Saville (eds), *Dictionary of Labour Biography, Vol. I* (London, Macmillan, 1972), pp. 350–51; Craig, *British Parliamentary Election Results, 1918–1945*, p. 538.
114. Craig, *British Parliamentary Election Results, 1918–1945*, p. 562; Morgan, *Rebirth of a Nation*, p. 191.
115. Labour assumed control of the RUDC, for example, in 1919. Williams, '"An able admistrator of capitalism"?', p. 22.
116. Craig, *British Parliamentary Election Results, 1918–1945*, p. 540.
117. B. Holton, *British Syndicalism, 1900–1914: Myths and Realities* (London, Pluto Press, 1976), pp. 79–81; M.G. Woodhouse, 'Rank and file movements among the miners of South Wales, 1910–1926', unpublished PhD. dissertation, University of Oxford (1969), p. 10; Kenneth Hilton, 'John Spargo, the Social Democratic Federation, and the 1898 South Wales coal strike', *Welsh History Review*, 16, 4 (1993), pp. 542–50.
118. For the formation of CPGB and role of the different South Wales' groups, see Woodhouse, 'Rank and file movements among the miners of South Wales', pp. 187–94.
119. D. Egan, 'Noah Ablett 1883–1935', *Llafur*, 4, 3, p. 22.

120. Holton, *British Syndicalism*, p. 81.
121. Fagge, *Power, Culture and Conflict in the Coalfields*, pp. 249–50.
122. Williams, *When Was Wales?*, p. 250.
123. Egan, 'Noah Ablett', pp. 27–8.
124. E.D. Lewis, *The Rhondda Valleys: a Study in Industrial Development, 1800 to the Present Day* (London, Phoenix House, 1959), p. 178.
125. Egan, 'Noah Ablett', p. 28.
126. URC, *The Miners' Next Step: Being a Suggested Scheme for Reorganisation of the Federation* (Tonypandy, 1912).
127. G. Foote, *The Labour Party's Political Thought: a History* (London, Croom Helm, 1985), p. 92.
128. *The Miners' Next Step*, p. 24.
129. Woodhouse, 'Rank and file movements among the miners of South Wales, 1910–1926', p. 73.
130. *Rhondda Socialist*, 11 May 1912, p. 4.
131. Egan 'Noah Ablett', p. 26; J.M. Bellamy and J. Saville (eds), *Dictionary of Labour Biography, Vol. 3* (London, Macmillan, 1976), p. 38.
132. M. Foot, *Aneurin Bevan, 1945–1960* (London, Paladin, 1975 edn), p. 17.
133. M. Foot, *Aneurin Bevan, 1897–1945* (London, Paladin, 1975 edn), p. 27.
134. A. Bevan, *In Place of Fear* (London, Heineman, 1952), p. 1.
135. P. Stead, 'Working class leadership in South Wales, 1900–1922', *Welsh History Review*, 6, 3 (1973), p. 342.
136. Presidential address before Annual Conference, 6–7 April 1914, SWMF Minutes, 1914, C.2.
137. Bellamy and Saville, *Dictionary of Labour Biography, Vol. 1*, p. 285.
138. C. Williams, 'The South Wales Miners Federation', *Llafur*, 5, 3, p. 49.
139. Williams, *The Welsh in their History*, p. 186; Stead, 'Working class leadership in South Wales', pp. 329–353; P. Stead, 'The language of Edwardian politics', in D. Smith (ed.), *A People and a Proletariat: Essays in the History of Wales, 1780–1980* (London, Pluto Press, 1980), pp. 148–65; Williams, '"An able administrator of capitalism"?', pp. 20–33; Williams, 'The South Wales Miners Federation', pp. 45–56. D. Smith, *Aneurin Bevan and the World of South Wales* (Cardiff, University of Wales Press, 1993), pp. 67–89.
140. Williams, *The Welsh in their History*, p. 186.
141. Stead, 'Working-class leadership in South Wales', p. 344; Williams, 'The South Wales Miners' Federation', pp. 51–2. Hartshorn even argued before the 1919 Sankey Inquiry that nationalization would be a useful defence against the growing tide of Bolshevism: *Minutes of Evidence of the Royal Commission on the Coal Industry* (Parl. Papers, 1919 Cd. 360, XI, 373), p. 363.
142. Macintyre suggested that the principal appeal of the Communists in the 'Little Moscow' at Maerdy was their ability to offer good leadership and to represent 'the sense of cohesion and common purpose that was a feature of such mining communities'. S. Macintyre, *Little Moscows: Communism and Working Class Militancy in Inter-War Britain* (London, Croom Helm, 1980), pp. 44–5; Stead, 'Working class leadership in South Wales', pp. 351–2.

Index

Compiled by Terry Wyke